The Life and Times of Fraser Mackintosh, Crofter MP

Ewen A. Cameron

Centre for Scottish Studies
University of Aberdeen

First published 2000
©Centre for Scottish Studies, University of Aberdeen
and the Author, jointly

ISBN 0 906265 28 2

Printed by Polestar AUP Aberdeen Ltd

Dedication

for Sally

Contents

Introduction		1
Chapter One	Charles Fraser Mackintosh and Local Politics, 1857-1867	15
Chapter Two	Charles Fraser Mackintosh and Parliamentary Politics, 1865-1874	35
Chapter Three	Charles Fraser Mackintosh in Parliament, 1874-1882	65
Chapter Four	Charles Fraser Mackintosh and the Crofters' Wars	91
Chapter Five	The Napier Commission	117
Chapter Six	Charles Fraser Mackintosh and Political Re-alignment, 1885-86	141
Chapter Seven	Political Twilight, 1886 to 1892	177
Chapter Eight	A Crofters' Party?	205
Conclusion	History, Politics and Antiquarianism	219
Bibliography		231
Index		247

Acknowledgements

I would like to record my gratitude to the Gaelic Society of Inverness and the Centre for Scottish Studies at the University of Aberdeen for generous financial support in the publication of this volume. I am also grateful to the Faculty of Arts at the University of Edinburgh for supporting the research for this volume in a variety of ways.

The staff of the following archives and libraries were unfailingly helpful and generous with their time: Aberdeen Public Library; Birmingham University Library; Bodleian Library, Oxford; British Library; Dundee University Library; Edinburgh Public Library; Edinburgh University Library; Glasgow University Library; Highland Regional Archive; Inverness Public Library; Mitchell Library, Glasgow; National Archives of Scotland; National Library of Scotland; Stirling University Library. Sir Donald H. Cameron of Lochiel and the Marquis of Salisbury permitted me access to their muniments.

Mr Hugh Barron was generous with his deep knowledge of genealogical matters relating to Charles Fraser Mackintosh. Dr Hugh Dan MacLennan and Dr John Bannerman provided a number of references and advice on Gaelic material. My colleagues in the Department of Scottish History at the University of Edinburgh put up with my frequent references to Charles Fraser Mackintosh with at least the appearance of interest. Successive groups of students in my Special Subject were similarly tolerant and they have influenced the outcome more than they know. In their (very) different ways, but with characteristic perception, Professor Donald E. Meek and Professor Allan I. Macinnes, provided me with a number of helpful suggestions relating to this project. I had many fruitful discussions, in a variety of locations, with my cosmopolitan research student Andrew G. Newby. Dr John S. Smith, in his inimitable way, and Mrs Margaret Croll prepared my untidy text for publication with great speed and efficiency. Mrs Lesley M. Ford, my literary agent, secured a lucrative deal with my publisher! My parents deserve thanks once again for their support, bed and board on research trips to Inverness and for living adjacent to Fraser Mackintosh's former residence at Lochardil House, Inverness. Once again, Sally has put up with much and this book is dedicated to her with much love and gratitude.

Introduction

The research for this book builds on my earlier study of Government policy in the Scottish Highlands in the decades after the Crofters' Act of 1886, work for which first brought me into contact with the figure of Charles Fraser Mackintosh, MP for the Inverness Burghs from 1874 to 1885, member of the Napier Commission in 1883-84, and MP for Inverness-shire from 1885 to 1892.[1] In examining newspaper sources such as the *Scottish Highlander*, I became aware of Fraser Mackintosh's weekly historical columns, 'Antiquarian Notes'; and in looking at the *Transactions of the Gaelic Society of Inverness*, I noted that Fraser Mackintosh was an important figure in the foundation of that venerable organisation, and published many papers in its *Transactions*. My view of his political career, however, was circumscribed by my concerns with the politics of the mid - 1880s and subsequent years. I did not think of him beyond the early campaigns to establish a Royal Commission to investigate the grievances of the Crofters and Cottars of the Highlands, and as a member of the Crofters' Party, whose arrival at Westminster in 1885 and 1886 had such a small impact on the Parliamentary debate on the Crofter question. Whilst I noted Fraser Mackintosh's Liberal Unionism after 1886, and his defeat at the hands of another Crofter candidate at the General Election in 1892, I did not deal with these issues in detail. I was compelled to take a more comprehensive overview of Fraser Mackintosh's career in writing a short notice about him for the *New Dictionary of National Biography*; this made me more aware of his earlier career in Inverness, in local politics and urban improvement, and the range of his historical publications.[2]

I began detailed work on his political career after spending a summer reading John Murdoch's extraordinary newspaper, *The Highlander*, published in Inverness between 1873 and 1882. One of the first things I came across in its columns was the adoption of Charles Fraser Mackintosh as an independent Liberal candidate for the Inverness group of Burghs in late 1873; this was followed quickly, almost too quickly for Fraser Mackintosh, by the General Election of 1874 at which he triumphed over the indolent sitting member, Aneas Mackintosh of Raigmore, and the amiable but ineffectual Angus Mackintosh of Holme, the Conservative candidate.[3] Fraser Mackintosh's protestations of independence from local cliques, and his subsequent activities in parliament, most notably over the question of the status of the Gaelic language in the Scottish school curriculum, stimulated me to undertake further research on his political career. This research formed the basis of a paper presented, appropriately enough, to the Gaelic Society of Inverness in late 1996.[4] At this stage the amount of material I had in hand encouraged me to think that further research would yield sufficient results to be able to write a short book about Charles Fraser Mackintosh. This volume represents the final outcome of this process.

Objectives
My aim in this study is to attempt to examine the entire range of Fraser Mackintosh's political activities rather than to take a snapshot of the years in the mid 1880s when he, and the Crofter issue, were prominent. A further aim is to set his political career, and the evolution of Highland politics in this period, in a wider context. Although the Highland land issue was highly distinctive, it was by no means unique, and the debates surrounding it did not take place in an ideological vacuum.[5] The passage of the Crofters' Act of 1886 and the activities of the Crofters' movement cannot be divorced from the wider political agenda; an appreciation of this is at least as important as understanding the local political cultures in the Scottish Highlands. The years of Fraser Mackintosh's parliamentary career, 1874 to 1892, span a crucial period in the development of politics in the United Kingdom and demonstrate this point with the utmost clarity. The 1874 election was the first to be conducted under the Ballot Act of 1872, which conferred secrecy on the voting process; the 1885 election was the first to be conducted after the reforms of 1884 and 1885 which had not only expanded the electorate - especially the rural electorate, a particularly salient fact in the Scottish Highlands - but had also redistributed seats and made further attempts to clean up the electoral process.[6] If this was not enough of a revolution in British politics there were further crucial events in 1886: William Gladstone, the Liberal Prime Minister, introduced his Irish Home Rule Bill which, although unsuccessful, led to division in the Liberal Party. Those Liberals who opposed the Bill (now calling themselves Liberal Unionists) entered into an electoral arrangement with the Conservatives at the General Election of 1886 and opposed their former colleagues. Fraser Mackintosh was returned unopposed at the General Election of 1886 as a Liberal Unionist/Crofter.

The Irish Home Rule Bill of 1886, which proposed the creation of a unicameral Parliament in Dublin and the removal of Irish MPs from Westminster, was among the most controversial events in British political history in the 19th century.[7] It led, as has been noted, to a re-alignment of the parties at the General Election of 1886, and to a new kind of politics. The constitutional structure of the United Kingdom was now a key political issue; further attempts to pass forms of Home Rule for Ireland, in 1893, 1912-14 and 1920 confirmed this impression. Unionists, who deprecated the potential for the break up of the Kingdom and, by implication, the Empire, opposed these bills; there was also a strand of opposition from social reformers who believed that the Irish issue, and the parliamentary time which it absorbed, were barriers to progress on important questions of social reform. Many Unionists were not diehard opponents of all forms of constitutional reform. Some, like Charles Fraser Mackintosh, argued, with varying levels of sincerity, that federal Home Rule, or 'Home Rule All Round', would be preferable to passing a measure dealing exclusively with Ireland. As one of the Liberal dissidents - although clearly not a major player - in this realignment, Fraser Mackintosh is worthy of study. To understand his position we must take a comprehensive view of his career, noting his views on the Irish question at earlier points, rather than merely taking a snapshot of his views during the heated period of debate in 1886.[8]

Although it is important to place Charles Fraser Mackintosh's career in a wider context, it is obvious that his principal concern was with issues relating to the Scottish Highlands. In the period prior to c.1880 these related mostly to questions revolving around language, education and the game laws. His activities on these issues were recognised and honoured by the Federation of Celtic Societies in 1877. The agenda broadened after the public campaign over the Leckmelm evictions in 1880; a coalition of individuals and organisations concerned with the Highland land question from a variety of perspectives began to gather and the issue achieved a greater prominence. The activities of Donald MacFarlane, MP for County Carlow, and Sir Charles Cameron, one of the Glasgow MPs, drew attention to the Highland land question in parliament; Fraser Mackintosh, as befitted his nickname, 'Member for the Highlands' was active with them.[9] It was this activity, and the utter respectability of his rhetoric, which led to his appointment to the Royal Commission chaired by Lord Napier in 1883.

A whole chapter is devoted to the Napier Commission and discusses

Fraser Mackintosh's role in having the Commission appointed, the membership of the Commission and the evidence which it heard. The Report of the Commission is subjected to analysis with the objective of drawing attention to the range of issues which it considered. The Napier Commission induced a crucial change in the way Fraser Mackintosh was perceived by his supporters and opponents. He was now more fully integrated with the burgeoning Crofters' movement, as was indicated by his Crofter candidature for the County of Inverness. This presaged the most contested part of his career as he was assailed by former colleagues and opponents accusing him of mendacity and inconsistency.[10] These accusations are meaningless unless an appreciation of Fraser Mackintosh's earlier career has been reached. Such an appreciation also serves to point out the diversity of the group of individuals who became known as the 'Crofters' Party', as well as the irony that the member most closely associated with the Highlands by birth, education and inclination, should be the most conservative of the group.[11]

The final phase of Fraser Mackintosh's career lasted from 1886, and his vote against Irish Home Rule, until his defeat in 1892: this was characterised by a growing detachment from the steadily disintegrating Crofters' movement.[12] It can be argued that Fraser Mackintosh's own career mirrors the rise and fall of the Crofters' movement, although it would be wrong to argue that there was any causal link between the two profiles. An attempt will be made to compare Fraser Mackintosh with the other Crofter MPs, particularly Gavin Clark and Donald MacFarlane. The contrast with Clark is particularly instructive: Clark had little or no personal contact with the Highlands but came to the Highland land question through involvement in a wide range of social issues, especially land nationalisation, temperance, and the Irish land and national questions. Perhaps it was Clark's physical and emotional detachment from the Highland past which allowed him to take a more radical view of the Highland land question. This is a direct contrast with Fraser Mackintosh, whose views were compromised by his idealised view of pre-1745 social relations in the Scottish Highlands. This is one area where brief analysis of Fraser Mackintosh's historical work has illuminated certain aspects of his political career.[13] A common theme in his rhetoric was the notion that the Highlanders were a loyal people, in contrast to Irish small tenants, and that this made the articulation of their grievances especially worthy. There is a sense in some of his speeches that one his concerns was to become involved in the Crofters' agitation in an attempt to prevent it from compromising this perception by becoming too aggressive or assertive.

A further aim is to note the extent to which Inverness was a centre of political activity related to the land agitation. As will be noted below, the town had a wide range of newspapers which contributed to a lively political culture. Inverness was a burgeoning town in this period and, it had a multifaceted orientation, towards the Highlands, the south of Scotland, and beyond, symbolised by its railway connections. The relationship between the town and the Highlands was far from simple: while it was an important service centre for the agricultural economy of the North (as indicated by the annual Wool Fair, which was an important political occasion in its own right) and it also profited from the traffic associated with the growing sporting estates of the north and west, there was also a relationship with the crofting community. The Inverness branch of the Highland Land Law Reform Association was one of the first to be formed in 1882, and even before this there were a number of important meetings concerned with the Leckmelm evictions, the event which began to bring together the coalition which formed the Crofters' movement. It is a subsidiary objective of this study to draw attention to, and place greater emphasis on, the Leckmelm evictions and the political events associated with them as a key event in the Crofters' War. Whilst most studies of the Crofters' War have paid a good deal of attention to groups of politically active Highlanders in the Scottish cities and in London, insufficient emphasis has been placed on the role of Inverness in the agitation.[14] The local political structure mirrors the situation in the Highlands as a whole; politics in the town moved from the uncontested return of moderate Liberal candidates, in the shape of Matheson of Ardross and Mackintosh of Raigmore, to the three way election from which Charles Fraser Mackintosh emerged victorious in 1874. Due to the extension of the burgh electorate in 1868, urban politics became contested at an earlier stage than Highland county politics, which did not benefit from increased enfranchisement until 1885. The political culture of the town was not dominated by the land question, however. This was demonstrated after Fraser Mackintosh moved to the representation of Inverness-shire; the contests in the Inverness Burghs were dominated by the Church issue and Fraser Mackintosh's successor was the Liberal Unionist and Free Church Constitutionalist, R. B. Finlay. Nevertheless, in the late 1870s and early 1880s, with the activities of Fraser Mackintosh and his supporters, John Murdoch and Alexander

Mackenzie, and the presence of clergymen, such as John Mactavish of the Free East Church, or Charles Macecharn of the Gaelic charge of the Church of Scotland, there was a coterie of radicals active in raising the profile of the Highland land question in the town.[15] In drawing attention to the political culture in the town use will be made of the cartoons, songs and poetry which added colour to local election contests.

Sources

In his work on Gladstone Professor Matthew has shown how much can be achieved by a skilled historian working with a comprehensive collection of papers relating to one individual.[16] The Gladstone Papers, including the diaries, represent the classic collection of papers of a Victorian politician. Gladstone, of course, was a politician of the first rank, and his eminence, position, and staggering range of interests attracted correspondents on a vast scale. The length of his political career, the number of offices he held, not least that of Prime Minister, which he held four times, ensures that his papers are a fruitful source of information to historians working on a bewildering variety of topics.[17] Equally, it has been noted that lesser politicians, constituency MPs for example, frequently leave little or no body of archive material behind.[18] It is not clear as to why this should be so, but what is clear is that none of the Crofter MPs, or others associated with the movement, left any substantial amounts of archive material behind.[19] Fraser Mackintosh is no exception in this regard, although it could be argued that he is better served than some of the other personalities who appear in this volume.

There are three main sources of personal material relating to Charles Fraser Mackintosh. The first of these is the Fraser Mackintosh Collection in the National Archives of Scotland: this collection is mostly made up of the historical materials which Fraser Mackintosh collected during his life, although there are some items of personal correspondence: the latter have been utilised here, where appropriate.[20] The second collection of use to the student of Charles Fraser Mackintosh are the Mackintosh Muniments, also in the National Archives of Scotland.[21] This is largely a collection of estate material but also contains some material relating to Charles Fraser Mackintosh by virtue of the fact that he acted as factor on this estate from 1869 to 1873. Of the Fraser Mackintosh material in this collection, much relates to the day-to-day activities of a factor on a Highland estate; nevertheless, there are revealing snippets of political and personal information. The third principal source of information are the Fraser Mackintosh Collections in Inverness Public Library. The bulk of this material is composed of the library of books which Fraser Mackintosh built up over his scholarly and political career. In addition to this material, which, in itself, forms a valuable resource for Highland history, there are some volumes of press cuttings kept by Fraser Mackintosh, and some extremely useful ephemeral material relating to the elections of 1874 in the Inverness Burghs and that of 1885 in Inverness-shire.[22] These sources allow some insight into the individual behind the public face, but they do not amount to a comprehensive collection of papers. This gap means that the student of Fraser Mackintosh's political career has to search in other sources: to some extent they can fill the gap left by the absence of private papers, but not wholly.

The principal source which has been consulted for this study has been the press. Inverness in the late-Victorian period had a vibrant culture of newspaper publishing and a wide variety of titles representing a broad range of political opinions.[23] The oldest established newspaper in the town was the *Inverness Courier* which took a moderate Liberal stance on most questions; as the Crofters' War developed it became very critical of the Crofters' movement. The *Inverness Advertiser* was also a Liberal newspaper, but it took a more advanced position than the *Courier*: the *Advertiser* was absorbed by the *Courier* in 1885. There are three other Inverness newspapers which are particularly worthy of mention: these are the *Highlander*, the *Northern Chronicle* and the *Scottish Highlander*.

The *Highlander*, edited by John Murdoch and published between 1873 and 1882, defies easy description or political categorisation. It was essentially a vehicle for Murdoch's distinctive ideas on subjects as diverse as personal hygiene, diet, and politics in Scotland and Ireland. In our context it is notable for the support it gave to Fraser Mackintosh during the 1874 Inverness Burghs election. The *Northern Chronicle* was the only Conservative newspaper published in what was a thoroughly Liberal Burgh. It was established in 1881, after an abortive attempt by the local Conservatives, including Fraser Mackintosh's former business partner Charles Innes, to buy over the ailing *Highlander* in the mid-1870s. The *Chronicle* continued until 1969 and, in our period at least, took a fairly standard Conservative line on most issues of the day. During the 1885 General Election, however, the *Chronicle* not only took an exceptionally partisan line in favour of the Conservative candidate,

Reginald MacLeod, but conducted a vitriolic and sustained assault on Charles Fraser Mackintosh. This campaign, conducted by Innes, attacked Fraser Mackintosh as a political turncoat, a convenient and insincere convert to the cause of the crofters, and sought to make political capital from actions, or alleged actions, carried out during his factorial career.[24] The third notable paper was the *Scottish Highlander*, published from 1885 to 1898 by Fraser Mackintosh's supporter Alexander Mackenzie. This newspaper appeared on the scene so fortuitously in time for Fraser Mackintosh's Crofter candidature in Inverness-shire in 1885, that many suspected that he had a hand in its foundation. The *Scottish Highlander* was certainly his most consistent supporter in the difficult final years of his career: although Mackenzie disagreed with Fraser Mackintosh on a number of issues, most notably Irish Home Rule, he continued to support him in the internecine disputes which troubled the Crofters' movement after 1886.[25] A final local newspaper worthy of mention is the *Highland News*: during the last phase of Fraser Mackintosh's political career the *News* was his most consistent opponent, constantly upbraiding him for his absences from Parliament, his record of voting with the government when he was there, and expressing exultation when he was defeated by Donald Macgregor in 1892.[26]

This wide selection of local newspapers has been the basic source for this study; they allow the historian to take a more or less comprehensive view of the public utterances and activities of Charles Fraser Mackintosh. The Victorian convention of reporting political speeches verbatim, replete, especially at election time, with comments - supportive and otherwise - from the audience, greatly facilitates this process.[27] Supported by other sources, such as *Parliamentary Debates*, the development of Fraser Mackintosh's political views and rhetoric over his parliamentary career can be traced. These sources give an excellent window on his public life and contribution to politics, but they can be uninformative, or even misleading, at certain junctures. For example, there is no doubt that some correspondence to and from Fraser Mackintosh would help to resolve issues such as his reasons for changing seat in 1885, or the precise motivations which induced him to vote against Irish Home Rule in 1886. The welter of newspaper comment, even if one is aware of the political angles from which the newspapers were coming, cannot amount to a complete view of these important turning points. This said, it should be emphasised that the absence of a collection of private papers cannot be advanced as a reason for not attempting a rounded study of Fraser Mackintosh's political career. Fraser Mackintosh, and the other Crofter MPs, operated in the public sphere and analysis of their activities in that sphere can help the historian to approach the material which helped to form contemporary perceptions.

Early Life
The final section of this introduction will sketch in the few facts we know about the early life of Charles Fraser Mackintosh. He was born in June 1828, the youngest of the four children of Alexander Fraser of Dochnalurg and Marjory Mackintosh, daughter of Captain Alexander Mackintosh of Borlum. His father was born in 1764 and was well known in the Inverness district as a noted farmer and fisherman: his book on the *Natural History of the Salmon* was published in 1833. He attended school at Dochgarroch from 1836 to 1840 and followed this up, it is suggested, with a year at a private adventure school, run by two brothers, John and Walter Gair, at Torbreck, near Inverness. In 1842, at the age of fourteen, he began his training as a lawyer in Inverness.[28] He matriculated at the University of Edinburgh for four sessions from 1849 to 1852, but does not seem to have graduated; this was not unusual for an apprentice solicitor in the years before the reforms of the Scottish Universities, the practice of graduation would have been seen as expensive and unnecessary.[29] He returned to Inverness after his time at University and continued to practice as a solicitor until we find him emerging into the public gaze at the General Election of 1857, as election agent for Campbell of Monzie and subsequently as an Inverness Town Councillor.[30]

Insufficient knowledge of his early life and experiences prevents us from reading too much into these events. One important point can be made, however: although he was a Gaelic speaking Highlander he did not come from the crofting community, his father was a tacksman and farmer. A further salient point concerning his early years, and this was something which was commented on by those who wrote about him during and immediately after his life, was the importance of his Jacobite heritage, on both his father's and his mother's side. Alexander Mackenzie, for example, comments on the fact that two of his great grandfather's brothers had been involved in the rebellion of 1715, were taken prisoner and transported to South Carolina.[31] As will be noted below, this heritage was important, it gave Fraser Mackintosh a fixed point in history which formed the basis of his frame of reference and induced the rather idealised view of the Highland past which characterised much of his thinking. This theme will be returned to at various points in the political narrative which forms the basis of this study. It is to politics, and local politics in Inverness in the 1850s and 1860s in particular, to which we must turn at the outset.

---

[1] E. A. Cameron, *Land for the People? The British Government and the Scottish Highlands, c.1880 -1925* (East Linton, 1996).

[2] I followed up some aspects of his early career in local politics and urban improvement in E. A. Cameron, 'The construction of Union Street, Inverness, 1863-65', *Scottish Local History Journal,* 44 (Winter, 1998), pp. 13-18.

[3] See E. A. Cameron, 'Embracing the Past: The Highlands in Nineteenth Century Scotland', in D. Broun, R. J. Finlay & M. Lynch (eds), *Image and Identity: The Making and Re-making of Scotland Through the Ages* (Edinburgh, 1998), pp. 204-6.

[4] E. A. Cameron, 'The Political Career of Charles Fraser Mackintosh, 1874-1892', *TGSI,* 60 (1996-98).

[5] E. A. Cameron, 'Politics, ideology and the Highland land issue, 1886 to the 1920s', *SHR,* 72 (1993), pp. 61-79; K.T. Hoppen, *The Mid-Victorian Generation, 1846-1886* (Oxford, 1998), pp. 549-50; M. Bentley, *Politics Without Democracy, 1815-1914: Perception and Preoccupation in British Government* (London, 1984), pp. 236-9; H. C. G. Matthew, *Gladstone, 1875-1898* (Oxford, 1995), p.243.

[6] N. Blewett, 'The Franchise in the United Kingdom, 1885-1918', *Past and Present,* No 32 (1965); pp. 27-56; M.E.J. Chadwick, 'The Role of Redistribution in the Making of the Third Reform Act', *Historical Journal,* 19 (1976), pp. 665-83; J. P. D. Dunbabin, 'Parliamentary Elections in Great Britain, 1868-1900: A Psephological Note', *English Historical Review,* 81 (1966), pp. 82-99; M. Dyer, *Capable Citizens and Improvident Democrats: The Scottish Electoral System, 1884-1929* (Aberdeen, 1996); H. J. Hanham, *Elections and Party Management: Politics in the Time of Disraeli and Gladstone* (2nd edition, Hassocks, 1978); K. T. Hoppen, 'The Franchise and Electoral Politics in England and Ireland, 1832 -1885', *History,* 70 (1985), pp. 202-17; M. Kinnear, *The British Voter: An Atlas and Survey since 1885* (2nd Edition, London, 1981).

[7] It is also deeply controversial in historiographical terms; A. B. Cooke & J. R. Vincent, *The Governing Passion: Cabinet Government and Party Politics in Britain, 1885-86* (Brighton, 1974); G. D. Goodlad, 'The Liberal Party and Gladstone's Land Purchase Bill of 1886', *Historical Journal,* 32 (1989), pp. 627-41; G. D. Goodlad, 'Gladstone and his rivals: popular perceptions of the party leadership in the political crisis of 1885-86', in E. F. Biagini and A. J. Reid (eds), *Currents of Radicalism: Popular radicalism, organised labour and*

party politics in Britain, 1850-1914 (Cambridge, 1991), pp. 163-83; W. C. Lubenow, *Parliamentary Politics and the Home Rule Crisis: The British House of Commons in 1886* (Oxford, 1988); W. C. Lubenow, 'The Liberals and the National Question: Irish Home Rule, Nationalism, and their Relationship to Nineteenth Century Liberalism', *Parliamentary History,* 13 (1994), pp. 119-42; P. T. Marsh, 'Tearing the Bonds: Chamberlain's Separation from the Gladstonian Liberals, 1885-6', in B. L. Kinzer (ed), *The Gladstonian Turn of Mind: Essays Presented to J. B. Conacher* (Toronto, 1985), pp. 123-53; A. O'Day, *The English Face of Irish Nationalism: Parnellite Involvement in British Politics, 1880-1886* (Dublin, 1977); R. Quinalt, 'John Bright & Joseph Chamberlain', *Historical Journal,* 28 (1985), pp. 623-46.

[8] The latter approach has been taken by B. W. Rodden, 'Anatomy of the 1886 Schism in the British Liberal Party: A Study of the Ninety Four Liberal Members of Parliament who voted against the First Irish Home Rule Bill', unpublished PhD thesis, Rutgers University, 1968, this work does have the virtue of containing snapshots of all the Liberals who voted against the Home Rule Bill.

[9] See chapters three and four.

[10] See chapters five and six.

[11] This is discussed in chapters six and eight.

[12] Chapter seven.

[13] I am very conscious that my examination of Charles Fraser Mackintosh's historical work is overly brief and superficial; my own lack of expertise in the areas in which Fraser Mackintosh was interested was the principal limitation in this regard.

[14] J. Hunter, *The Making of the Crofting Community* (Edinburgh, 1976), p. 143; I. M. M. MacPhail, *The Crofters' War* (Stornoway, 1989), pp.9-10, 90-92; other studies have played down the role of groups of Highlanders in the cities, J. Mackenzie, 'The Highland community in Glasgow in the nineteenth century: a study of non assimilation', unpublished PhD thesis, University of Stirling, 1987, pp. 293-348; C. W. J. Withers, *Urban Highlanders: Highland-Lowland Migration and Urban Gaelic Culture, 1700-1900* (East Linton, 1998), pp. 191-3.

[15] More detail will be provided in chapter four.

[16] H. C. G. Matthew, *Gladstone, 1809-1874* (Oxford, 1986); Matthew, *Gladstone, 1875-1898.*

[17] There is much information on the making of the *Crofters' Holdings (Scotland) Act* in the Gladstone Papers in the British Library, see, Cameron, *Land for the People?,* pp. 16-39.

[18] I. G. C. Hutchison, 'Politics and Society in mid-Victorian Glasgow, 1846-1886', unpublished PhD thesis, University of Edinburgh, 1974, introduction.

[19] One exception is John Murdoch's diary, the original can be read in the

manuscripts' department of the Mitchell Library in Glasgow; some of it, with associated material, has been published, see J. Hunter (ed), *For the People's Cause: From the Writings of John Murdoch, Highland and Irish Land Reformer* (Edinburgh, 1986).

[20] NAS, Fraser Mackintosh Collection, GD128.

[21] NAS, Mackintosh Muniments, GD176.

[22] A Catalogue of this library was prepared for Fraser Mackintosh in 1885, copies of which can be found in the National Library of Scotland and Inverness Public Library, Reference Room; the latter location has a fuller card index of the contents of the library in 1921 when it came into the hands of the Inverness Public Library. *Catalogue of the Library at Lochardil, and London, belonging to Charles Fraser Mackintosh of Drummond, Inverness,* (London, 1885), [National Library of Scotland, T.6.f]. I was first alerted to the existence of this source by, H. Barron, 'Books belonging to a Highland Tacksman', *Scottish Gaelic Studies,* 12 (1971), pp. 56-58; see also J. MacNaughton, 'Burgh M.P. went on to champion the causes of the crofters in the Highlands', *Inverness Courier,* 19 Jan 1993.

[23] MacPhail, *Crofters' War,* pp.10-12; E. Barron, 'The Printed Word', in L. Maclean (ed), *The Hub of the Highlands: The Book of Inverness and District* (reprinted, Edinburgh, 1990), pp. 291-305; J. Noble, *Miscellanea Invernessiana: with a bibliography of Inverness newspapers and periodicals* (Stirling, 1902); E. M. Barron (ed), *A Highland Editor: Selected Writings of James Barron of the "Inverness Courier"* (Inverness, 1927), pp. 29-92; MLG, John Murdoch Autobiography, volume iv, pp. 77-99.

[24] For the attempted takeover of the *Highlander* by the Tories see NAS, Innes and Mackay Papers, GD296/156-8; for the role of the *Chronicle* in the 1885 elections see below, chapter six.

[25] There was no secret about the fact that Fraser Mackintosh was a Director of the Scottish Highlander Company, Ltd., see, 'Abridged Prospectus of the Scottish Highlander Company, Ltd.', *Scottish Highlander,* 25 Nov 1886.

[26] *Highland News,* 16 July 1892.

[27] For some background on the press and politics in this period see, Matthew, *Gladstone, 1875-1898,* pp. 43-9.

[28] A. Mackenzie, *History of the Frasers of Lovat* (Inverness, 1896), pp. 606-8; Barron, 'Highland Tacksman', p. 57; H. Barron, 'Notes on the Ness Valley', *TGSI,* 43 (1960-63), pp. 152-170; J. N. MacLeod, 'Charles Fraser Mackintosh M.P. - A True Friend of the Highlands', *Northern Chronicle,* 5 Aug 1953.

[29] Edinburgh University Library, Matriculation Roll of the University of Edinburgh, iv, 1830-58, pp. 1271, 1286, 1303, 1318; Inverness Public Library, Charles Fraser Mackintosh Collection, Lectures by John Schank More on the law of Scotland, in the session of 1849/50, as taken down by Charles Fraser, FM 3260; Lectures on conveyancing, 1851, MS Lecture notes, taken down at

Edinburgh University by Charles Fraser, FM 3528; Civil Law Class, 1852-53, MS of five essays written by Charles Fraser at Edinburgh University, FM 3261; Rhetoric Class, 1851-52, Charles Fraser's work-book at the University of Edinburgh, FM 3262.

[30] K. D. Macdonald, 'Life of the Author', in Charles Fraser Mackintosh, *Antiquarian Notes: A series of papers regarding families, and places in the Highlands* (2nd edition, Stirling, 1913), pp. xiii-xiv.

[31] Mackenzie, *Frasers of Lovat,* p. 605.

Chapter One

Charles Fraser Mackintosh and Local Politics, 1857-1867

Introduction
The rather general remarks which have been made by historians about Fraser Mackintosh's political career have not included any assessment of his involvement in local politics in Inverness in the 1850s and 1860s.[1] The implication is that he appeared on the political scene in 1874, when he was first elected to parliament for the Inverness group of burghs, or even in the early 1880s, with the successful campaign to have a Royal Commission of Enquiry into crofting conditions established. Fraser Mackintosh's early career is of interest not only for the light it casts on the way local politics were conducted in a Scottish burgh, but also for the clues it gives to controversies which arose in Fraser Mackintosh's subsequent career. For example, at the General Election of 1885 when Fraser Mackintosh changed his party label - from "Liberal" to "Crofter"- and forsook the Burgh seat for the wide expanses of Inverness-shire, he was accused by his opponents of political inconsistency and opportunism and of having been a Tory in his earlier career. It is only by an examination of the early years of his political life that these later debates can be understood.

This chapter will look at three phases of Fraser Mackintosh's involvement in the public affairs of the town of Inverness in the 1850s and 1860s. The first is his involvement in the parliamentary elections of 1857 and 1859, when he acted as agent for the Liberal Candidate, Alexander Campbell of Monzie, who challenged the sitting member, Alexander Matheson of Ardross. The second is Fraser Mackintosh's election, in the autumn of 1857, to Inverness Town Council. Local politics were not divided along party political lines but Fraser Mackintosh's candidature and his subsequent activity on the Council did have a definite political objective which will be explored below. Thirdly, the chapter will examine his involvement in the building of Union Street in the early 1860s. Along with two other local solicitors, Donald Davidson and Hugh Rose, and a Civil Engineer, George G. Mackay,

Fraser Mackintosh purchased an area of undeveloped land between Academy Street and Church Street and turned it into a prominent public thoroughfare which soon became a source of civic pride, and of considerable profit for the men who had projected the construction of the street. Also in this period Fraser Mackintosh purchased two properties, Ballifeary and Drummond, on the fringes of the town and cashed in by selling off feus upon which large villas were built.

The General Elections of 1857 and 1859 in the Inverness Burghs
Alexander Matheson of Ardross was the sitting MP for the Inverness Group of Burghs (which also included Nairn, Forres and Fortrose), the seat he had held since 1847.[2] He was generally thought to be a Whig, but his inactivity as an MP made it difficult for his precise political identity to be established. In addition, this was a confused period in party politics as the coalition of interests which would eventually emerge as the Liberal Party in the 1860s was still coming together. Matheson was the nephew of Sir James Matheson, the fabulously wealthy proprietor of Lewis and MP for Ross-shire, and he, like his uncle, had made a substantial fortune from his involvement in the trading activities of Jardine Matheson.[3] Among these trading activities was involvement in the opium trade, this was often held up against Sir James Matheson: Disraeli had famously described him as '. . . a dreadful man! richer than Croesus, one McDruggy, fresh from Canton with a million of Opium in each pocket, denouncing corruption, and bellowing free trade': it was free trade rather than opium which the waspish Disraeli objected to.[4] Accusations concerning the opium trade would also be a factor in Alexander Matheson's political career; at the General Election of 1859, for example, he had to deny current involvement in the opium trade and the *Inverness Advertiser* commented:

> . . . had Mr Matheson been still deriving profit from the trade he would have laid himself open to a most serious objection to being sent up to parliament as a legislator on questions relating to the welfare of India. Even as it is, his fitness to give an impartial vote on such questions must be a matter of grave doubt.[5]

Matheson was scarcely reticent about his involvement in the opium trade as the gateposts at Ardross were adorned with representation of poppies![6]

Matheson spent huge sums of money on purchasing over 200,000 acres of land in Ross-shire and Inverness-shire and even greater sums of money on building and laying out grounds at Duncraig Castle, near Plockton, and at Ardross Castle in Easter Ross. His other enthusiasm was railways: he was prominent in projecting the Dingwall and Skye Railway and was Chairman of the Highland Railway Company.[7] It was felt by some that his seat in parliament was primarily for the purpose of promoting railway schemes.

At the General Election of 1857 Alexander Campbell of Monzie came forward to challenge Matheson, and Charles Fraser, as he then was, acted as his agent. This was the first challenge Matheson had faced since commencing the representation of Inverness in 1847. Campbell of Monzie had begun his political career as a Conservative; however, he was a strong Free Churchman, having left the Conservative party over their treatment of the Church of Scotland in the years which culminated in the Disruption of 1843. He had been MP for Argyll between 1841 and his resignation in September 1843. He went on to stand as a Liberal-Conservative against T.B Macaulay in Edinburgh in 1852; unfortunately, on that occasion he came bottom of the poll.[8] Campbell was a dedicated field sportsman and had married into the Highland landowning class in 1844 in the shape of the daughter and heiress of Sir Duncan Cameron of Fassifern.[9] His political identity in Inverness in 1857 was unclear. The *Inverness Courier*, a supporter of Matheson, commented:

> the struggle was personal not political - both candidates were Palmerstonians. A certain portion of the sectarian feeling mingled with the contest, one of the candidates being a member of the Established Church and the other a member of the Free Church.[10]

The result of the election was a majority of only 47 for Matheson, out of a poll of 717, and the *Courier* reflected that the result 'should operate as a stimulant to the sitting member':

> We should hint to the sitting member that he must mingle more familiarly with his constituents and visit them oftener. No one denies his solid and valuable qualities, but he must add to them the recommendation of a liberal personal intercourse.[11]

The *Inverness Advertiser*, which supported Campbell, was much more aggressive in its criticism of Matheson. It was noted that Matheson's vulnerability had been exposed by a candidate who was scarcely known to the electors when he came forward for the contest. The reason for this, it was argued, was that Matheson had:

> so grossly abused the confidence of the electors by his repeated - we fear we must say systematic - absences from Parliament, that people who were not tied to him by the bonds of self interest thought his exclusion from public life was a just and necessary punishment.[12]

At this election Fraser Mackintosh admitted that he was a Conservative, but he may well have been absorbing political lessons which he would put into practice in 1874, when he came forward as a parliamentary candidate himself. He cannot have failed to notice the opportunity which was available to a candidate promising a more active representation of the Burghs against a sitting member who was perceived as indolent and merely self-interested.[13] It was in the aftermath of this election that Fraser Mackintosh put himself forward as a candidate for the Town Council and he carried his antipathy to Matheson into the Council Chamber, as will be explored below.

The 1859 election was not such a closely fought contest but many of the same criticisms of Matheson were heard. The *Advertiser's* opening remarks on the campaign are instructive as to their view of Matheson: 'Mr Matheson has again chosen to breast the flood-tide of popular indignation which at the last election had well nigh overwhelmed him'.[14] Campbell of Monzie opposed him once again and Fraser Mackintosh acted as his agent.[15] The *Courier* complained of attempts to 'arouse sectarian prejudices . . . personal animosities and to excite popular violence'.[16] Remarking on Matheson's strengthened majority of 103, it was felt that it was due to his 'successful exertions in promoting railway communication in the North'.[17] Some insight into his career is provided by Joseph Mitchell, the railway engineer who had encountered him on railway business. Despite this close association he damned him with faint praise:

> Mr Matheson had an unhappy shyness and coldness of manner. Of course he possessed much intelligence and shrewdness . . . to the general public his manner was uncongenial, and his want of facility in public speaking was much against him, and it has only been by the great services he has rendered to the country that a more favourable public appreciation of his good qualities and patriotism has been established.[18]

At the end of his career as MP for Inverness Burghs the *Advertiser* softened its line, arguing that his attention to his parliamentary business had been greater and:

> of late years the enormous benefits he has conferred upon the town by encouragement to railways, by buildings, by opening up new roads, and in other ways, have in the opinion of most people thrown any demerits of his completely into the shade.[19]

It is noticeable that very few substantive issues were debated at these elections and the political identities of the candidates were unclear. The contest was essentially over Matheson's value as a MP; with one side declaring that 'he has proved himself incompetent to the last degree' and the other congratulating the constituency on 'securing the services of a representative of sense, experience, character and influence'.[20] It is also noticeable that any distinctive political culture which did exist in Inverness at this time was not in evidence at the Parliamentary level. More colour was evident, however, at the level of Town Council politics. It was to this arena that Fraser Mackintosh devoted his political energies in the years from 1857 to 1862.

Town Council Politics, 1857-1863

One of the themes of the parliamentary elections of 1857 and 1859 was the way in which Matheson's influence stretched into the Town Council in the shape of his agent, George Macpherson, who was a prominent councillor. The defeat of Matheson at a parliamentary level, it was felt by some, would also end the malign influence of Macpherson in the Town Council. Macpherson's opponents felt that he controlled a self serving clique on the Council, they supported each other in electing the Bailies and made strenuous attempts to keep Councillors from outwith the clique outside the Magistracy.[21] A rather unexpected retirement in the Third Ward (which was west of the River Ness) created an opening for Charles Fraser Mackintosh. He was elected in second place with 103 votes, George France headed the poll with 104 votes.[22] This was a surprisingly good performance for a candidate at his first attempt: Fraser Mackintosh was cashing in on the prominence he had achieved during the recent parliamentary election. The new Council now had a recognisable 'popular party' and both Fraser Mackintosh and George France would be prominent members of it over the next five years.

Trouble started almost as soon as the new council was elected; initially debate focused on the election of the Magistrates. The Provost, Colin Lyon-Mackenzie, proposed that the Magistrates be elected as a party group. George G. Mackay, Fraser Mackintosh's future partner in the Union Street scheme, was at the forefront of the opposition to this scheme; he declared:

> I am sorry to find here a party - a close bigoted, sectarian, domineering party, whose councils are not held openly at this board, but are secretly held behind certain scenes which shall be nameless, and whose conclusions are brought up here for ratification by the votes of the unconsulted but sworn attachees of the party.[23]

Fraser Mackintosh seconded this motion, but it was defeated by 12 votes to seven. This unaccustomed activity on the normally rather staid Council caused the *Advertiser* to remark that: 'the minority has been kicking up its heels most unmistakably, striking right and left in a very wild fashion'.[24] There was more to come, however. At the next meeting of the Council some of the antipathies of the recent parliamentary election campaign became evident. Fraser Mackintosh attempted to introduce a motion which would have resulted in both the exclusion of Matheson's agent, George Macpherson, from the Council and the prohibition of Council employees from participating in municipal elections. He made it clear that his real target was Macpherson and that his objections to him related to his use of municipal politics to bolster the position of the MP. Fraser Mackintosh remarked:

> His theory of Parliamentary representation was that the member was the free choice of the constituency. The candidate came down, canvassed the electors and polled the electors. When the contest was over, he should stop all proceedings and influences that had been at work; there was nothing more to be done by him, nothing more he had a right to do than attend to the register. But when a member finds himself weak with the constituency he is obliged, or his agent for him, to enter upon another course of action to keep him right in his seat. He must be ever on the watch to strengthen himself. He must watch the municipal elections, secure a majority in the Town Council, and have the making of magistrates. He said that this had been done in Inverness, and that there had been in Inverness interference with the free choice of the people.[25]

Those who spoke against Fraser Mackintosh accused him of being a Tory, an accusation which would trouble him throughout his political career. His agency for Campbell of Monzie was also problematic in this regard, as Monzie had been a Tory MP earlier in his career. Indeed, Fraser Mackintosh's position, as the agent for the defeated candidate, was not a particularly strong one from which to complain about the presence of agents in the Town Council as it smacked of sour grapes. His opponents in the Council also attempted to argue that the Council should remain non-political: the Provost remarked that

> it had always been understood and acted out that parties returned to the Council were fit to sit at that Board and that when there, threw politics overboard and joined to see what they could do in improving the town and managing its funds.[26]

The *Courier*, which had supported Matheson at the parliamentary election, was strong in its condemnation of Fraser Mackintosh's motion, labelling it 'absurd and reprehensible' and 'repugnant to law, common sense, and justice.' Macpherson was described as 'a warm hearted obliging man, and an active, successful law agent.'[27]

There is no doubt that local politics in Inverness quickened after the controversies of the 1857 election campaign. There was now a group of Councillors, including Fraser Mackintosh and George G. Mackay, who seemed determined to act as a 'popular party' in the Council Chamber; one commentator even called them 'reformers'.[28] An indication of the resentment which Fraser Mackintosh, in particular, stirred up, can be seen by an attempt to have his election to the Council declared void because he was entered on the voters' roll as Charles Fraser, but had been elected as Charles Fraser Mackintosh![29] The new Councillor continued in assertive vein throughout 1858, pressing, for example, for a new valuation of the town's property because he felt 'they were getting deeper and deeper into debt' and no valuation had been carried out since 1842. Later in the year the theme of financial mismanagement was continued as a motion of no confidence in the Provost and his party was attempted.[30] At the election of 1859 Fraser Mackintosh topped the poll in the third ward with 122 votes.[31] In the new Council the 'popular party' turned their attention to Councillor John Cook who was accused, not only of being a member of the 'clique' but also that as a publican he had breached the Forbes Mackenzie Act.[32] Indeed, he had been questioned by a Royal Commission on this matter.[33] It was not possible for such a small group of Councillors to sustain controversies and by 1860 and 1861 Town Council politics had returned to their customary soporific state. The 'popular party' attempted to revive things at the election of 1861: Fraser Mackintosh and James Simpson, his fellow candidate in the third ward, issued a joint address to the electors. At this election Fraser Mackintosh came within six votes of the Provost, Colin Lyon-Mackenzie. Almost immediately Fraser Mackintosh opposed the re-election of Lyon-Mackenzie as Provost, but to no avail.[34]

Fraser Mackintosh's career on the Town Council came to an end in May 1862 with his sudden resignation. This came as a surprise even to his colleagues in the 'popular party', to whom he apologised for his failure to inform them of his action. He gave as the reasons for his resignation 'the gradual increase in his private business' which he said made it 'necessary for him to abstain entirely from public affairs'. He went on to refer to some of the controversies which he had engendered during his time on the Council:

> Many exciting discussions had taken place during the five years he had been in the Council, and it was probable he might have given offence to members. If he had done this, and, in particular, if he had gone beyond legitimate parliamentary bounds with reference to the Provost, he would now express his regret, and tender his hearty apology.[35]

His biographer, K. D. Macdonald, who was his agent when he was a Liberal Unionist M.P from 1886 to 1892, put a positive spin on this speech:

> This little scene in the Town Council is typical of Mr Fraser Mackintosh's whole public life. He could, and did when the occasion demanded, as it frequently did during the Whig dominance in Inverness, hit hard, but he sought no personal quarrel with his opponent, and nothing was further from his wish than to leave a rankling wound. When the public controversy was over he was willing, nay anxious, to shake hands.[36]

Whilst it is likely that the 'increase in his private business' to which he referred was the early stages of the Union Street project, the resignation statement as a whole gives some insight into themes which would become more evident as Fraser Mackintosh's political career developed. The most important of these is his rather ambivalent position regarding the 'establishment', in this case the Town Council. Throughout his career Fraser Mackintosh often laid great emphasis on his status as an 'outsider' or as 'independent' (see his label as an Independent Liberal at the 1874 election, for example) but was equally careful not to place himself entirely outside the bounds of 'respectability'. He was keen that his independence should be recognised but he was equally keen to avoid being thought of as a anti-establishment figure or as a rebel. Further, political opportunism was another charge frequently laid at his door. This, it could be argued, was relevant here as well. Did he use the Town Council as a device to try and weaken Matheson's position in the parliamentary constituency? Perhaps he was as guilty of manipulating the business of the Council to further the interests of the candidate for whom he acted as agent as Macpherson was, certainly some other councillors thought so. It is noticeable that his activity on the Council tailed off after the election of 1859 when Campbell of Monzie was defeated for a second time. It was certainly evident that he used the Council as a vehicle to elevate his own prominence in the town. The information and experience he gained while a Councillor, especially through his work on the Improvements Committee, stood him in good stead for the next important element of his activities in Inverness in this period. Indeed, he may have been keen to mollify the 'establishment' on the Council as he required their backing for his next project.

'Modern Inverness dates from the 1860s':[37] The construction of Union Street, 1863-65

The 1860s were an important decade in the history of Inverness, seeing important developments both in railway communications and in the built environment of the town.[38] The line from Perth reached Inverness via Forres and Nairn in 1863 and this new element in the development of the town was symbolised by improvements to the Railway Station in 1863 and 1864.[39] This was an important event not only in the development of the town but also of the Highlands more generally, as the *Courier* noted:

> Beyond Inverness and on the shores of the Moray Firth there is a large populous and fertile country, to which speedy connection with the South is a matter of the utmost importance.[40]

The *Advertiser* also recognised the importance of these changes, commenting more specifically on the people and trade which the railway brought to the town.[41] Thus, in the early 1860s Inverness began to think of itself in rather more grand terms than in previous decades. The traffic brought by the railway extended the reputation of the town more widely than ever before and prominent citizens realised that the adornment and improvement of the town could go hand in hand with personal profit.

In early 1863 it became known that Fraser Mackintosh, in association with Donald Davidson, George G. Mackay and Hugh Rose purchased, for £6000, an area of land opposite the railway station and stretching west to Church Street. Further land was purchased from the Inverness Incorporated Trades for over £3000; the intention of the buyers was to build a prestigious street, a project which, it was estimated, would cost over £40,000. The buildings on the land which had been purchased yielded a rent of only a little more than £600 and were valued at around £400.[42] Such a street would open a thoroughfare from the Railway Station to the Caledonian Hotel on Church Street.[43] The local press, caught up in the notion of the greater prestige of the town, went into paroxysms of delight when Fraser Mackintosh and his colleagues presented their plans for the new Street. The respectability of the street was established by the fact that no licensed establishments were to be permitted; the *Advertiser* commented that Union Street was 'designed to initiate one of the greatest improvements Inverness has seen during the present century'. The *Courier*, warming to Fraser Mackintosh compared to their coverage of his Council career, commented on the plans which he and his colleagues had presented:

> The steps they have hitherto taken promise that the scheme will be judiciously prosecuted and on a scale of great liberality. They contemplate one of the greatest improvements ever made in the town, and we heartily wish them success.[44]

The street would be mostly taken up with business premises with apartments on the upper levels and on the north side of the street, on the corner with Church Street, the Bank of Scotland purchased a site for a new branch.[45] Spirituality and entertainment were also to be catered for on Union Street with the construction of a new Church for the United Presbyterian congregation and the erection of a new public hall. The latter would require £7,000 of capital to be raised in shares of £10 each.[46]

The promoters of the scheme were conscious that the Town of Inverness would profit greatly from their entrepeneurship and in mid-1863 they approached the Town Council for assistance. They pointed out that the valuation of the property in the town would be much increased by the Union Street project and they noted that: 'There can, of course, be no more legitimate application of the public funds than for a great public improvement'. Discussion of the matter was deferred and responsibility was passed over to the Improvement Committee, but the Dean of Guild did remark that any contribution would be dependant on the opening of an entrance to the Council's covered market, which lay immediately to the north of the new street. George Mackay said provision had been made for this.[47]

The newspaper reports from 1863 and early 1864 record rapid progress being made on the construction of Union Street, so rapid, in fact, that a partial opening of the street was made in early February 1864.[48] The construction of the street was not without its problems, however. The early months of 1864 were plagued by strikes of the stonemasons and joiners working on the street. The initial cause of the stonemasons' strike, which began in late February, was a controversy over a number of 'non-unionists' in the employ of Arnott and Fraser, the contractors who had won the contract to build the public hall on Union Street. This was relatively quickly resolved, but disputes over pay proved to be more problematic. The Inverness Lodge of the United Operative Masons Association of Scotland demanded a wage rise of three shillings per week on the grounds of the increased costs of provisions. By mid-March there had been no resolution to the dispute, the employers offered an increase of 1s, but this was not sufficient to end the strike. An end to the problems came only with a deal which involved the employers advancing a 3s increase for six months, in return for a promise that there would be no further strikes.[49] No sooner was this dispute resolved than the joiners struck, over wages and the right to a half day holiday on Saturday. This dispute was resolved much more quickly with the granting of a 2s increase in wages but no concessions over shorter working hours.[50] There were further strikes towards the end of 1864 and the *Courier* noted that: 'The number and arbitrary nature of the "strikes" by workmen engaged in the erection of Union Street have been extremely embarrassing to the contractors'.[51]

This climate of industrial assertiveness among the tradesmen of Inverness was put down by some commentators to the very fact that there were so many improvements ongoing in Inverness in the mid-1860s. This condition left the tradesmen in a very strong position *vis-à-vis* their employers, especially when the latter were under so much pressure from promoters of schemes, such as Fraser Mackintosh and his colleagues, to finish the job so that they could begin to see a return on their investments.[52] Certainly, it was the case that there were a significant number of major projects under way in the town at this time.

Not to be outdone by his political opponents, Alexander Matheson of Ardross had bought a substantial area of land on the west side of the river and proceeded to lay out a number of streets, most notably Ardross Street, which ran from the west bank of the river to Glenurquhart Road. It was handed over to the Town Council in September 1864.[53] To these works can be added the improvements at the Railway Station and the Caledonian Hotel and improvements to the east bank of the river at Douglas Row, an area very prone to flooding. The latter improvement was carried out using materials which had been excavated in the course of the construction of Union Street.[54]

The final controversy relating to the Union Street project involved the Council's attitude to taking over the street once it was completed. In 1866 the proprietors were still responsible for the maintenance of the roadway. The Council was refusing to take it over until it was put into 'thorough working order' and also demanded that the proprietors give up the ground in perpetuity. George G. Mackay felt that this was gross ingratitude towards the promoters of the project, on the part of the Council and his feelings may have reflected that the efforts on behalf of the town expended by he and his colleagues had not received sufficient recognition.[55]

The scale of the Union Street project can crudely be gauged by comparing the valuation of the property before and after the street was constructed. Prior to the purchase by Fraser Mackintosh and his colleagues the property owned by Miss Ettles and the Incorporated Trades was valued at £450. After the construction of Union Street and Drummond Street (a short street extending from the North side of Union Street to Baron Taylors Street, which ran parallel to Union Street) the property was valued at £2700. Thus, Fraser Mackintosh and his colleagues became the proprietors of substantial amounts of property. Fraser Mackintosh alone was the proprietor of property worth over £580.[56]

The Purchase of Drummond Estate
The Union Street project was not Fraser Mackintosh's only foray into the property market in the early 1860s.[57] In October 1863, again in partnership with George G. Mackay, he purchased the 270 acre estate of

Drummond, previously worked as two farms, on the outskirts of the town. The estate was put up for auction in Edinburgh for £8,500 and Fraser Mackintosh's legal partner, Charles Innes, bid on his behalf against Alexander Matheson's solicitor. The Edinburgh correspondent of the *Advertiser* remarked that Innes 'was determined to have the place at any price'; eventually he secured the property for £13,450. Such determination was not only motivated by business considerations but also by political antipathy to Matheson, as Innes was a leading Conservative in Inverness.[58] The intention of Fraser Mackintosh and his partner was to sell feus for small acreages to individuals wishing to build houses on the land. Leaving aside the small number of workers cottages which were constructed, the bulk of the property, which stood on high ground overlooking the river and with outstanding views to the west, was soon covered in substantial villas for the wealthier classes in the town. The *Courier* remarked that Drummond:

> ... now wears the aspect of a suburb of the town. The villas built or building on every part of the estate quite enliven the scene, and the views of the surrounding scenery from the terraces and the various roads and walks are of the finest description.[59]

In 1865 Fraser Mackintosh purchased the forty acre estate of Wester Ballifeary, on the west side of the river Ness, also with the intention of feuing it for building purposes. Despite later criticisms that these projects operated largely for the benefit for the middle classes, they brought a large amount of work to the building trade in Inverness. Indeed, when the water works at Drummond were opened in March 1865 the *Courier* reported that there was a toast to Fraser Mackintosh and one of the labourers was alleged to have remarked that 'he has been a good friend to the working men of Inverness'.[60] This statement may or may not actually have been uttered, but it was the kind of thing which allowed Fraser Mackintosh, when he was standing for parliament in 1874, to present himself as the candidate most favourable to the working class.

Conclusions

Whilst there was much comment in the local press welcoming these improvements to the infrastructure and property of the town, a critical note was sounded on occasion. These criticisms referred to the consequences of the improvements, particularly those at Union Street, for the working classes of the town.

The *Advertiser* struck a more critical note on the development of the town in late 1864 when it pondered the wider significance of the recent changes. It was noted that the improvements at Union Street, Drummond Street, Ardross Street and on the Drummond estate just outside the town, served to show that 'the middle classes are quite alive to their own interests, and that there is no lack of funds when a fair investment can be carried out'. The article went on, however, to deplore the lack of housing for the working classes and to suggest that they should be more proactive. It was noted that the building works in the town had brought 'hundreds of workmen with their families' to the town but that 'we can scarcely point to the erection of a single additional dwelling house suitable for their accommodation'.[61] Indeed, it was probably the case that the developments at Union Street had *depleted* the stock of cheap rented accommodation. A number of cheap cottages had been cleared away before the building works had started and the apartments above the business premises on Union Street were certainly not within the spending power of the working classes.[62] Although some cheap cottages had been included in the recent developments, most notably by Matheson at Kenneth Street and Tomnhurich Street on the west side of the river, they were insufficient to cope with the demand. A more positive note was sounded early in 1865 when it was noted that on the Drummond estate, some workmen had taken lots with the intention of building cottages for themselves.[63] The *Advertiser* was worried about the consequences for the town:

> The consequence of this state of things has been most disastrous in every way - in raising rents and in overcrowding families, thus leading to uncleanliness, disease and that increased mortality in the town which we all have to deplore.[64]

It was advocated that the remedy for such a state of affairs was to build substantial numbers of cheap cottages for the working classes and an answer was found to those critics who argued that such a scheme would not pay, by pointing to the working class houses recently built in Edinburgh. The *Inverness Advertiser* was not the only voice in Scotland expressing such sentiments of course. The themes raised by this article, celebration of urban improvements alongside a palpable fear of the deleterious effects of the unchecked growth of the working class, were mid-nineteenth century shibboleths.[65]

The 1860s saw a number of attempts to deal with these problems; the permissive, although important, Lindsay Act of 1862 increased the potential powers of local government to deal with problems relating to sanitation and overcrowded housing. The City of Glasgow Improvements Act of 1866 gave a newly created City Improvement Trust the power to purchase and redevelop areas of the city centre which were deemed in need of improvement. This involved the purchase and redevelopment of 88 acres of the city centre and included the destruction of the homes of over 15,000 people. The initial objective was 'sanitary rather than philanthropic' and the ideal was for the private sector to provide the investment for the new buildings. This broke down in the aftermath of the depression caused by the failure of the City of Glasgow Bank in 1878, but provided a powerful incentive for the municipal authorities to begin their own provision of working class housing.[66] In Edinburgh similar forces were at work. The publisher William Chambers, Lord Provost of the City between 1865 and 1869; the city's Medical Officer of Health, Dr James Littlejohn; and the pamphleteer George Bell, combined to implement a City Improvement Act of 1867. The motivations of this group varied widely, from personal vanity on the part of Chambers, to Littlejohn and Bell's desire to improve the public health of the city. Several important streets were widened but the most 'spectacular result' was the creation of Chambers' Street. This was designed not only to improve east-west communications in the city, but also to improve the flow of air in the city, as contemporaries believed in the 'miasmic' theory of the spread of disease, which held that the stench from decomposing waste was an important progenitor of disease in the urban environment.[67] This theory has been proven to be mistaken, but the innovations stimulated by it, notably improved drainage and waste disposal, did much to improve public health in nineteenth century cities.[68] The improvements occasioned by this legislation in the major Scottish cities had a positive effect on mortality, mostly because of reduced population densities, but had the major drawback of being the engine of destruction of large numbers of working class dwellings which were not replaced in sufficient quantity or in equally convenient locations. The commonality between these two projects was fear, specifically fear of the disease, squalor and filth generated by overcrowded working class districts in the centre of major cities. A further factor, as evidenced by the vanity of people like Chambers, was the desire of the middle class to put their stamp on the urban environment.

Morris, in his study of the Chambers Street improvement scheme in Edinburgh, has suggested that:

> This was one street in one, albeit important city but the same complex set of processes was at work in other towns. There are many other streets in Scotland which can and should be 'read' in this way.[69]

How can Union Street be 'read'? Clearly, Inverness did not face the same social problems, either in nature or extent, as major cities like Glasgow and Edinburgh. The article in the *Advertiser* provides evidence that the classic mid-nineteenth century fear of the deleterious effects of the working class was present in even such a small provincial town as Inverness. This was ample demonstration of its greater integration into Scottish life, symbolised by the railway developments which were a source of such pride. In 1866, for example, the Rev David Sutherland of the Free East Church, chaired a public meeting on the question of sanitary reform and 'the elevation of the masses', where he remarked of the improvements promoted by Matheson on the west side of the river:

> The population which these improvements had displaced must have gone somewhere, and created an overcrowding incompatible with moral prosperity and physical and sanitary considerations. He thought the community should desiderate a complete scheme of sanitary reform, and not only the erection of handsome streets, but workmen's houses in suitable locations, combining an abundant supply of pure air, light and water.[70]

Some insight into the objectives of those who promoted Union Street can be gained from Mackay's letter to the press in January 1866 when he complained of the attitude of the Council towards the street. In the course of this letter he remarked:

> It is, perhaps, unnecessary to say that, before joining in the erection of Union Street, we satisfied ourselves that there was urgent need for a great thoroughfare in this locality, and that the investment of the money necessary would be remunerative. But, at the same time, we felt that a great advantage would thus be conferred on the town; and, as we were all born and brought up in Inverness, we were not without the ambition of doing something for the good of Clachnacuddin.[71]

The most important 'reading' of the Union Street project, it is suggested here, is the ambition of a group of middle class notables in the town recognising that the economic and social context of Inverness had changed irrevocably. Railway communication provided great opportunities to profit from the new situation if facilities for appropriate economic activity could be provided. The business premises and public buildings of Union Street provide evidence of their attempt to do just that.

The extent to which Fraser Mackintosh had been successful in building his reputation in the town and his personal fortune can be gauged from two related events in 1867. The first was the fact that he was able to retire from private and legal business, he spent most of 1867 and 1868 travelling on the continent. The second event was a public dinner in his honour, hosted by prominent figures such as Charles Waterston, the Manager of the Caledonian Bank and the purchaser of a feu on Drummond. As Macdonald remarked: 'This was a remarkable testimony of esteem to a man who was still under 40 years of age and who had only been about 14 years in business in the town.'[72] It is perhaps even greater testimony to Fraser Mackintosh's careful cultivation of his own reputation. As Waterston remarked at the dinner, Fraser Mackintosh and his colleagues were able to:

> seize the opportunity ... and then to form Union Street - an enterprise alike creditable to them as patriotic citizens desirous to improve and ornament the town, and as men of business, intent upon carrying out a profitable speculation.[73]

The *Courier,* certainly no friend of Fraser Mackintosh during his days on the Council, even went as far as to remark that the dinner was a fitting tribute to 'one who has made himself so much respected as a private gentleman and improver of the town'.[74]

Thus, in the ten years from 1857 to 1867, Fraser Mackintosh had cut his political teeth as the agent for a parliamentary candidate, served on the Town Council, and had been involved in sufficient property business in and around Inverness to allow him to retire at the age of thirty nine: an enviable state of affairs. Beneath this level of public success, however, we can detect some themes which would recur in his later political career. His careful attempts to manage his own reputation and try to appear as all things to all men were relatively successful in this period. Further, and equally important, was the vagueness about his political identity. He had been very careful not to let his activities as a member of the 'popular party', or his often inflammatory remarks in the Council chamber, dominate the perception of him by other leading Invernessians. He had acknowledged his Conservatism, had acted for a former Conservative MP, and had entered business with one of the leading Conservatives in the town, Charles Innes: it is, therefore, scarcely surprising that he was to some observers a less than convincing Liberal candidate in the 1870s and 1880s.

---

[1] One exception is K. D. Macdonald, 'Life of the Author', in Charles Fraser Mackintosh, *Antiquarian Notes: A series of papers regarding families, and places in the Highlands* (2nd edition, Stirling, 1913), pp. xiii-xxxi.

[2] For the background to the election see, Macdonald, 'Life of the Author', p.xiv-xv.

[3] M. Keswick (ed), *A Celebration of 150 Years of Jardine Matheson and Company: The Thistle and the Jade* (London, 1982), pp. 16-25.

[4] B. Disraeli, *Sybil; or, The Two Nations* (1845, reprinted Harmondsworth, 1980), p.74

[5] *Inverness Advertiser,* 26 Apr 1859.

[6] N. Newton, *The Life and Times of Inverness* (Edinburgh, 1996) p.121.

[7] A. Mackenzie, *History of the Mathesons with Genealogies of the Various Families* (2nd edition, Stirling and London, 1900), ed, A. MacBain.

[8] M. Stenton, ed, *Who's Who of British Members of Parliament, Volume I, 1832-85* (Sussex, 1976), p.63. I. G. C. Hutchison, *A Political History of Scotland, 1832-1924: Parties, Elections and Issues* (Edinburgh, 1986), pp. 17, 25, 64, 68-9, 84; G I. T .Machin, *Politics and the Churches in Great Britain, 1832 to 1868* (Oxford, 1977), pp. 136-42, 248; J. C. Williams, 'Edinburgh Politics, 1832 -1852', unpublished PhD thesis, University of Edinburgh, 1972, pp. 321-33.

[9] *Inverness Courier,* 14 Jan 1869.

[10] *Inverness Courier,* 2 Apr 1857.

[11] *Inverness Courier,* 2 Apr 1857.

[12] *Inverness Advertiser,* 10 Aug 1858.

[13] *Inverness Advertiser,* 31 Mar 1857; *Inverness Courier,* 2 Apr 1857.

[14] *Inverness Advertiser,* 12 Apr 1859.

[15] *Inverness Advertiser,* 15 Mar 1859, 3 May 1859.

[16] *Inverness Courier,* 28 Apr 1859.

[17] *Inverness Courier,* 5 May 1859.

[18] J. Mitchell, *Reminiscences of my Life in the Highlands, (1883) volume 1,* (reprinted, Newton Abbot, 1971), p. 276.

[19] *Inverness Advertiser,* 11 Jul 1868.

[20] *Inverness Advertiser,* 12 Apr 1859; *Inverness Courier,* 5 May 1859.

[21] Macdonald. 'Life of the Author', p. xiv.
[22] *Inverness Advertiser,* 10 Nov 1857.
[23] *Inverness Advertiser,* 10 Nov 1857.
[24] *Inverness Advertiser,* 17 Nov 1857.
[25] *Inverness Advertiser,* 29 Dec 1857, 5 Jan 1858.
[26] *Inverness Advertiser,* 5 Jan 1858.
[27] *Inverness Courier,* 7 Jan 1858.
[28] Macdonald, 'Life of the Author', p. xiv.
[29] *Inverness Advertiser,* 12 Jan 1858.
[30] *Inverness Advertiser,* 9 Nov, 16 Nov 1858.
[31] *Inverness Advertiser,* 1 Nov 1859.
[32] The Forbes Mackenzie Act had been passed in 1853 and was the first attempt to control the opening hours of licensed premises in Scotland; see, T. C. Smout, *A Century of the Scottish People, 1830-1950* (London, 1986), p. 137.
[33] *Inverness Advertiser,* 8 Nov 1859.
[34] *Inverness Advertiser,* 15 Feb, 18 Oct, 29 Oct, 8 Nov, 12 Nov 1861.
[35] *Inverness Courier,* 8 May 1862.
[36] Macdonald, 'Life of the Author', p. xvi.
[37] Macdonald, 'Life of the Author', p. xvii.
[38] A. Mackenzie, *Guide to Inverness, Historical, Descriptive and Pictorial* (Inverness, 1893), pp. 9-11.
[39] J. Thomas & D. Turnock, *A Regional History of the Railways of Great Britain, Volume XV, The North of Scotland* (Newton Abbot, 1989), pp. 232-5; E. F. Carter, *An Historical Geography of the Railways of the British Isles* (London, 1959), p. 329.
[40] *Inverness Courier,* 3 Sept 1863.
[41] *Inverness Advertiser,* 9 Dec 1864.
[42] NAS, VR42/5, Inverness Burgh Valuation Roll, 1859-60; *Inverness Courier,* 14 May 1863.
[43] *Inverness Courier,* 12 Feb, 5 Mar 1863; *Inverness Advertiser,* 6, 10 Feb 1863.
[44] *Inverness Advertiser,* 10 Feb, 7 Mar 1863; *Inverness Courier,* 5 Mar 1863.
[45] R. Saville, *Bank of Scotland: A History, 1695-1995* (Edinburgh, 1996), 'Appendix 8, 'Branches and Sub-Branches of the Bank of Scotland, 1774-1939', p.876, records the Union Street Branch opening in 1775.
[46] *Inverness Courier,* 14 May 1863; *Inverness Advertiser,* 17 Nov 1863, for details of the 'Prospectus of the Inverness Public Hall Ltd', giving the names of those on the Provisional Committee for the project.
[47] *Inverness Courier,* 4 Jun 1863.
[48] *Inverness Courier,* 25 Jun, 30 Jul, 27 Aug, 15 Oct, 10 Dec 1863, 28 Jan, 4 Feb 1864; *Inverness Advertiser,* 14, 31 Jul, 1 Dec 1863.
[49] *Inverness Courier,* 25 Feb, 10, 17 Mar 1864; *Inverness Advertiser,* 4, 8, 15 Mar 1864.

[50] *Inverness Courier,* 7, 14 Apr 1864; *Inverness Advertiser,* 5, 12 Apr 1864.
[51] *Inverness Courier,* 22 Dec 1864.
[52] *Inverness Advertiser,* 28 Apr 1865; *Inverness Courier,* 17 Mar 1864.
[53] *Inverness Courier,* 8 Sept 1864; *Inverness Advertiser,* 9 Sept 1864.
[54] *Inverness Courier,* 27 Oct 1864, 26 Jan 1865; *Inverness Advertiser,* 1 Dec 1863.
[55] *Inverness Courier,* 18 Jan 1866, Letter to the Editor from George G. Mackay.
[56] NAS, VR42/5, Inverness Burgh Valuation Roll, 1859-60; VR42/1 Inverness Burgh Valuation Roll, 1864-65, ff.30-33; VR42/12, Inverness Burgh Valuation Roll, 1866-67, f.35.
[57] Macdonald, 'Life of the Author', p. xvii.
[58] *Inverness Advertiser,* 16, 20 Oct 1863. Innes's antipathy to the Mathesons can be seen in his defence of the Bernera rioters in 1874. The partnership with Mackay lasted until March 1864 when Fraser Mackintosh became the sole proprietor; see *Inverness Courier,* 10 Mar 1864.
[59] *Inverness Courier,* 26 Jan 1865.
[60] *Inverness Courier,* 9 Mar 1865.
[61] *Inverness Advertiser,* 9 Dec 1864.
[62] *Inverness Advertiser,* 26 Jan 1864; NAS, VR42/11, Inverness Burgh Valuation Roll, 1865-66, ff.30-33.
[63] *Inverness Advertiser,* 3 Mar 1865.
[64] *Inverness Advertiser,* 9 Dec 1864.
[65] R. J. Morris, 'Urbanisation and Scotland', in W. H. Fraser & R. J. Morris (eds), *People and Society in Scotland, Volume II, 1830-1914* (Edinburgh, 1990), pp. 73-102;. Smout, *A Century of the Scottish People,* pp. 32-57.
[66] C. M. Allan, 'The genesis of British urban redevelopment with special reference to Glasgow', *Economic History Review,* 18 (1965), pp.598-613, esp 604.
[67] R. J. Morris, 'Death, Chambers Street and Edinburgh Corporation', *History Teaching Review Year Book,* 6 (1992), pp. 10-15.
[68] A. S. Wohl, *Endangered Lives: Public Health in Victorian Britain* (London, 1984), pp. 87-8.
[69] Morris, 'Chambers Street', p. 14
[70] *Inverness Courier,* 20 Mar 1866.
[71] *Inverness Courier,* 18 Jan 1866.
[72] Macdonald, 'Life of the Author', p. xviii.
[73] *Inverness Courier,* 9 May 1867.
[74] *Inverness Courier,* 9 May 1867.

Chapter Two

Charles Fraser Mackintosh and Parliamentary Politics, 1865-1874

Introduction
This period would see substantial developments in Fraser Mackintosh's career. He was involved in parliamentary contests in the burgh seat, culminating in his own election as member for the group of burghs in 1874; but discussion must begin with the election contest in Inverness-shire in 1865. Fraser Mackintosh was only tangentially involved in this election, as a supporter of the Conservative candidate, but it is worthy of examination for two reasons. Firstly, it can be used to gauge the changes in the political company kept by Fraser Mackintosh at various stages in his career. In 1865 we find Angus Mackintosh of Holme, his Tory opponent in 1874, and Charles Innes, his chief tormentor in 1885, alongside Fraser Mackintosh in support of Henry Baillie. It was this kind of activity which gave substance to those who accused him of being a political opportunist when he appeared before the electorate as an Independent Liberal in 1874, and as a Crofter candidate in 1885. Secondly, a brief examination of political conditions, the make-up and geographical distribution of the electorate and the issues which were debated in 1865, demonstrate the extent of the changes which were wrought in the political culture of the Highlands by the Reform Act of 1885.

The General Election of 1865 in Inverness-shire
The 1865 contest was interesting as there had not been a contested election in the county since 1837, and the seat had been represented by a Conservative since 1835. Indeed, Inverness was one of the few Scottish county seats which had a tradition of returning a Conservative member. The sitting MP, and local landowner, Henry J. Baillie, had represented the County since 1840 and had been returned unopposed on six occasions since then. He had been associated with Disraeli in his younger days; indeed, he had almost been Disraeli's second in a duel with Morgan O'Connell, son of Daniel. He was an 'intermittent supporter' of

Young England, and had held minor office in the 1850s.[1] The Liberal candidate who came forward to face Baillie was another landowner, Sir George Macpherson Grant of Ballindalloch. His election address was rather bland, limiting itself to vague generalities about the record of Palmerston's government, the desirability of extending the franchise and the positive benefits of free trade.[2] Since there had not been a contest for so long it was not at all clear to the supporters of either candidate what the political conditions in the County were like. In 1837 there were 753 electors, of whom 552 polled; by 1865 the electoral roll had increased to 878.[3] There had also been substantial changes in landownership and while this was not such an important consideration as it had been prior to 1832, it was still relevant to the nature of politics in Inverness-shire. The *Courier,* which was still a broadly Liberal paper, reflected at length on these changes in the run up to the election. Putting the best possible construction on the changes in landownership, it was noted that prominent Liberals like Sir Edward Ellice, the MP for the St Andrews Group of Burghs; Campbell of Monzie, the 1857 and 1859 candidate for the Inverness Burghs; and Captain William Fraser had purchased or inherited large estates. It was also felt that the Chisolm and Macdonald family interests 'will be with the new candidate'.[4] This information was all only partly relevant and chose to avoid the fact that there were still very large portions of the County which were in the hands of Conservative proprietors, most notably the Lovat and Mackintosh estates. Furthermore, these estates were concentrated in the wealthier eastern and central portions where most of the electors were concentrated. There were only eight electors in Kilmuir, north Skye, where Fraser's estate was located for example. Of the 878 electors on the roll, there were only 187, or 21.3 per cent, in the coastal and insular districts.[5] This would have important repercussions, not only for Macpherson Grant's campaign in 1865, but also for Fraser Mackintosh in 1885, when the electorate in the under-represented west was so massively expanded. The nature of the constituency was fundamentally altered from a Conservative seat dominated by the interests of the east of the County, to a very promising seat for a Crofter candidate as the expansion of the crofter electorate had made their interests predominant.

In 1865, however, Fraser Mackintosh had a long political road to travel before he would appear before the electors as a Crofter candidate. At the election of 1865 we find him on the 'Committee for Promoting the Election of Mr Baillie' and present in support of Baillie at the nomination. Interestingly, in the light of antipathies which would emerge in 1885, we also find Charles Innes present at the nomination on the same side.[6]

In the wider Scottish context the 1865 election in rural seats was dominated by two issues: hypothec and the operation of the game laws. Tenant farmer disaffection over these two issues contributed to significant Tory losses in rural Scotland at the General Elections of 1865 and 1868. Hypothec gave landlords the power to sell the assets of a tenant in any attempt to recover unpaid rents. The game laws prevented farmers from protecting their crops against the depredations of hares and rabbits, as landowners increasingly sought to profit from commercialised sporting activities.[7] This served to drive a wedge between landowners and tenant farmers, and may have contributed to the high Liberal vote in Inverness-shire in 1865, despite the dominance of Conservative landowners in the east of the County. In other parts of the country tenant farmers came forward as candidates, against their own landlords as in the case of the contest between George Hope of Fenton Barns and Lord Elcho in East Lothian in 1865. In the north east of Scotland cattle disease added to the grievances of the tenant farmers and produced political action in the shape of the victory of the famous cattle breeder William McCombie at the General Election of 1868 in West Aberdeenshire.[8] Some of these grievances were evident in Inverness-shire as well. The *Inverness Advertiser*, slightly less Whiggish in its Liberalism than the *Courier*, declared in June 1865:

> No County in Scotland perhaps draws more revenue from game than our own; and a clear distinction must be drawn between the fostering of game in pastoral districts and its maintenance on arable holdings. It may be a question whether or not it is prudent to displace sheep and cattle by deer and grouse; but that is a point which may be left to our landlords, and to the sportsmen who visit the north, and who circulate much money in it.[9]

Baillie tried hard to respond to the demands of the tenant farmers in the county, as he had to if he was to stand any prospect of being elected; he was in favour of giving farmers the right to kill hares and rabbits and generally disposed towards 'such measures as are calculated to beneficially increase the farming interests'.[10] In the event his efforts were sufficient, the result of the election being a victory for the Conservatives by 336 votes to 297, with the poll of 633 being the greatest ever recorded in the County.[11] After Baillie's death it was said that he had gained much support in the Long Island as he had chartered a steamer to take voters to Broadford for polling. Given the small number of voters in the Long Island this would seem to have been a very expensive way of gaining votes, but given the small majority it may have been a significant factor. Baillie was a strong opponent of the extension of the franchise and the writer of his obituary speculated that his retiral in 1868 may have been because 'he did not care to go back to the House of Commons after the 1868 Reform Act!'[12] The fact that the Liberals came within 40 votes of unseating Baillie gave them great heart and, although they struggled to find a candidate to stand again in the County until Kenneth Mackenzie of Gairloch stood against Donald Cameron of Lochiel in 1880, they felt that they had a good chance of taking the seat if a suitable candidate could be found.

The 1868 General Election in the Inverness Burghs
In 1868 the sitting member for Ross-shire, Sir James Matheson, retired suddenly and his nephew, Alexander Matheson, replaced him as member for that county. This left a vacancy for the Inverness Burghs seat (which encompassed the Burghs of Inverness, Fortrose, Nairn and Forres), a vacancy which was filled by the unopposed return of Aneas Mackintosh of Raigmore. Fraser Mackintosh was taken by surprise by the speed of these events and his campaign to contest the seat was still-born.[13] It is the purpose of this section to reflect on these events for what they can tell us about Fraser Mackintosh's later political behaviour, most obviously in 1874 when he did get his act together in time to stand for the Burghs at the General Election.

After the initial events of Sir James Matheson's retirement from Ross-shire and it becoming clear, in early July 1868, that his nephew Sir Alexander Matheson would succeed him as candidate, and, most likely, member, in Ross-shire, there was some doubt as to what would happen in the Inverness Burghs.[14] The local press, elements of which were quite critical of Matheson and had promoted the candidacy of Monzie in the late 1850s, credited him with making a clean break with the constituency and avoiding the temptation of fixing up the seat for a successor.[15] It would seem that Aneas W. Mackintosh of Raigmore came forward of his own volition as the Liberal candidate. Mackintosh was a well known figure in the locality: he had been educated privately and at Oxford and had been called to the Scottish Bar in 1849. Three years earlier he had succeeded to his father's estates and the income from this source meant that he did not have to practise law. He was an associate of Matheson in railway enterprises, beginning with the initial line from Inverness to Nairn and then later in the *Highland Railway Company*, eventually becoming its chairman in 1890. He was also, like Fraser Mackintosh, a considerable owner of property in Inverness. In particular he was involved in the laying out of Queensgate, north of Union Street and running parallel to it.[16]

The context of politics in urban Scotland was greatly changed in 1868 compared to previous elections. The burgh electorate had been greatly expanded by the Reform Act of 1868. In Inverness this meant that the electoral roll was increased from 1,022 in 1865 to 1,995 in 1868.[17] This increase was not solely due to changes in the franchise, but also to the growing wealth and population of the town of Inverness. The major national issues of the 1868 election were the prospect of the Disestablishment of the Church of Ireland, and the Game Laws. Raigmore declared himself to be in favour of the Disestablishment of the Church of Ireland; he had nothing to say, however, about the game laws.[18] The *Inverness Advertiser*, the more advanced of the Liberal papers in the town, criticised him for this stand, remarking that the game laws were:

> a subject which cannot be overlooked by the electors of the Inverness Burghs, who must do their best to rectify the grievance of their neighbours all round about, if unhappily the latter are not able to help themselves.[19]

This was slightly disingenuous, there was another side to Raigmore's silence on this important issue. This relates to the growing trade in Inverness connected to the growth of commercialised sport, Raigmore may have been reticent on the issue in an attempt to avoid alienating electors who had an economic interest in the sporting industry. Indeed, in 1874 Fraser Mackintosh was very clear on this point drawing attention to the contribution of the sporting industry to the town and being very careful indeed as to his statements on the game laws.

The rapidity with which Raigmore announced his candidacy casts some doubt on the notion that that he was not acting in league with his predecessor, or at least with some prior knowledge of his actions. Nevertheless, this speed of movement meant that it was very difficult for other candidates to come forward to claim the Liberal label. The reforms of 1868 had confirmed the Inverness Burghs as a Liberal stronghold. The *Courier* mentioned two other possible candidates, Joseph Mitchell, the railway engineer, and Charles Fraser Mackintosh, and remarked that 'it was all but certain that Raigmore will not be allowed to keep possession of the field intact'.[20] Indeed, it seemed that Fraser Mackintosh was the more likely threat to Raigmore, as by mid July a requisition was compiled encouraging Fraser Mackintosh to come forward as a candidate. At this juncture, the *Courier* thoroughly approved of him as someone who had a made great practical contribution to the town, and concluded that he was 'an estimable citizen of Inverness'.[21] This uncontroversial statement aside, there was, as ever, doubt about the political identity of the potential candidate. The *Advertiser* remarked:

> Respecting his political views, we can at this moment say nothing definite . . . but we are entitled to assume from his position as agent for a Liberal during the last two contests for the Burgh with Mr Matheson, no less than from the reforming tendencies he showed whilst in the Town Council, that he will not be a whit behind his opponent in his statement of Liberal principles.[22]

The *Courier* noted that Fraser Mackintosh was a 'popular townsman' but it did not share the confidence of its contemporary in Fraser Mackintosh's Liberalism, going as far as to remark:

> . . . it is uncertain to what political party he is likely to attach himself. His name appears on the list of Mr Baillie's committee as a Conservative at the last county election; but on the other hand, he acted as political agent for the Radical opponent of Mr Matheson in the last two occasions on which there was a contest in the Inverness Burghs.[23]

It might also have been added that since his return to the town in early 1868 he had been employed as the factor on the estates of the Mackintosh of Mackintosh, a landowner who was one of the most prominent Conservatives in the county. The young Mackintosh wrote to Fraser Mackintosh from Cambridge, where he was an undergraduate, lamenting the fact that two Liberals were elected in 1868 for that borough in place of two Conservatives. He commented that this was 'Sad!': he also commented on the Liberal success north of the Border, where they won 51 out of the 58 seats in 1868, with the opinion that 'Scotland is disgraceful'.[24]

By the end of July 1868 it became clear that Fraser Mackintosh had decided not to accept the invitation to stand as Liberal candidate; indeed, he had published an address 'To the Electors and the Ratepayers about to be Enfranchised, of the Royal Burghs of Inverness, Forres, Nairn and Fortrose' stating his reasons for not coming forward. This document asserted that his absence from the country (he was travelling abroad) when Matheson announced his decision not to stand again for the Burgh seat, combined with the fact that Raigmore had already come forward and had secured pledges from many of Fraser Mackintosh's 'intimate and personal friends', compromised his potential candidacy. He remarked that the simultaneous departure of Matheson and appearance of Raigmore was 'by arrangement, I presume'. Possibly the man reason for Fraser Mackintosh declining to stand in 1868 emerges from a letter to his employer, The Mackintosh of Mackintosh, in January 1872. In this letter he finally admitted to being in quite serious debt. Fraser Mackintosh hinted that he should have been more open about this fact but in the belief it was not 'canny' to admit debts he had always 'kept very silent about it'. The extent of his financial embarrassment was such that he feared that he would have to sell substantial amounts of his property. From the point of view of the political situation in 1868 the important point is that the peak of his debts had come in July 1868 when he owed £20,000.[25] Thus at the time of the election Fraser Mackintosh was burdened with a massive debt. This may have been the reason why in that year he accepted paid employment from the Mackintosh, to whom some of the money may have been owed, rather than try to take up the unpaid and expensive role of Member of Parliament for the Inverness Burghs.

> An important theme which emerges from the address, and which would form an important part of his stance in 1874, was the need for the electorate to: 'exercise the undoubted right of selecting themselves a Representative from among their number, instead of, as has hitherto been too often the case, submitting to the dictation of a party.[26] The *Advertiser* regretted his decision not to stand and remarked that he would 'without question have been a formidable opponent to Raigmore, with a creed equally Liberal'.[27]

The explanation for Fraser Mackintosh's actions in 1868 may well be related to a lack of confidence that he could win the seat. If he harboured long term political ambitions it would have been inauspicious had he stood in 1868 only to lose to a candidate as limited as Raigmore. Lessons were learnt, however, and in the run up to the next General Election Fraser Mackintosh was careful to prepare the ground for his appearance as a candidate. With this in mind, it is ironic that he was almost caught out once again, having to issue his initial election address from Algiers!

Fraser Mackintosh spent the years from 1869 to 1873 as Commissioner, or Chief Factor, on the estates of Aneas Mackintosh of Mackintosh.[28] Fraser Mackintosh accepted this post with a typical rhetorical flourish, remarking: 'Upon consideration, the strong feeling of clannish attachment which I believe is notably apparent in the kin of Clan Chattan to their Chief and head'. His biographer presents this period as:

> four years of earnest and successful endeavour for the improvement of the vast estates under his charge and for the amelioration of the condition of the tenantry, most of them kin of the Clan. A great deal was accomplished during those years.[29]

The evidence presents a picture which is a little more complex than this. Whilst the tenantry gave a dinner in his honour when he ended his period of office in 1873, his factorial past came back to haunt him at the General Election of 1885, when it was used by his Tory opponents in an attempt to tarnish his credentials as a Crofter candidate.[30]

The 1874 General Election in the Inverness Burghs

> No general election since the time of the first Reform Bill has created a greater amount of stir and excitement in Scotland than that which is now imminent. The suddenness of the call to the exertion, far from abating, has rather, as it would seem, tended to augment and intensify, the eagerness and interest. From Maidenkirk to John O' Groats the whole country is in an inflammatory state.[31]

There were three surprising elements of the 1874 General Election, the first, as the quote indicates, was the alacrity with which it was called; Gladstone surprised all but his closest colleagues with his dissolution. A number of reasons have been advanced for the manner in which the election was called; ranging from the deteriorating position of the Liberal party in the House of Commons after a number of by-election losses, disunity in the cabinet and even the possibility that Gladstone may have been concerned at the possibility of his own Greenwich seat being declared vacant as he had not called a by-election when he added the office of Chancellor of the Exchequer to that of Prime Minister.[32] Gladstone attempted to turn the election into a crusade to unite the Liberal Party around the issue of fiscal reform: a strategy which was strikingly unsuccessful.[33] The second surprise was the Conservative victory; although, with hindsight, the increasing disunity in Liberal ranks and the efforts the Conservatives made to institute party organisation, were telling factors in their victory. Liberal disunity was clearly seen in the number of double Liberal candidatures across the country, including the Inverness Burghs, of course. The third surprising factor in the election was the geographical spread of Conservative gains. The Conservatives had performed so badly in Scottish seats, especially urban seats, in the elections of 1865 and 1868, that their capture of twenty Scottish seats, including three burghs, was striking. These gains were modest, however, compared to the advances made in the urban areas of England where the real basis of the new Conservative majority lay. In Ireland both the Liberals and the Conservatives lost ground to the Irish Home Rulers, although the Liberal losses were the greater. The overall result was a Conservative majority of 48, their first since 1846.[34]

In the Inverness Burghs, Fraser Mackintosh was determined not to repeat the mistake he made in 1868 when he had been caught out by speedy and possibly secretive developments and was unable to come forward as a candidate for the county seat. Thus, the politics which led to his victory in the election of 1874 began in 1873. The Mackintosh of Mackintosh had encouraged him to 'have a shy at the Inverness Burghs as a Moderate Tory' and expressed the belief that he thought such a candidature would be successful.[35] In April 1873 it would seem that Fraser Mackintosh had already decided to stand, he remarked in a letter to the Mackintosh of Mackintosh:

> I would prefer if there were no dissolution this year. It would be in my favour if I were absent for a while. The change from leaving an office in Union Street to go to St Stephens would be too much to swallow by many. However, come what will, if I get a fair prospect I will not throw it off.[36]

Fraser Mackintosh left the town in September to travel in Europe and North Africa, thus making himself 'absent for a while', a strategy which backfired when the election was called unexpectedly early. This letter also demonstrates that Fraser Mackintosh was aware that he could be embarrassed by a sudden appearance as an Independent Liberal soon after a spell as a factor and a lawyer. In the event he was correct in his fears, the change was 'too much to swallow' for many, and not just in 1874 but throughout his political career, especially after his further transmogrification into a Crofter candidate in 1885.

Fraser Mackintosh had resigned his factorship of the Mackintosh estates in July 1873 and had been succeeded in that position by George Malcolm, who, in the 1880s and 1890s, would be one of the most articulate defenders of private landowners and deer forests. The *Inverness Courier* remarked that Fraser Mackintosh's administration of the estate had been characterised by even handed treatment of both landlord and tenant. Fraser Mackintosh's retirement was marked, in early August 1873, with a dinner in his honour attended by the tenants of the Mackintosh estates. In his speech on this occasion he remarked:

> The times with [the tenantry] are rather hard as I well know. Labour is scarce and dear, and the seasons are fickle, but they must rely on themselves and not listen to any officious meddlers, who will promise everything, but can fulfil nothing.[37]

Before going on to examine the election it is important to appreciate that the context of politics had changed markedly, both in a national and a local context, in the years since 1868. Firstly, the extension of the franchise had been complemented by the introduction, in 1872, of secret voting. This was an important innovation, even with an enlarged electorate, but the initial level of trust in the secrecy of the ballot was not high and voters required reassurance on the subject at the General Election campaign of 1874. Secondly, the enlargement of the electorate was an important fact; the Burgh electorate had increased to 2,419 by 1874. In the wider context the period between 1868 and 1874 was one of clear bi-partisanship. The issues which had cut across party lines, such as the implications of the Disruption in Scotland, or which had divided parties, such as the Free Trade issue, had been worked through. The Free Trade (or Peelite) wing of the Conservative party was now fully integrated with the Liberal Party. This integration was capped, of course, with Gladstone, who had been Peel's Chancellor of the Exchequer in the 1840s, emerging as leader of the Liberal Party and Prime Minister between 1868 and 1874. This is not to say that the political parties of the Mid- Victorian era were the homogeneous entities of the twentieth century. There were still important distinctions to be made within the Liberal party; for example, between Radicals and Whigs. As we have seen, there were a number of single issues which could challenge the unity of the coalition of interests which meant to make up the Liberal Party; these would include the farming issues discussed above, the movement to disestablish the Church of Scotland and, in the 1880s, as will be discussed below, the grievances of the Crofters. None of these issues, however, were holistic challenges to the ethos of Liberalism. This is not to say that such issues could not be very damaging indeed, as the controversy over Irish Home Rule in 1886 would demonstrate very clearly.

John Murdoch and *The Highlander*
In a local context there had also been important changes since 1868. In this period public meetings and reports of public meetings in newspapers were the most important means of communication between parliamentary candidates and the electorate. This process of communication became much more important with the enlarged electorate and the secret ballot. As we have seen the two main newspapers in Inverness, the *Courier* and the *Advertiser* were both Liberal in their political outlook, even if the *Courier* was slightly more inclined to a Whig point of view. Neither were particularly challenging in their attitude either towards the successive members for the Burgh, Alexander Matheson and Aneas Mackintosh of Raigmore, or the restrictive politics which operated in the Town Council. The same limitations can be seen in their comments on wider changes taking place in the Highlands and Islands in this period. These points serve to emphasise the distinctiveness of the additional newspaper which was being published in Inverness by the time of the 1874 campaign: John Murdoch's *Highlander*, the first issue of which appeared in May 1873.[38]

Murdoch was a distinctive figure with a highly individualistic perspective on conditions in the Highlands, the constitutional position of Scotland, the Irish question, organised religion, and much else besides, including temperance, vegetarianism and the virtues of frequent bathing. Throughout his career in the excise service he had been a prolific journalist and pamphleteer; his most important contributions to the Irish and Scottish press had been on the land issue.[39] One author has described him in the following terms:

> ... of all the indigenous leaders Murdoch has the grandest scope of political vision, one that encompassed the theory and practice of land reform, Ireland's struggle for national liberation, Celtic political and cultural brotherhood, Scottish nationalism and - however broadly it may be defined - socialism.[40]

Another contemporary remarked: 'I once heard him declaim upon the land question with a fervour which would have made me tremble for my future had I owned but as much as a flower-pot of earth'![41]

Consideration of these views requires an examination of the career of John Murdoch. In many ways Murdoch was the pioneer of the Crofters' movement. He was born in the Highlands, at Ardclach in Nairnshire in 1818.[42] His outlook was heavily influenced by a formative period spent on the island of Islay where he associated with the family of the laird, Walter Frederick Campbell, one of whom was the future folklorist John Francis Campbell. Murdoch would support Campbell's Liberal candidature in Argyll in 1878, but it seems that Campbell did not approve of Murdoch's political views, which he later deprecated as 'socialism'. It was not so much this Gaelic background which gives Murdoch his pioneering role in the Crofters' movement, but his experiences in different corners of the British Isles and Ireland over the course of his career in the excise service. Like many of the Crofter M.P.s in the 1880s, although not Fraser Mackintosh, Murdoch was influenced by political and cultural experiences garnered from the observation of social change in urban and industrial areas in the mid-nineteenth century. Much has been made of his experiences in Ireland in the 1850s, but his exposure to religious revivalism in Kilsyth in the late 1830s and early 1840s was also important. Murdoch's religion was fundamental, in the literal sense. Fundamental to his own outlook, not least on the land question, as will be shown; fundamental also in that he drew his inspiration not from organised religious denominations, which he viewed with suspicion, but directly from scripture.[43] The 1830s and 1840s were a period of ecclesiastical discord which was marked by a deep internecine and sectarian dispute in Scottish Presbyterianism which resulted in, and was exacerbated by, the Disruption of 1843. Murdoch remarked that 'Churches have become like shops competing for customers for themselves instead of being agents of Christ'.[44] This remarks sums up, almost as neatly as is possible, the ecclesiastical atmosphere of the period when the new Free Church of Scotland was seeking to establish its status, partly by impressive fund raising efforts.

Murdoch also spent time in the early 1840s in Armagh, in Ulster, and in Lancashire. Hunter has argued that although Murdoch was appalled by working and living conditions in industrial areas he was not sanguine about the possibilities of improving the conditions of these workers 'without re-establishing their connection with the land'.[45] With this idea he provides a link not only with the Crofter's movement of the 1880s, but beyond them to the Edwardian Liberals who thought that land reform and the creation of small holdings was a panacea for a wide variety of social ills.[46]

During his sojourn in Lancashire Murdoch also came into contact with Chartists whose radicalism was informed by a belief in the iniquities of the land system. This was a view particularly associated with Feargus O'Connor who believed in the notion, drawn from William Cobbett, of national vitality stemming from a healthy rural population. A rural population who owned their own land would also be an independent population, a population not bound to landowners or employers. The Chartist Land Plan sought to create co-operative small holding communities to achieve this end. Many Chartists viewed it as a distraction from the more important political objectives inherent in the Charter, and very little progress was made.[47] Nevertheless, it does establish an important strand of thinking about the land question which linked rural and urban injustice and saw concentrated landownership and capitalist exploitation as part of the same problem. These ideas were taken up by later thinkers, such as Henry George, Michael Davitt and Gavin Clark, who sought to make common cause between rural small tenants and industrial workers. This was also a common theme in John Murdoch's thinking as he made clear in many of his editorials in the *Highlander* in the 1870s. He sought to demonstrate to the citizens of the Highland Capital that they were not immune from the effects of rural injustice.[48] Murdoch noted that 67 per cent of the paupers in Inverness were from rural areas and he appealed to their self interest and morality by noting that the sense of 'superiority' which townspeople affected over country people, effectively meant that they were 'winking at the work of desolation and pauper making which is going on in the country parishes', the ultimate effect of which was to drive up poor rates in the town.[49]

An additional strand was added to Murdoch's thinking by his posting to Dublin in the 1850s. Ireland had changed greatly since Murdoch's posting to Armagh a decade earlier: the trauma of the famine had been experienced and 1848 had seen a small scale nationalist uprising in

Tipperary. Murdoch, it seems, came into contact with some of the Young Irelanders who had been involved in this episode and imbibed some of their ideas, most notably those of James Fintan Lalor and Thomas Davis. Something also needs to be said about the political atmosphere of Dublin in the 1850s. Since Catholic emancipation and the reform of burgh politics in Ireland in the late 1820s and early 1830s local politics in Dublin had taken on a distinctly nationalist hue. Daniel O'Connell had been elected Lord Mayor in 1841 and partly used his year of office, in the words of his biographer, as a 'first trial in self government'.[50] Dublin in the 1850s was not the anglicised Ascendancy city of caricature; it had a vibrant nationalist culture exemplified by the publication of nationalist newspaper *The Nation,* founded by the former Young Irelander, and future Prime Minister of Victoria, Charles Gavan Duffy. [51] Later, the *Nation* would notice with approbation the efforts of Murdoch's *Highlander* to draw attention to issues of language and land reform in both Scotland and Ireland. The editor of the *Nation* did perhaps exaggerate when he declared that the efforts of the *Highlander* indicated 'evidence that the Home Rule cause is making friends among our Celtic brethren in the neighbouring island'.[52] It should be noted that the *Highlander* was very much a voice in the wilderness, certainly in the Highlands, in commenting positively on Irish affairs.

It was in this paper that Murdoch published his first thoughts on the land question in a pan British context. In these articles he argued that the British legislature was 'as alien to the people of Great Britain as to the people of Ireland' and that it had been responsible for foisting a feudal system of land tenure onto the people of the British Isles and Ireland. He excoriated the people of lowland Scotland and England for becoming degraded in the face of landlord exactions. He went on to argue that it was not religious or racial animosity between Britain and Ireland which was the obstacle to a pan - British campaign against this state of affairs but:

> the irritation to which we refer is traceable to the land laws which drive the downtrodden people to seek employment from others when they ought to be working for themselves on the land which God gave them; and that it is to the removal of the feudal system which we must look for the removal of those hostilities which have been unjustly ascribed to the blood and creed.[53]

This was an ambitious programme which, although Murdoch long cherished it, never came close to fruition: even during the Crofters' wars of the 1880s tension between Scotland and Ireland was as evident as fellow feeling between the Celtic brethren. Certainly Murdoch's sojourn in Ireland was important in the development of his thinking but we should also note the possibility of an Islay influence in this regard.[54] In a projected article about Islay and the Irish connection Murdoch argued that the

> Irish channel was a ready means of communication at many points, where now it is truly a water of separation. The people of Donegal and Antrim communicated directly with those of Kintyre and Islay and even now with a mail packet station at Donaghadee and Portpatrick, there is not half the intercourse between the people of Galloway and those of Antrim and Down that there was before the steamboats were constructed or even the Post Office established.[55]

The separation of Gaeldom into national zones was a longstanding historical process, and one unlikely to be countered by John Murdoch, but beneath the idealism he touched on an important point in explaining the continued separation.[56] The facilities of modern economic life, such as steamboats; and the influences of the state, such as the postal service; had a profound effect in breaking down older loyalties and accelerating the process of cultural uniformity. While Murdoch's radicalism should certainly be noted, an idealistic view of the past was at least as important an element in his outlook as the more modern 'left wing' radicalism with which some have identified him.[57]

The *Highlander* promised an independent and assertive approach to Highland social, economic and linguistic questions. Murdoch declared in February 1873:

> A primary object of the *Highlander* will be to awaken an intelligent and vigorous public spirit and afford opportunity and encouragement to the inhabitants of the Highlands and Islands to be heard on their own behalf and in matters on which they are best able to judge. Highland interests, however, will be advocated and Highland ideas ventilated in no narrow spirit, but in the conviction that Highlanders have duties to perform as well as rights to defend.

In terms of politics the *Highlander* was intended to be free from strict party affiliations, promising that 'the actions of political parties [will be] subjected to independent criticism'.[58] The early editorials in the

Highlander expressed similar sentiments and Murdoch's rigid adherence to these principles set the tone for the short and financially troubled history of the newspaper until its demise in 1881.[59] There is no doubt that the *Highlander* was more critical of landowners than most other newspapers in the 1870s, and that in this it performed an important function in laying the foundations for the more active anti-landlordism of the 1880s. Cameron of Lochiel remarked in 1876, perhaps additionally embittered by his failure to buy the *Highlander* over and give it a Conservative editorial line, that 'the whole tone of the paper is . . . calculated to cry down landlords and to produce a spirit of communism'.[60] While it was in circulation the wider political conditions for its success were not propitious, the anti landlord message which emanated from it was rather isolated, and those to whom it was directed did not have ready means of responding to its message, or of converting Murdoch's rhetoric into action. Charles Fraser Mackintosh did not appear to espouse many of Murdoch's ideas at this stage in his political career, but the support of the *Highlander* did bring him into contact with ideas of land reform and anti-landlordism.

The Humiliation of Mhairi Mhor nan Oran

A further event which brought Fraser Mackintosh into the realm of Gaelic activism, was perhaps the occasion of his initial contact with Murdoch, and one which certainly provided him with one of his most faithful supporters, was a little noticed case in the Inverness Police Court in 1872. The *Inverness Courier* recorded the following details under the heading 'Heartless*Robbery'

> A very painful and disgraceful case came before Baillie Simpson at the Police Court on Monday. A Nurse named Mary Macpherson was engaged to attend a lady lying ill of fever. The lady, comparatively a stranger in Inverness and living with her family in lodgings, unhappily died, and the nurse took advantage of the her position in the House to pillage her wardrobe. While the funeral service was being read at the Cathedral, she was ransacking the boxes of her deceased mistress. The charge was fully proved and the prisoner was sentenced to 40 days imprisonment.[61]

Mary Macpherson, or *Mhairi Mhor nan Oran*, as she would become known, was a native of Skye and had spent around 25 years in Inverness at the time of her conviction, which occurred when she was 51 years of age. Whilst suffering this traumatic humiliation she began to use poetry, in the words of one critic, 'as a therapy aimed at calming her own mind'. Meek goes on to argue that her poetry was characterised by a 'deep sense of personal outrage, and a marked grudge against the establishment . . . the peaks and troughs of her own emotions are all too clearly reflected in the uneven texture of her verse'.[62] It is said that John Murdoch arranged her legal representation for her trial in Inverness in 1872: a prominent feature of this trial was the fact that it was conducted in English, a language which the accused did not understand. This was a grievance to which Murdoch occasionally drew attention in the *Highlander*.[63] It may have been in this context that she came into contact with Fraser Mackintosh, a well known figure in legal circles in the town. Mhairi left Inverness after her imprisonment and qualified as a nurse in Glasgow. In Glasgow she was involved in the community of emigre Gaels who had congregated in that city and came into further contact with Murdoch, especially after a meeting of the Highland Society of Glasgow in February 1875 which provided the context for her poem "A Choinneamh Chaidreach" (The Friendly Meeting) where she describes Murdoch as '. . . the hero who stands by your side in such a manly way trying to shift the mill-stone placed about the necks of the stalwarts'.[64] John Murdoch also drew attention to this meeting in the *Highlander:* he felt that the fact that the entire proceedings as well as all of the publicity were in Gaelic was particularly significant. He went to point out:

> The proceedings having been entirely in Gaelic, a report, in Gaelic also, will be found on our third page. Those who cannot read that report must submit to have it read for them: and those who cannot understand that must be content to have the report interpreted for them. They will have a small taste of the inconvenience and loss to which some of our people have been subjected from want of current Gaelic literature.

In his speech at this meeting Murdoch exerted the members to 'put their heads together . . . to form an opinion which would induce the legislature to put an end to the malign power which sent them out of their own loved land'.[65] It would be much later in the decade, however, before the Gaelic and Highland societies in lowland Scotland would accept Murdoch's recommendation.[66]

The Election Campaign

Throughout the election campaign Fraser Mackintosh had to contend with two arguments. Firstly, the charge that he was a Tory in disguise, and, secondly, that his candidature merely served to divide the Liberal interest. This was the view taken by *The Inverness Courier,* the most Whiggish of the Inverness newspapers. Fraser Mackintosh himself remarked in September 1873 'I hear I am shown up right and left by the *Courier* . . . all this does me no harm'.[67] Fraser Mackintosh presented himself to the constituency as a candidate free from the influence of the local cliques which, he claimed, had propelled Raigmore to power in 1868. This was a theme at which he had hinted in his abortive campaign of 1868, but which was developed to its fullest extent in 1874. He had the support of the more radical of the local newspapers, *The Inverness Advertiser,* which described his appearance as 'creditable' and which immediately began the effort to counter the accusations of his opponents that he was a Tory; the *Advertiser* declared that the accusation was: 'neither fair nor honourable - for it is a thorough mis-representation of the fact'.[68] The *Courier*, however, had raised the spectre in some detail, reminding its readers of Fraser Mackintosh's early political career:

> . . . we are certainly astonished to find Mr Fraser Mackintosh suddenly converted to "Liberal and Progressive measures". He has always been considered a Conservative; he has been, we are assured, a member of Conservative clubs, and as a Town Councillor he was a strenuous in opposing the Liberal agent, Mr Macpherson, as having too much influence in the burgh from his position as agent for Mr Matheson.

This was a prominent theme in the campaign and it crops up in a variety of different forms of material associated with the election. One cartoon caricatures Fraser Mackintosh as a 'Quack Political Doctor' selling 'Higglers Blood Purifier' which was capable of curing 'scruples of conscience' and was 'warrented (sic) to root out consistency, honour and self respect and all other diseases of the body politic.'[69] A poem published by Fraser Mackintosh's opponents during the election lampoons him from a similar perspective: entitled 'A Candidates Candid Confession', it includes the following verse

> My p'litical principles aint nothin particular
> They aint horizontal nor yet perpendicular
> But glide down the long slant from High Tory prerogative

To the bottomless pit of political negative
My principles are, as it were, universal
On this side or that, none or both, quite impartial.[70]

The *Courier* went on to articulate the second charge against Fraser Mackintosh, that if he was a sincere Liberal his candidacy would have no other effect than to divide the Liberal vote and 'sow dissension for no public object whatever'. The attack was rounded off with the veiled accusation that he had merely adopted the Liberal label for opportunistic reasons as: 'The Inverness Burghs are decidedly Liberal, and we are certain would not knowingly elect a Conservative'.[71] The theme of Fraser Mackintosh's Tory past was also evident in the comments which the national press made on the contest in the Inverness Burghs.[72] A further element of this controversy was his alleged membership of the Carlton Club. Fraser Mackintosh denied being a member of that club, which was closely associated with the Conservative party, but admitted to being a member of the Junior Carlton Club, although he declared that he had never used the facilities of the Club.[73] In the aftermath of their success in the General Election of 1874 the Conservative Party made an effort to investigate the causes of their unexpected success and to think about how they could capitalise upon it. During these investigations Charles Innes was interviewed about politics in the North of Scotland. In the course of his remarks he noted that Fraser Mackintosh had been a Conservative but had switched his allegiance after 'not having any prospect of place held out to him by the Party before the last General Election'.[74] This may have been sour grapes from Innes and it is not consistent with Fraser Mackintosh's contemplation of a candidature at the 1868 election. What is clear is that at some point between the general election of 1865 and late 1873 Fraser Mackintosh ceased to think of his political career prospering under Tory colours.

Fraser Mackintosh argued that the secret ballot gave the reformed electorate real independence for the first time, and he drew attention to this in his election literature.[75] Fraser Mackintosh's most extravagant journalistic support, on this and other points, came from John Murdoch's *Highlander*; Murdoch had commented that secret ballot would 'break through the old habit of being afraid'.[76] This was in line with the objectives he had set out for the newspaper. He was intent on encouraging Highlanders to take responsibility for their own destinies, and firmly believed that they had 'duties' to perform. One of those duties, clearly, was the development of an independent political perspective and an end to the practice of meekly voting for candidates presented to them by political machinations and fixes. Murdoch, in his inimitable rhetorical style, flayed the 'parcel of shopkeepers, sartorial bailies and the like' who, he argued, controlled the political life of the constituency.[77] Further, Murdoch approved of Fraser Mackintosh's attitude to the Highlands;

> Apart altogether from his more political views, Mr Fraser Mackintosh has in a variety of ways, and over a long course of years, proved himself a real representative man as regards the Highlands and Highland capital. He has never sneered at Gaelic, at Highland sentiment or polity. On the contrary, he is a Highlander not only by blood but by feeling and sentiment.[78]

This clearly reflects one of Fraser Mackintosh's most obvious public roles at this point in his career, that of antiquarian and historian as well as his involvement in the establishment of the Gaelic Society of Inverness in 1871.

The *Courier* could find nothing to complain of in Raigmore's career as MP, and it poured scorn on Fraser Mackintosh's protestations of political independence, describing them as 'so vague ... as to mean anything or nothing', concluding that an 'independent member means a member on whom no party can depend . . . he is practically useless as a member of the House of Commons'.[79] There was little expectation in Inverness, or in Nairn, that Fraser Mackintosh was a serious candidate at this stage. There were accusations that Raigmore had not been the most active Member, but he had his defenders in the press in both towns. Raigmore does seem to have been a remarkably indolent Member, never once speaking in the House of Commons during his six years as member for the Inverness Burghs. Indeed, one cartoon from the 1874 election campaign entitled 'Dream of Bygone Days' satirised Raigmore's laziness.[80] The *Courier* emphasised Raigmore's experience as an Oxford educated member of the Scottish Bar and the sitting member and contrasted it with Fraser Mackintosh's inexperience and his tendency to make vague and unrealisable promises

> Mr Fraser Mackintosh simply selects a few Liberal Questions, without assigning a single reason for supporting them, and promises, as an independent member to press local claims and schemes upon the

attention of government. He would abolish the Income Tax, but has no suggestion to make up the deficiency; he would give us railways to Badenoch and Fort William; He would ask for a grant to Nairn harbour; he would get a railway made to Fort George; he would assist the Black Isle to obtain a railway; and he would not forget the Forres Post Office. Mr Fraser Mackintosh speaks as if these schemes - such at least as are reasonable - were never attempted before.[81]

Similar criticisms were voiced in Nairn where the local press commented that Fraser Mackintosh's candidature should be treated with 'suspicion' due to his inexperience, his protestations of independence and the contrast between his Tory past and his current Liberal identity. They concluded: 'that a more barefaced attempt to hoodwink the electors of any burgh has seldom or ever been made.[82]

When the election was called in January 1874 Fraser Mackintosh was caught by surprise in Algiers on the latest leg of a 'grand tour' he was undertaking after his retirement from the Mackintosh estates; indeed, he issued his election address from that city.[83] The election campaign was novel for a number of reasons; firstly, it was the first contested election in the Burghs since 1859; secondly, it was the first election since the passage of the *Ballot Act* of 1872. The presence of two Liberal candidates was not a particularly novel feature, there were eight double Liberal candidatures in Scotland at the election of 1874 and 34 seats across the UK where there were more Liberal candidates than seats available, it has been estimated that the Liberals lost thirteen seats as a result. One of the most glaring examples was in Glasgow where four Liberals competed for three seats allowing a Tory to gain the third seat.[84]

The platform on which Fraser Mackintosh stood is worthy of some examination. Some of the more notable ideas included quinquennial parliaments (as opposed to the existing septennial arrangements), the assimilation of the county and burgh franchise (the burgh electorate had been enlarged by the Reform Act of 1868, the county suffrage would remain unreformed until 1885); he advocated votes for female taxpayers (women were already enfranchised for School Board elections). He supported limited reform of the game laws, a key political question in Scotland in the 1860s and 1870s. In this area he supported reducing the protection given to ground game but he was not in favour of the total abolition of the game laws due to the importance of commercial sport to the Highland economy. He remarked during the election campaign:

> We all know how valuable game is to the Highlands; how sportsmen come here in the season to shoot our game, and leave a great deal of money behind them. Indeed, there is scarcely a town or a village in the Highlands which does not benefit more or less from sportsmen coming to this part of the country.[85]

We have already seen how Raigmore's silence on the game issue in 1868 was related to the contribution which the sporting industry made to the economy of Inverness and of the Highlands more generally. As an independent Liberal, and in the context of politics in the mid- 1870s, before the Highland land issue became politically prominent Fraser Mackintosh could enunciate such views safely. As a Crofter candidate, and in the more febrile atmosphere of Highland politics in the mid-1880s, Fraser Mackintosh's views on commercialised sport and deer forests were considerably more radical, although, as we shall see he became more ambivalent in the 1890s, towards the end of his political career. This is only one example where a careful examination of his views over his entire career can lead to the conclusion that his years as a Crofter MP were the exception. Because he was most visible during these years attempts to generalise from such a snapshot of his overall career produces only a partial, or even distorted, picture of his political views.

He advocated improvements to the communications network through state control of the railways and extension of postal and telegraph facilities throughout the Highlands. The latter proposals sound rather prosaic but they would form one of the most continuous themes throughout Fraser Mackintosh's political career. In this context it is interesting that the Conservative government of 1886 to 1892, which Fraser Mackintosh, as a Liberal Unionist broadly supported, advocated and partly implemented such policies.

The two most prominent themes underlying Fraser Mackintosh's campaign in 1874 were his political inexperience and his political independence. The two themes were related in that they were part of an attempt by Fraser Mackintosh to establish that he was untainted by party politics. He returned to these themes repeatedly. At a meeting in the Music Hall in Inverness in the course of the campaign he declared; 'It is perfectly true that men can sit and take an independent position in Parliament without being slaves of either party'.[86] He went on to say;

> I say again, there is a great principle at stake in this election, that is

whether you have not a right to return your own MP. The political life and independence in these burghs have been rendered worse ... the machinations of some few men have been able to keep the political life and independence down, they have not succeeded altogether in stifling your political liberty.[87]

At this stage, as in the previous Autumn, the *Courier* and the *Nairnshire Telegraph* derided these ideas. The latter paper referred to his address as 'rash and crude' and was confident that Raigmore would triumph.[88] The *Courier* was similarly dismissive of Fraser Mackintosh's ideas and confident of his defeat.[89] In a less strident manner than the *Highlander* the *Advertiser* supported Fraser Mackintosh and was highly critical of Raigmore's performance as an M.P., going as far as to say that: 'he has been found lamentably deficient in the capacity to discharge effectively the grave and responsible duties of our Parliamentary Representative'. It was felt that Fraser Mackintosh's election would lead to 'the emancipation of these burghs from the system which has prevailed of the retiring member nominating his successor.'[90]

Fraser Mackintosh, however, triumphed at the election with a majority of 255 over Aneas W. Mackintosh of Raigmore, with Angus MacKintosh of Holme, the Conservative candidate, receiving only 16 votes.[91] It has been suggested that Fraser Mackintosh's 1134 votes included a substantial number of Tory voters.[92] The extremely small Tory vote adds some credence to this notion. Tories may have voted tactically to get rid of Raigmore or may have been attracted to Fraser Mackintosh by virtue of his connections with Conservatism. It is unlikely, however, that this was a significant factor in his victory. Inverness had not been represented by a Tory since 1835 and the last unequivocally Tory candidate to stand was John Fraser at a by-election in 1840.[93] As has been noted, Inverness Burghs was a thoroughly Liberal seat at this time, especially with the increased franchise and the prosperity and growth of the town.

His opponents put Fraser Mackintosh's victory down to the readiness with which he made promises to his constituents, in an effort to 'ingratiate' himself with the working classes.[94] The *Courier*, seeming to miss the point of reforming the franchise, remarked;

> The successful candidate, in fact, has been returned by the mass of the electors recently enfranchised, who wished to enjoy the luxury of returning a representative of themselves, a man of the people.

A major factor in the victory was the efficient organisation of his campaign. The *Courier* made an important point when they commented in the aftermath of the election; 'Speaking Gaelic, as most of them did, the canvassers found a direct way to the affections of a great number of the electors'. Fraser Mackintosh concentrated his attentions on the working class districts on the west side of the river where most of his supporters were to be found. It also seems clear that he made moves towards courting the sizeable temperance vote in the Burghs. There was also some evidence of religious feeling in the election; something was made of Raigmore's Episcopalianism and he was accused of breaking the Sabbath as some of his election literature was put into the Post Office late on a Saturday evening with the result that the postmark was of Sunday morning.[95] In Nairn, where Raigmore may have had more supporters than in Inverness, the *Telegraph* failed to hide its bitterness remarking: 'we would rather be on the losing side than on the other side with victory purchased at the cost of honest principle and integrity'.[96]

Fraser Mackintosh concluded his campaign with a speech from the window of the Royal Hotel to a boisterous crowd packed into Station Square. He declared; 'I am an Inverness man. I am one of yourselves, I have no interest in going to Parliament, except to do the best for your interest'.[97] Thus concluded the most bitterly fought election campaign that Inverness had seen since the late 1850s.

Conclusion

The careful groundwork laid by Fraser Mackintosh paid off in the election of 1874. Organisation was the key to his victory: he had adapted to the realities of the new context of politics far better than his opponent. Indeed, Raigmore's obituary recorded that:

> His hold on the burghs would probably have been permanent if he had chosen to assert himself, but he came on the scene at a time of transition, just before the necessity for organisation and for stimulating local agencies had made itself manifest.[98]

The themes of Fraser Mackintosh's election campaign were consistent with many of his statements since he entered public life. He had, after all, opposed the 'clique' and Matheson's agent in the late 1850s and early 1860s, and argued that political life in the Burghs should be opened up. His enterprises on behalf of Inverness, as he presented them, also stood him in good stead. We can also examine the 1874 election in the light of later events. Fraser Mackintosh was never able to fully shake off the accusation that he was a Tory. Charles Innes pursued this theme remorselessly in 1885 and the issue of his membership of the Carlton Club cropped up once again at that very hotly contested election. Whilst there was little evidence of any interest in the land issue or Crofters' grievances in his rhetoric in 1874, we need not necessarily be surprised at this. This was, after all, a Burgh election and the grievances of the Crofters would only really become an issue in the late 1870s and early 1880s. It is interesting, however, to bear this silence in mind when we examine the metamorphosis of Fraser Mackintosh from Independent Liberal to Member for the Highlands over the course of the next ten years.

---

[1] F. W. S. Craig, ed, *British Parliamentary Election Results, 1832-1885* (London, 1977), p.588; H. J. Hanham, *Elections and Party Management: Politics in the time of Disraeli and Gladstone* (2nd edition, Hassocks 1978), p.160. M. Stenton (ed), *Who's Who of British Members of Parliament, Volume I, 1832-85* (Sussex, 1976), p.17; R. Blake, *Disraeli* (London, 1966), pp.126, 172, 176.
[2] *Inverness Courier*, 22 Jun 1865, 19 Dec 1885.
[3] Craig, *Election Results, 1832-1885*, p.588.
[4] *Inverness Courier*, 22 Jun 1865.
[5] Calculated from figures published in *Inverness Courier*, 22 Jun 1865.
[6] *Inverness Courier*, 13, 20 Jul 1865.
[7] I. G. C. Hutchinson, *A Political History of Scotland, 1832-1924: Parties, Elections and Issues* (Edinburgh, 1986), pp.103-4.
[8] I. Carter, *Farm Life in Northeast Scotland, 1840-1914: The Poor Man's Country* (Edinburgh, 1979), pp. 165-66.
[9] *Inverness Advertiser*, 27 Jun 1865.
[10] *Inverness Advertiser*, 27 Jun 1865.
[11] Craig, *Election Results, 1832-1885*, p.588; *Inverness Courier*, 27 Jul 1865.
[12] *Inverness Courier*, 19 Dec 1885.
[13] *Inverness Advertiser*, 11 Jul, 21 Jul, 24 Jul, 1868; *Inverness Courier*, 25 Jun, 23 Jul, 30 Jul 1868.
[14] In the event Matheson was returned unopposed in 1868, 1874 and 1880; he resigned in 1884, precipitating a by-election. See, Craig, *Election Results, 1832-1885*, p. 602.
[15] *Inverness Advertiser*, 11 Jul 1868.
[16] *Inverness Courier*, 19 Jun 1900.
[17] Craig, *Election Results, 1832-1885*, p. 551.

[18] Raigmore's election address was published in the *Inverness Courier*, 23 Jul 1868.
[19] *Inverness Advertiser*, 11 Jul 1868.
[20] *Inverness Advertiser*, 11 Jul 1868.
[21] *Inverness Advertiser*, 21 Jul 1868.
[22] *Inverness Advertiser*, 21 Jul 1868.
[23] *Inverness Courier*, 23 Jul 1868.
[24] NAS, Fraser Mackintosh Collection, GD128/21/6/1, The Mackintosh to Charles Fraser Mackintosh, 17 November 1868; same to same, 11 Dec 1868; NAS, Mackintosh Muniments, GD176/1993, List of Noblemen and Gentlemen members of the Inverness-shire Conservative Association, July 1873.
[25] NAS, Mackintosh Muniments, GD176/2287/6, Charles Fraser Mackintosh to The Mackintosh of Mackintosh 18 Jan 1872.
[26] *Inverness Courier*, 30 Jul 1868; for the address see, *Inverness Advertiser*, 24 Jul 1868; the address is reproduced in Appendix I.
[27] *Inverness Advertiser*, 24 Jul 1868.
[28] NAS, Fraser Mackintosh Collection GD128/21/4, Factory of Commission by Alexander Aneas Mackintosh of Mackintosh in favour of Charles Fraser Mackintosh, 8 Sept 1868.
[29] K. D. Macdonald, 'Life of the Author', in Charles Fraser Mackintosh, *Antiquarian Notes: A series of papers regarding families, and places in the Highlands* (2nd edition, Stirling, 1913), p. xviii.
[30] Macdonald, 'Life of the Author', p. xviii.
[31] *North British Daily Mail*, 28 Jan 1874; the *Aberdeen Free Press*, a leading Liberal newspaper in the North of Scotland also intimated its surprise at the dissolution: see, *Aberdeen Daily Free Press*, 26 Jan 1874.
[32] W. H. Maehl, 'Gladstone, the Liberals, and the election of 1874', *Bulletin of the Institute of Historical Research*, 36 (1963), pp. 53-69. During this period when M.P.s accepted a government post they were obliged to resign their seats and stand for re-election to the House of Commons.
[33] E. F. Biagini, 'Popular Liberals, Gladstonian Finance, and the debate on taxation, 1860-1874', in E. F. Biagini and A. J. Reid (eds), *Currents of Radicalism: Popular radicalism, organised labour and party politics in Britain, 1850-1914* (Cambridge, 1991), pp. 154-62; H. C. G. Matthew, *Gladstone, 1809-1874* (Oxford, 1986), pp. 220-27.
[34] Hutchison, *Political History of Scotland*, p.103; K. T. Hoppen, *The Mid-Victorian Generation, 1846-86* (Oxford, 1998), pp. 611-12; R. Shannon, *The Crisis of Imperialism, 1865-1915* (London, 1976), pp. 96-7.
[35] NAS, Fraser Mackintosh Collection, GD128/21/6/6, The Mackintosh to Charles Fraser Mackintosh, 18 Mar 1873.

[36] NAS, Fraser Mackintosh Collection, Charles Fraser Mackintosh to The Mackintosh, 16 Apr 1873; another copy of this letter can be found at: NAS, Mackintosh Muniments, GD176/2307/7.
[37] *Inverness Courier*, 24 Jul, 7 Aug 1873; see also, A. M. Mackintosh, *The Mackintoshes and Clan Chattan* (Edinburgh, 1903), pp. 360-1.
[38] For brief comments on the *Highlander* see; E. Barron, 'The Printed Word', in L. Maclean (ed), *The Hub of the Highlands: The Book of Inverness and District* (reprinted, Edinburgh, 1990), p. 301; J. Noble, *Miscellanea Invernessiana: with a bibliography of Inverness newspapers and periodicals* (Stirling, 1902), pp. 198-200.
[39] J. Hunter, ed, *For the People's Cause: From the Writings of John Murdoch, Highland and Irish Land Reformer* (Edinburgh, 1986) provides a short biography of Murdoch with a selection of his journalism and autobiography; Fionn, 'John Murdoch, *The Highlander*', *Celtic Monthly*, 8 (1899-1900), p.5; N. Maclean, *The Former Days* (London, 1945), p. 82.
[40] I. F. Grigor, 'Crofters and the Land Question (1870-1920)', unpublished PhD thesis, two volumes, University of Glasgow, 1989, p. 198.
[41] *Quiz*, 1 Jun 1883, p.12.
[42] The details, although not necessarily the interpretation, of John Murdoch's life have been drawn from Hunter, *People's Cause*, pp. 9-40.
[43] D.E. Meek, 'The Land Question Answered from the Bible; The Land Issue and the development of a Highland Theology of Liberation', *SGM*, 103 (1987), pp. 85-7.
[44] Hunter, *People's Cause*, pp.15-16.
[45] Hunter, *People's Cause*, pp.18.
[46] E. A. Cameron, *Land for the People? The British Government and the Scottish Highlands, c.1880 to 1925* (East Linton, 1996), p. 144; J.F. McCaffrey, *Scotland in the Nineteenth Century*, (London, 1998), pp. 110-17.
[47] A. M. Hadfield, *The Chartist Land Company* (Newton Abbot, 1970); D. Read & E. Glasgow, *Feargus O'Connor: Irishman and Chartist* (London, 1961), pp. 108-12; J. MacAskill, 'The Chartist Land Plan' in A. Briggs (ed), *Chartist Studies* (London, 1959), pp. 304-41; M. Chase, 'Out of Radicalism: The Mid-Victorian Freehold Land Movement', *English Historical Review*, 106 (1991), pp.319-45.
[48] E.A.Cameron, 'Embracing the Past: The Highlands in Nineteenth Century Scotland', in D. Broun, R. J. Finlay & M. Lynch (eds), *Image and Identity: The Making and Re-making of Scotland Through the Ages* (Edinburgh, 1998), p. 205.
[49] *Highlander*, 9 Aug 1873, see also 23 May 1874, 4 Sept 1875.
[50] O. MacDonagh, *O'Connell: The Life of Daniel O'Connell, 1775-1847*

(London, 1991), p.484.
[51] For a brief synopsis of Duffy's career see R. F. Foster, *Modern Ireland, 1600-1972* (London, 1988), p. 311.
[52] *The Nation,* 2 Sept 1876 quoted by M-L. Legg, *Newspapers and Nationalism: The Irish Provincial Press, 1850-1892* (Dublin, 1999), p.100.
[53] Hunter, *People's Cause,* p.98.
[54] D. E. Meek, 'The Role of Song in the Highland Land Agitation', *Scottish Gaelic Studies,* 16 (1990), pp.5-6, explores this point; see also C. Whyte, 'William Livingstone/Uilleam Macdhunleibhe (1808-1870): a survey of his poetry and prose', unpublished PhD thesis, University of Glasgow, 1991, pp. 40-1.
[55] NLS, MS 14986, 'The Queen of the Hebrides' by Finlagan.
[56] J. Dawson, 'The Gaidhealtachd and the emergence of the Scottish Highlands', in B. Bradshaw & P. Roberts (eds), *British consciousness and identity: The making of Britain, 1533-1707* (Cambridge, 1998), pp. 259-60.
[57] J. D. Young, 'Murdoch, John (1818-1903)' in J. Baylen & N .J. Gossman (eds), *Biographical Dictionary of Modern British Radicals, Volume 3: 1870-1914, L-Z* (London, 1988), pp. 607-8.
[58] NAS, GD296/158/16, Innes and Mackay Papers, 'Prospectus. "The Highlander" Newspaper, to be published in Inverness, Editor - John Murdoch, Inverness, 11th February 1873'.
[59] *Highlander,* 16 May 1873; see also Cameron, 'Embracing the Past', pp. 204-5.
[60] NAS, Innes and Mackay Papers, GD296/157, Lochiel to Charles Innes, 10 May 1876.
[61] *Inverness Courier,* 11 Apr 1872.
[62] D.E. Meek, 'Gaelic Poets of the Land Agitation', *TGSI,* 49 (1974-76), p.314.
[63] *Highlander,* 24 Jan 1874, 18 Apr 1879.
[64] Meek, 'Gaelic Poets', pp. 322, 365.
[65] *Highlander,* 13 Feb 1875.
[66] C. W. J. Withers, *Urban Highlanders: Highland-Lowland Migration and Urban Gaelic Culture, 1700-1900* (East Linton, 1998), pp. 190-3.
[67] NAS, Mackintosh Muniments, GD176/2307/15, Charles Fraser Mackintosh to the Mackintosh of Mackintosh, 18 Sept 1873.
[68] *Inverness Advertiser,* 5 Sept 1873, 16 Sept 1873.
[69] 'The Quack Political Doctor' in An Album of twelve cartoons by various artists, 9 on the 1874 Inverness Burghs election campaign, 3 on the 1885 Inverness County election, Inverness Public Library, Charles Fraser Mackintosh Collections, FM 1074.
[70] Parliamentary contest for Inverness District of Burghs 1873-4, Album of

miscellaneous election material, Inverness Public Library, Charles Fraser Mackintosh Collections, FM 2915.
[71] *Inverness Courier,* 21 Aug 1873; see also *Inverness Courier,* 28 Aug 1873.
[72] *North British Daily Mail,* 28 Jan 1874; *Scotsman,* 27 Jan, 4 Feb 1874; *Aberdeen Daily Free Press,* 27 Jan 1874.
[73] *Nairnshire Telegraph,* 4 Feb 1874.
[74] B. L. Crapster, 'Scotland and the Conservative Party in 1876', *Journal of Modern History,* 29 (1957), p. 358.
[75] 'The Coming Election - To the Working Men of Inverness', in Parliamentary contest for Inverness District of Burghs 1873-4, Album of miscellaneous election material, Inverness Public Library, Charles Fraser Mackintosh Collections, FM 2915.
[76] *Highlander,* 24 May 1873.
[77] *Highlander,* 6 Sept 1873.
[78] *Highlander,* 23 Aug 1873.
[79] *Inverness Courier,* 21 Aug, 28 Aug, 4 Sept, 1873.
[80] *PD,* 3rd Series, volumes 194-217; 'A Dream of Bygone Days' in An Album of twelve cartoons by various artists, 9 on the 1874 Inverness Burghs election campaign, 3 on the 1885 Inverness County election, Inverness Public Library, Charles Fraser Mackintosh Collections, FM 1074; 'New M.P. Kept cartoonists busy' *Inverness Courier,* 9 Feb 1993.
[81] *Inverness Courier,* 4 Sept 1873, 18 Sept 1873.
[82] *Nairnshire Telegraph,* 3 Sept, 10 Sept, 17 Sept 1873.
[83] *Inverness Courier,* 29 Jan 1874.
[84] Craig, *Election Results, 1832-1885,* pp.535-607; Maehl, 'Gladstone, the Liberals and the election of 1874', p.67; Hutchison, *Political History,* p.103.
[85] *Highlander,* 7 Feb 1874.
[86] *Inverness Courier,* 5 Feb 1874.
[87] *The Highlander,* 7 Feb 1874.
[88] *Nairnshire Telegraph,* 4 Feb 1874.
[89] *Inverness Courier,* 5 Feb 1874.
[90] *Inverness Advertiser,* 27 Jan 1874.
[91] Craig, *Election Results, 1832-1885,* p.531.
[92] E. M. Barron (ed), *A Highland Editor: Selected Writings of James Barron of the "Inverness Courier"* (Inverness, 1927), p. 49.
[93] Craig, *Election Results, 1832-1885,* p. 551. Craig labels Campbell of Monzie as a Conservative candidate at the elections of 1857 and 1859, but as we have seen in chapter one, this is not strictly correct.
[94] *Nairnshire Telegraph,* 11 Feb 1874.
[95] *Inverness Courier,* 12 Feb 1874.

[96] *Nairnshire Telegraph*, 11 Feb 1874.
[97] *Inverness Courier*, 12 Feb 1874.
[98] *Inverness Courier*, 19 Jun 1900.

Chapter Three

Charles Fraser Mackintosh in Parliament, 1874-1882

Introduction

Fraser Mackintosh's parliamentary career can be divided into four stages; the first, from 1874 to 1882, will be examined in this chapter; the second was dominated by the Crofters' Wars from 1882 to 1885; the third was characterised by personal and general political realignment in 1886; and the fourth ran from the passage of the Crofters' Act down to his defeat in 1892. The first stage saw Fraser Mackintosh establish his parliamentary reputation and solidify his position in his constituency, but can be treated as a preliminary to the later periods. Indeed, after the hyperactivity of the previous stage of his career, his early years in parliament represent something of a lull in activity. Whilst he was certainly a more active parliamentarian than his mute predecessor, he was scarcely prolix. He frequently asked questions and put down motions but his speeches were infrequent. This was perhaps understandable for someone who had been accustomed to recognition as a substantial figure in his own locality but would be a more anonymous figure on the larger stage.

Examination of three important issues can help us to understand some of the developments in the later part of his career: these issues are the Gaelic language, the Game Laws and the Irish controversy. This chapter will also seek to illuminate the atmosphere of the late 1870s with regard to the land issue. Although this issue did not have its greatest impact until the years after 1882, there were a number of important events in the previous decade which helped to build the coalition of Highland, urban and political interests which would dominate the Crofters' movement in the mid-1880s. The Bernera Riot of 1874 and, perhaps more important, the Leckmelm evictions of 1879, stand out in this regard. In many ways, however, the crucial years from 1874 to 1882 remain under-researched. It is not the purpose of this chapter to provide a detailed account, merely to note that the dramatic events of the 1880s cannot be understood without some understanding of the important themes current in the 1870s. Partly it was a decade of rising confidence and cultural assertiveness, with the publication of the *Highlander* in 1873, the formation of the Gaelic Society of Inverness in 1871, and Fraser Mackintosh's election in 1874. Nevertheless, the Bernera Riot, the Leckmelm evictions and the difficult economic conditions at the end of the decade served to emphasise the tenurial and economic insecurity of the crofting community: insecurities which could not be assuaged by the publication of idealistic newspapers with limited circulation, the formation of scholarly societies, or the election of a new MP for the Inverness Burghs. Despite this, the way in which the trial of the Bernera rioters was turned into an indictment of the factor on Sir James Matheson's estate in Lewis; or the campaign on behalf of the evicted tenants of Leckmelm, led by the local Free Church minister, demonstrated that, with leadership, assertiveness in the crofting community could have an impact.[1]

A number of important changes occurred over this period in Highland county politics, the most important of which was their increasingly contested nature. For many years these seats had been in the control of various land-owning families. The contests which did take place, in Argyll-shire in 1878, where Colonel Malcolm of Poltalloch challenged the ducal interest as a Conservative candidate; or in Inverness in 1880, where Kenneth Mackenzie of Gairloch came forward as a Liberal candidate in opposition to the sitting Tory MP, Cameron of Lochiel, were contests within well recognised boundaries. They could be nothing else given the limited franchise in the counties at this time: this was demonstrated in Ross-shire in 1884, when, after the retirement of Matheson of Ardross, Dr Roderick Macdonald came forward as a crofter candidate and received less than 250 votes.

The Gaelic Language
Already well known for his advocacy of Gaelic before his entry to Parliament, through his historical work and his involvement in the establishment of the Gaelic Society of Inverness in 1871, Fraser Mackintosh pursued this issue in Parliament in the 1870s.[2] He had two motivations for his activities on behalf of the Gaelic language, neither of them relating to the preservation of the language as a living, spoken entity. The first motivation was scholarship and the rehabilitation of the Highlander in historical perspective: in a speech to the annual dinner of the Gaelic Society of Inverness in 1872 he outlined some of his thinking. He felt that the most important role of the Society was to remove 'by

every legitimate mode, the idea that the Highlands was a barbarous country, and the people little better than savages'. He then went on to point out the means by which this could be done:

> ... the more original documents are searched out, the more it will be found ... that the general character of the Highlander was peaceful and the undoubted painful events which are scattered over history will be traced to the fact that the people and their immediate masters were driven to desperation by the grinding encroachments of strangers from the south and west. ... We in the Highlands are perhaps the most peaceable, law abiding people in the world, and if we wish our posterity to think well of is, as all of us must do, then it is not only our duty, but we ought to esteem it our privilege, to rehabilitate our predecessors, by giving them the justice they have not hitherto received.[3]

There are some interesting themes here which are worthy of brief examination as they will crop up in later examples of Fraser Mackintosh's rhetoric. The most obvious is his desire to rehabilitate the Highlander, not only in the interests of justice, but also of respectability. This was uncontroversial in the 1870s, but by the 1880s, with the Highlands in what many people considered to be open rebellion, the situation was very different. Fraser Mackintosh and others who regarded themselves as opinion formers, would see it as their job to maintain the perception of the respectability and loyalty of Highlanders. This was especially important in comparison with Irish small tenants, who were perceived to be in rebellion, not only against unjust tenurial arrangements, but also against British rule in Ireland. This was an important consideration for those who wished to glory in the martial exploits of the Highlander in the service of the British empire. Fraser Mackintosh saw no contradiction between celebrating this theme in Highland history alongside the Jacobitism of the pre-1746 period. Thus, in this context, the revival of Gaelic can be seen as a vehicle for establishing the respectability and British identity of the Highlander. A further important theme here is that of race: this was a defining characteristic of nineteenth century thinking about identity. In the later decades of the century a strand of this thinking was devoted to what has been called 'a patriotic Celticist counter current to Teutonic racialism'.[4] This had as its objective a more respectable philological contextualisation of the Celts, although, for some, it ran over into anti-

Saxon aggression.

The second motivation for his interest in Gaelic was educational: one historian has called him an 'indefatigable campaigner' for Gaelic in the schools.[5] The 1872 *Education (Scotland) Act* was the culmination of a long controversy over the reform of the Scottish Education system. There had been a number of attempts since the 1850s to pass a Scottish education bill but these attempts had foundered on the sectarian squabbles among the Scottish Presbyterian Churches, and a lack of attention to Scottish business in the mid Victorian House of Commons. The 1872 Act, as it eventually emerged, was regarded as unsatisfactory by many interests; It took the administration of the education system out of the hands of the Churches and placed it in the hands of a new structure of locally elected School Boards. Further, it demanded compulsory attendance by children between the ages of five and thirteen. One of the areas where the Act was held to be unsatisfactory was in its failure to make any provision for Gaelic in the School curriculum. This was significant, not only of prevailing attitudes to the language, but also of the moribund and submissive nature of the Gaelic movement, if such a thing could be said to exist at this period. The Gaelic Society of Inverness had been formed in 1871, but its initial interests were more scholarly and philological, even sentimental. Indeed, the early *Transactions* of the Society give the impression of a movement merely intent on seeing that something be preserved from the death of the language. As the 'Introduction' to the first volume of *Transactions* noted:

> The Highlands owe it to the world of letters and philosophy, that whatever the Gaelic language, traditions, legends, poetry, sentiments and philosophy contain which is of value should be preserved by those who know them, and handed over as valuable contributions to the stock of materials out of which human learning must be built up. Whether the Gaelic language is destined to die or not, the above is due from Highlanders; and it is all the more imperative upon them if there be reason to fear that the language will shortly cease to be spoken. The more it is felt that such a calamity is imminent, the more active we should be to rescue from oblivion whatever is liable to perish along with the language.[6]

This was scarcely a very assertive argument and its minimal nature can be seen by reference to some of the views of dedicated opponents of

Gaelic who had no difficulty with the kind of activity proposed by the Gaelic Society of Inverness. William Chambers remarked in 1877, in the course of a strident article entitled 'The Gaelic nuisance', referring to the campaign for the Chair of Celtic at Edinburgh University: 'Let Celtic like any other ancient language, by all means, be cultivated among the higher aims of philology'.[7]

The passage of the 1872 *Education Act* and the absence of any mention of Gaelic in its provisions, gave the Gaelic lobby a cause to campaign for and, in Charles Fraser Mackintosh, they had a man ideally suited to pursuing that campaign. The Act itself was concerned with educational administration rather than curricular matters, but the annual Education Codes produced by the Scottish Education Department dealt with such issues and the campaign was aimed in this direction. Indeed, it was the educational issue which helped to lift the perspective of organisations like the Gaelic Society of Inverness to a more practical level. Initial pressure was exerted by the Society, but by 1875 only the most minimal of concessions had been granted. One of the problems in this era was the lack of reliable information on the demand for Gaelic teaching in schools. Although the administration of education was not formally in the hands of the Churches, clergymen remained an important influence on the new School Boards, and few of them were advocates of Gaelic in schools. There had long been myriad problems with Highland education, the limited rate income from Highland land meant that educational facilities were very poor and the most highly qualified teachers could not be attracted. This problem was exacerbated by the fact that, due to lack of wealth in Highland society and irregular attendance by scholars, fee income for teachers was minimal. A further problem was the difficulty of recruiting teachers who were able to teach Gaelic which was, in turn, a consequence of the minimal provision for Gaelic in the Universities and teacher training colleges in Scotland. With these problems in mind, the Privy Council organised an enquiry into the use of Gaelic in schools in 1876. This enquiry revealed that there was a demand for Gaelic teaching in the insular areas. The vast majority of School Boards were in favour of the idea of a special grant for Gaelic teaching and, surprisingly, only 14 Boards admitted to any difficulty in recruiting teachers who were able to instruct in Gaelic.[8] This was seen by many as a surprisingly positive response from the Highland School Boards; indeed, Fraser Mackintosh was later to remark that he 'had a pretty strong opinion that if it were thought that the returns would be so favourable to the teaching of Gaelic, the circular in question would never have been issued'.[9] Beyond this, Fraser Mackintosh viewed the results of this circular as an indication of the scale of the task facing those in favour of Gaelic education:

> From the returns it appeared that there were upwards of 20,000 children who ought to be instructed in Gaelic, but who are at present deprived of the great advantages which would accrue from such instruction.[10]

Two further minimal concessions were granted by the government, with their application still in the hands of the School Boards; indeed, it was the policy of the Scottish Education Department in this period to devolve as much responsibility as possible for Gaelic education onto the School Boards as they were reluctant to enter into any kind of compulsion.[11] This fact, essentially devolved power to the ratepayers who funded the School Boards and to those who elected the members of the School Boards. This electorate, it should be noted, was much larger than the parliamentary electorate; the franchise was based on a £4 property qualification and included women. This meant, as the Rev Alex Macgregor argued, that it was imperative that 'the proper men are returned at the next election of School Boards, men pledged to have our native language taught in our own schools, throughout the Highlands and Islands'.[12] The concession which had been obtained by all this activity was very minimal. Gaelic had been recognised by the Education Code, but its teaching was not funded by any special grant, and, as a one prominent HMI remarked:

> ... they should not be too sanguine in their expectations from teachers in view of the recent concession. It carried no money value with it, and the old standard tests had still to be passed in other subjects as before, and they required all the time and attendance teachers could give, to secure good results. If they expected too much they would certainly be disappointed, to the joy of their enemies and the sorrow of their friends.[13]

The government, however, were unwilling at this stage, to make it a special subject and thereby award special grants for its teaching.[14] Gaelic was eventually made a specific subject in 1885.[15]

Fraser Mackintosh was, like many in this period, 'utilitarian' in his attitude to the revival of the language.[16] This was the common view of Gaelic activists in the late nineteenth century; the language was defended on scholarly grounds or, in the educational field, as an aid for very young children to education in English. As one commentator has noted:

> ... although the various organisations working in Highland education in the 19th century made different educational uses of Gaelic, virtually no one, with the exception of some members of *An Comunn,* advocated the use of the schools in an attempt to preserve the language.[17]

This attitude was also dominant among those campaigning for the establishment of a Chair of Celtic in the University of Edinburgh. They were in favour of the use of Gaelic as an educational tool to assist the linguistic development of Gaelic speaking children, and as a necessary skill for advances in philological and historical study but were more circumspect on the issue of its rehabilitation as a living and developing language. Fraser Mackintosh's views are neatly encapsulated by a remark he made in 1876 in the course of a speech to his constituents in Inverness:

> ... what could be said or thought when we find a Highland School Board prohibiting the use of Gaelic . . . They who were in favour of Gaelic in Schools did not object to English, but rather looked on a knowledge of the one as helping the other.[18]

It was Fraser Mackintosh's efforts in parliament on behalf of Gaelic which lay behind expressions of gratitude to him at a 'Great Celtic Demonstration' in Inverness in 1878.[19] This was on the occasion of the founding of an body called the 'Federation of Celtic Societies' which was intended to be a coalition of all the existing Celtic, Highland and Gaelic societies.[20] John Murdoch was a persistent advocate of such a move; he had long felt that the Celtic and Gaelic societies were insufficiently assertive on the political questions which faced Highlanders.[21] The 'Federation of Celtic Societies', however, did not have a substantial impact; indeed, it proved reticent to engage in serious politics, restricting its activities to vague statements of intent and rather inconclusive meetings. Even John Murdoch, who had high hopes for the Federation, was extremely disappointed in its inactivity.[22]

A further element of Fraser Mackintosh's activity on behalf of the Gaelic language was his involvement in the campaign to have the census of 1881 produce an enumeration of the number of Gaelic speakers in Scotland. Fraser Mackintosh had enquired as to the possibility of such a census in August 1880, when he asked a parliamentary question on the subject. In making the case for a Gaelic census he cited the example of the Irish census of 1861 where such a linguistic question had been asked. He remarked, comparing the Highlanders favourably to the Irish, that he 'spoke on behalf of a peaceable and orderly people who seldom obtruded their wishes on the House'.[23] In this, as in many other areas, for Fraser Mackintosh, it was the civility and loyalty of the Highlanders which was their most pressing claim on the attentions of government. The campaign was initiated at a late stage, in January 1881, when the Gaelic Society of Inverness sent a memorial to the Home Secretary which argued:

> Its (the G.S.I.) experience leads it to believe that a census of the Gaelic speaking population of Scotland, such as has more than once been taken of the Irish speaking population of Ireland, would be of great practical value in connection with several important questions affecting the Highlands, and would hereafter be considered a valuable historical record.[24]

This petition had followed another rejection by the Home Secretary of a parliamentary demand by Fraser Mackintosh for a Gaelic census.[25] A concession was eventually granted by the Home Office after additional pressure from Fraser Mackintosh, and there was an attempt in the census of 1881 to enumerate the number of 'habitual' speakers of Gaelic in Scotland. Many, including Fraser Mackintosh, felt that this wording of the question under-estimated the number of people who had the facility to speak the language but did not do so 'habitually'.[26] The Lord Advocate, in response to a question by Fraser Mackintosh on this matter, felt that the census was best left to habitual speakers, he said he did not see 'what the legitimate purpose of . . . including in the census persons who merely possessed a literary acquaintance with the language'.[27] The concession had been won so late in the day that the Census schedules had been printed. Instructions, however, were issued to enumerators that they could include people who could speak Gaelic 'fluently'. As Fraser Mackintosh remarked: 'this covered all conscientious persons as might hesitate to return themselves habitually speaking Gaelic, though fluent in it'.[28] Nevertheless, the presence of the question on the census schedule was an important victory and it was refined in succeeding censuses.[29]

Sport, Game and the Highland Economy

The Game Laws were one of the key political questions in Scotland in the 1870s and had been the subject of a major parliamentary enquiry in 1872-73.[30] In the Lowlands it was largely a grievance of tenant farmers unable to control the ravages of ground and winged game on their crops. It had been the basis of political campaigns by famous tenant farmers such as George Hope of Fenton Barns and William McCombie of Tillyfour in the 1860s, as we have noted in an earlier chapter.[31] This aspect was present in the Highlands, but there was an extra element in the shape of the perception that commercial sport was a major prop of the Highland economy. This had been emphasised during the 1865 election in Inverness when George Macpherson Grant of Ballindalloch, owner of large sporting estates, stood as a Liberal candidate.[32] At this early stage in his political career this was the aspect which Fraser Mackintosh chose to emphasise; he did so with great clarity during the 1874 campaign and would continue to do so throughout the 1870s.

During a parliamentary debate Fraser Mackintosh pointed out the advantages, direct and indirect, of the Game Laws to the Highlands. Among the former were the increased rents which sporting tenants paid, as well as the boost to the rateable value of property. He went on to articulate some of the more indirect benefits;

> ... sportsmen going to the Highlands and spending large sums of money in our railways and steamers, and among our posting masters and merchants. In fact ... in Scotland alone, during the months of August, September and October, a sum of not less than £1,000,000 was spent on or in connection with game.[33]

This was not an isolated statement. Examination of Fraser Mackintosh's rhetoric in this period reveals many similar examples. One of the first controversial issues which he encountered in parliament was the Game Bill proposed by J. W. Barclay, a famous Deeside tenant farmer and Liberal MP for Forfar. Barclay's Bill would have given winged game no protection whatsoever, allowing farmers to protect their crops against such predators with impunity throughout the year. Fraser Mackintosh opposed this, while agreeing that ground game, such as hares and rabbits, should be protected, on the grounds that winged game, such as grouse and pheasant, were important for the sporting industry which contributed so much to the Highland economy.[34] The limitation of Fraser Mackintosh's radicalism can clearly be seen in comparison with Barclay;

the latter saw the Game Laws as a powerful rural injustice and condemned deer forests as 'an entire mistake'.[35]

Modern economic historians have questioned the extent of commercial sport's injections of cash into the Highland economy. Some evidence can be presented which suggests that large sums of money were spent on shooting lodges and improvements to estates, often bringing employment to the relevant locality or providing opportunities for migrant labour. These projects, while they may have provided some initial work, did not provide long term employment on a large scale, and the deer forests were notoriously minimal in their labour demands. Indeed, solitude was their biggest asset.[36] On a larger scale, however, sporting proprietors, such as Matheson of Ardross or the Duke of Sutherland, were substantial investors in the railway network of the Highlands. On the other hand, substantial amounts of money flowed out of the Highlands; by no means were all of the sporting rents re-invested in the local economy. Evidence presented to the Game Laws, Napier and Deer Forest Commissions from the 1870s to the 1890s, suggest that the extent to which sportsmen patronised grocers and other suppliers of essential goods in towns like Inverness, Dingwall or Oban, can be overestimated.[37] The value of the positive material contributions of the sporting industry can be questioned if one considers the overall impact on the Highland economy. As has been argued:

> The expenditure on estate roads, shooting lodges and other items connected with sport was essentially a form of conspicuous consumption and had little multiplier effect. While it may have created employment and encouraged local tradesmen, it did not provide the kind of stimulus required to solve the economic problems of the crofting counties and, therefore, merely helped to perpetuate the under-development of the area and confirm it in its role as a labour reserve for external interests.[38]

Certainly, by the time of the Crofters' War of the 1880s the exclusive, recreational use of land which deer forests represented, adjacent to extreme land hunger in some crofting communities, was one of the most obvious injustices of the land system which the Crofters' movement attacked. Thus, Fraser Mackintosh's support for the sporting industry in the 1870s, whilst understandable from the point of view of the MP for the Inverness burghs, was a long way from the views which it was necessary for him to express as the Crofter MP for Inverness-shire in the very different political atmosphere of the 1880s. There is no denying, however, that the positive contribution of the sporting industry to the Highland economy was a strong belief of Fraser Mackintosh and his contemporaries. By the early 1880s, as will be noted in a later chapter, Fraser Mackintosh's views developed as he became more interested in the land question in the Highlands. The *Advertiser* declared this to be a 'agreeable process of conversion'.[39]

The complaints from tenant farmers became more vociferous in the 1870s as the prosperity of the 1860s gave to way to enduring agricultural depression. Agricultural depression was not a theme which was confined to the Highlands, of course; indeed, it had its greatest impact on the high farming areas of the south east of England, where the collapse in the price of wheat had a devastating effect. Scotland, with its more diverse, mixed farming economy was able to weather the storm to a much greater extent.[40] Highland economic problems in this period have been most often discussed in relation to the way in which the Crofters' War emerged in the late 1870s and early 1880s.[41] Certainly, the late 1870s were difficult decades for crofters and farmers alike. Severe weather at harvest time in 1877 significantly damaged the economic prospects of the North of Scotland.[42] The following year, in agricultural terms, was a great improvement, with much better weather, and a greatly improved harvest.[43] The economy of the North was dealt a severe blow, however, when the *Caledonian Bank* was forced to close in the wake of the dramatic crash of the *City of Glasgow Bank*. Fraser Mackintosh, incidentally, was one of the ordinary Directors of the Bank, holding 180 shares.[44] The Bank opened again in 1879, but its deposits had been decimated by the loss of confidence caused by the problems of the previous year: an important source of capital for the Northern economy had been badly damaged and the bank was eventually taken over by the *Bank of Scotland* in 1907.[45] The late 1870s were peak years for banking failures, although some economic historians have argued that the consequences of these failures were contained and general panic and runs on banks were avoided, the consequences in an area like the North of Scotland, where sources of capital were limited, should not be underestimated.[46] Alexander Mackenzie went as far as to argue that: 'The fall of the *Caledonian Banking Company* is, not excepting the Highland Clearances, the greatest calamity that ever befell the North of Scotland'.[47]

Examination of the press of the period reveals a substantial agitation by tenant farmers in the 1870s; admittedly most of this agitation took place in a restrained and respectable manner, and most of it originated in the eastern Highlands. Neither of these points mean that it was unimportant, and both go some way towards explaining why, in the political context of the late 1870s, people like Fraser Mackintosh found it difficult to balance the interests of sportsmen, who were viewed as economically influential, and tenant farmers who were undoubtedly electorally decisive in the county seats, and not without influence in burghs like Inverness, which serviced the surrounding agricultural economy.[48] Indeed, Fraser Mackintosh made a speech to the *Inverness Farmers' Society* in 1879 where he rejected the farmers' calls for protection as a potential solution to the prevailing agricultural depression and advocated rent reductions instead.[49] His views on the Game Laws would cause controversy among the Liberal activists in the Burghs once again in 1880. Fraser Mackintosh had advocated the rejection of a Bill which would have given tenant farmers the inalienable right to protect their crops against hares and rabbits. This was a bill which was broadly approved of by farmers in the North, as meetings in Tain, Dingwall and Inverness testified. There was considerable disquiet over his position on this issue, so much so that a meeting of Liberal electors was held to condemn the Burgh member. In a sign of things to come, Alexander Mackenzie, in his short lived journal *The Invernessian,* was a lone voice in defence of Fraser Mackintosh.[50] This allowed the *Inverness Courier* to poke some fun at Fraser Mackintosh before concluding: 'was ever a Parliamentary Representative dealt with like this'.[51] As we have seen, Fraser Mackintosh's position here was the one he had held throughout the 1870s, it would be the next decade before his views on this issue started to change.

Ireland
Given his actions in 1886 on Irish Home Rule, it is important to examine the development of Fraser Mackintosh's views on this issue. No-one who was remotely familiar with his rhetoric can have been surprised that he voted against Irish Home Rule. In his annual speeches to his constituency in the late 1870s we can see very clear statements of his views on the matter. The late 1870s saw the Irish issue rise up the political agenda. As we have noted, the 1874 General Election in Ireland saw the election of a fifty-nine MPs who were described as the 'Home Rule Party'.[52] This description is deceptive: a third of them had been Liberals in the previous

parliament and their commitment to 'Home Rule' has been questioned. Isaac Butt's *Home Rule League*, of which many, although not all, were members, was not a tight party organisation. Nevertheless, there was a hard core of seriously committed Home Rulers in the group, a core which was augmented by by-election results, not least the election of Charles Stewart Parnell for Meath in 1875. Prior to Parnell's election the Ulster MP, Joseph Biggar was the most prominent Irish MP who argued that the best tactic to use was traditional parliamentary obstruction. Tension grew over this issue, with Butt, who had once been a Conservative MP, having profound misgivings over the idea of obstruction. Obstructive tactics were used selectively in 1876 and 1877 and sympathy for the tactic grew within the party before an eventual confrontation between Butt and Parnell and his supporters in 1877.[53] Although the obstructive tactics of Parnell, Biggar, and their supporters have been eulogised by later Nationalist historians, there was nothing particularly novel about the tactics used, nor were they especially effective as the rules of the House of Commons were soon adapted to cope with them and the advent of the land war in 1879 moved the focus of Irish Nationalism away from parliament. Nevertheless, the actions of this group of Irish MPs attracted opprobrium from British observers.[54] As early as 1876 Fraser Mackintosh contrasted the considerable attention given to Irish business in the House of Commons compared to the comparative neglect of Scottish issues: 'hardly a night had passed without some Irish question being discussed though in the end there was really very little Irish legislation'.[55] As the Irish MPs became more determined and more disruptive Fraser Mackintosh became more and more irritated with them.[56] In 1880, after the 'New Departure', where Parnell, John Dillon and Michael Davitt welded the causes of Irish nationalism and the land issue together, Fraser Mackintosh became almost apoplectic. Of the Irish nationalist MPs who had been returned in even greater number at the General Election of 1880, he complained, 'they have at the bottom the intention of dissevering themselves, if possible from this country and disintegrating the Empire'. He did not doubt the reality of agrarian grievances in Ireland, but with the Irish Land War at its height, he declared;

> I could not for one moment say one single word with reference to the present state of Ireland except in condemnation ... the first duty of government as to Ireland is the preservation of order.[57]

At a meeting in Nairn in 1881 he condemned the Land League as 'obnoxious' and the ingratitude of the Irish in responding to 'that great remedial measure - the Land Act'.[58] He was constantly at great pains to contrast the behaviour of the Irish tenants with that of the Highlanders despite the government's lack of interest in them; in 1882, after the passage of the Irish Land Act of 1881, he remarked:

> I am quite aware that there are many among the Irish members who live by agitation and by agitation alone. Of course, they will not be satisfied with any settlement; the moment there is a settlement their occupation is gone. I do not look to these people, but to the great majority of the people, the tenants of Ireland, who have now security for fair rents and tenure, a security for which, or for anything nearly so good, the people in the Highlands would be very thankful.

He went on to raise the prospect that if such neglect continued, that the 'members for the Highland counties will be exactly of the same class are those for the great counties of Ireland'.[59]

These were further statements of Fraser Mackintosh's belief that the Highlanders, whatever their grievances might be, were loyal British subjects who could be contrasted markedly with the disloyal Irish. It was the perceived disloyalty of the Irish, in a decade paranoid about Fenian conspiracies, which added to the vitriol of the response to the Irish MP's obstructive tactics in the Westminster parliament: it was the Irishness as much as the obstruction which was objected to.

Contesting Highland Politics

The 1880s would see Highland constituencies contested to a greater degree than ever before, especially with the expansion of the electorate and the advent of Crofter candidates at the General Election of 1885. The late 1870s and the General Election of 1880 provide some indication that the parties were less prepared than in earlier years to allow their opponents undisturbed occupation of seats. This became evident in Argyll in 1878, when, at a by-election, in a seat which was generally considered to be in the control of the Duke, Colonel Malcolm of Poltalloch, a Tory, came forward to challenge the Duke's son, Lord Colin Campbell, who was seeking to succeed his brother, the Marquis of Lorne, who had just been appointed Governor General of Canada.[60] Whilst Lord Colin was a Liberal, as his father was at this stage, this was a contest within the recognised rules of the old system. Neither candidate could be said to have come forward in response to any demand on the part of the electorate. John Murdoch in the *Highlander* particularly lamented this aspect of the election, although other elements of the Liberal press in the Highlands were happy enough with the result, which saw Lord Colin triumph with a majority of 335. Indeed, the *Inverness Courier* seemed to deprecate election contests, remarking of Lord Colin that: 'Having secured the seat after such a struggle he has every prospect of being left to enjoy it undisturbed'.[61]

In September 1880 at a 'Great Liberal Demonstration' in Inverness Lord Lovat, looking back on the election of that year and forward to the future remarked: '. . . no man can tell what the circumstances may be at the time of another election. We do not know what may be, and we do not know what may arise before that . . .'.[62] The election of 1880 in Inverness-shire is worthy of our attention as it can help to demonstrate how much political conditions had changed by 1885 when Fraser Mackintosh stood for the seat. We have the advantage over Lord Lovat in knowing the way in which politics developed and we can see the election contest in Inverness-shire in 1880 as part of a transition in Highland politics. The official Liberal candidate was the same on both occasions, Sir Kenneth Mackenzie of Gairloch. In 1880 he came within 29 votes of beating Cameron of Lochiel, gaining 779 votes (49.1 percent); in 1885 he received 1897 votes, but with the enlarged electorate this was only enough to put him in third place with a share of the vote of 25.4 per cent. Traditional Highland Liberalism, as expressed by Mackenzie, was a strong enough force with the smaller electorate in 1880. By 1885 the ideas it propounded seemed to have been rapidly overtaken: they would make a comeback, however, once the febrile political conditions of the mid-1880s had passed.

Inverness-shire county politics were slightly more open than those in Argyll, there was no one dominant landed family which controlled the constituency. The seat was held, however, by one of the few Conservatives MPs in the North, Donald Cameron of Lochiel. The Liberal press in the Highlands was affronted by this and the prospect of a challenge to Lochiel was a perennial topic of discussion. Like Mackintosh of Raigmore, Lochiel was not thought of as the most active of Members, even in Tory ranks in the county there was disquiet over his languid approach.[63]

In mid-1878 reports began to circulate that Lochiel did not intend to contest the County again and that two other local landowners, Lord

Reidhaven and Mackintosh of Mackintosh had been mentioned as possible Tory candidates. John Murdoch felt that one factor which was inhibiting candidates coming forward, either in the Liberal or the Tory interest, was the cost of a contested election in such a large county as Inverness.[64] Murdoch regarded the way in which candidates spent money at elections as 'an attempt at corruption, an insult to the electors', his solution was to conduct politics in a different manner, with the electors at the forefront of activity, acting with sufficient boldness to vote against the sitting candidate for honest political reasons. He felt that the 'first plank in the platform be that the candidates shall not be allowed to expend money in any way connected with their canvass'.[65] This was typical of Murdoch's idealism. He made a more telling point when he argued that representation was not simply a matter of personality, he emphasised that the habitual return of landlord candidates meant that the legislature danced to the tune played by landlords. If crofters and farmers wished redress of grievances with their form of tenure or with the agricultural depression, they should bring forward other parliamentary candidates.[66]

An additional worry for the Conservatives, and the factor which partly lay behind Lochiel's reluctance to declare himself as a candidate, was the potential expense of a contest. The size of the county and the enlargement of the electorate since the last contest in 1865 made the potential cost of the election very large. Lochiel's indecision over this matter drove his agent, Charles Innes, to distraction. Innes was well aware that there was little likelihood of being able to secure many pledges of support for the Conservative party if they were not even able to say who their candidate was, thereby conceding a considerable advantage to the Liberals.[67]

In early 1880 the County Liberals met in Inverness, with Colonel Fraser of Kilmuir in the Chair, and agreed to seek a candidate to come forward in the Liberal interest. It soon became clear that the candidate the party had in mind was Sir Kenneth Mackenzie of Gairloch and in due course a requisition signed by 435 electors was presented to him. A General Committee was formed to promote his candidature and a canvass took place.[68] Lochiel countered with the publication of a list of a General Committee in his support with 650 names. It seems that the purpose of the publication of this list was twofold: firstly, as Innes remarked, 'to agitate the other side a bit' and, secondly, to try and raise some money to defray Lochiel's expenses which, it was feared, would run to about £5000.[69] This tactic, however, worried the *Courier,* a staunch supporter of Sir Kenneth:

> What parliament intended in passing the Ballot Act was practically to put an end to this sort of announcement of how one intends to vote; but here every farmer and crofter is made to understand that he is expected to add his name publicly to the Committee of the sitting member. There are numerous electors who will not venture to refuse the invitation.

The *Courier* comforted itself with the thought that this tactic was unlikely to be very effective: 'the Committee is public, the voting is secret'.[70] Further, the size of the electorate added strength to this view; whilst there had only been 878 electors at the last contest in 1865, there were now 1,851.[71] Sir Kenneth was regarded as one of the most open minded and humane landowners in the north. So much so, indeed, that he was even approved of by John Murdoch:

> He has the largest crofter population in the Highlands, and he has never evicted one of them. He has granted them, when he came into possession, leases of twelve years. When these expired he had the crofts re-valued, and then granted them new leases which are now current. He has taken a most active and intelligent interest in getting Gaelic recognised in Highland schools, and in securing the special grant for education in the Highlands, which has so materially benefited the ratepayers throughout the North, especially the western portions of the county. He supported the teaching of Gaelic in the schools on his own estate in the West, long before Professor Blackie and others.

Murdoch, of course, was not in the habit of penning such eulogies of Highland landowners, but he saw a more lasting political advantage to be gained from Mackenzie's election. It would:

> . . . strengthen the hands of Mr Charles Fraser Mackintosh, now working single handed in the interest of our race, language and literature, and by so doing help to secure for us what is our due.[72]

Sir Kenneth's address concentrated on Foreign Policy; throughout the election he argued that it was his distaste at Disreali's imperial adventures which had turned him 'from a moderate Liberal to a very decided party man'.[73] This was the tone of the whole election: a tone which had been set by Gladstone's criticisms of Disreali's foreign and financial policies in two series of speeches in the course of his contest for the constituency of Mid-Lothian.[74] Beyond this, Mackenzie's address was the customary raft of policies designed to attract tenant farmers to the Liberal cause: reform of entail, succession, hypothec and the game laws.[75] A further issue which Mackenzie used to good effect was that of Disestablishment. Although the Free Church was strong throughout much of the constituency, there was an equally strong adherence to the principle of establishment, a principle which was central to the Free Church in its early years, and which endured in the Highlands longer than elsewhere. On the eve of the election the *Courier* was confident of a victory, declaring that: 'Sir Kenneth will not only be elected but elected by a decisive majority'.[76] This was not to be, however, as Lochiel triumphed by a mere 29 votes.

The Conservatives' organisation in the County was stronger than that of their opponents and Lochiel had the additional advantage of having a power base in the county, in Lochaber where his estates lay, and where he seemed to have been popular. Mackenzie was not enthusiastically supported by the leading Liberals in the constituency, Edward Ellice, for example, was unenthusiastic.[77] Lochiel had referred to his opponent's Ross-shire origins and claimed that 'Inverness-shire should be represented by an Inverness-shire man, not one from Ross-shire', and one potential Liberal supporter claimed to have been deterred from voting for Sir Kenneth as he felt it was 'discreditable to such a county as this that the Liberal party should go to Ross-shire for a candidate'.[78] Thus, it can be seen that the level of political debate in Highland County politics at this time was not very refined, although it has been noted that 'a landlord usually fought where he had estates'. At this stage the Liberals took great care to bring forward landed candidates to fight Tory landlords; the circular promoting Sir Kenneth's candidature referred to this issue pointing out that the Committee was 'aware' that Sir Kenneth had 'peculiar claims' on his native county but that owing to the fact that Sir Alexander Matheson was such an 'excellent member' in the 'prime of life physically and intellectually' and a 'staunch Liberal' it was justifiable to invite Sir Kenneth to come forward in the neighbouring county.[79] This was partly due to a wish not to put their own candidates at a disadvantage, but also it hints at the limits within which political debate was conducted prior to the great reforms of 1884-5.

The Liberals learned some important lessons from this election defeat. In September 1880 a 'Great Liberal Demonstration' and a banquet for Sir Kenneth Mackenzie was held in Inverness. The Chairman on this occasion, Lord Lovat, gave some of his own reasons why he felt that the Liberals had lost the recent contest in Inverness-shire; these were, lack of organisation and attention to the register, and an overconfidence which caused some of Sir Kenneth's supporters to stay at home on polling day. Sir Kenneth concurred in the view that organisation was an important factor but he added that 'the influence of a great many proprietors were on the other side'. He felt that this would be a less important factor in the future as 'increasing knowledge confers on the electors higher feelings of confidence'. Overall the party was confident of future success as Sir Kenneth claimed to have discovered a 'marked under-current of Liberal opinion in the County'.[80] The Liberals responded to the failings of their organisation by establishing a Liberal Association in the County.

Fraser Mackintosh's sole contribution to this election was rather ill-judged and scarcely liable to raise the level of political discourse. A week before the election he published a letter in the *Inverness Advertiser* criticising Lochiel for accepting office as a Groom - in - Waiting in the Royal Household, an office which he had held since 1874. Since this was a position in Lord Beaconsfield's government a by - election had to be called in Inverness-shire, which was duly won by Lochiel without a contest in March 1874. Fraser Mackintosh attempted to argue that this was a demeaning office for someone bearing such a proud Highland name as Cameron to accept. Not surprisingly, Lochiel took exception to this accusation. Fraser Mackintosh returned to the attack, this time arguing that 'the member for the great county of Inverness should not hold so insignificant a post'.[81]

Fraser Mackintosh did not face a contest at the election of 1880; although at one point it looked as if he would have an opponent, in the shape of Mr Campbell of Saddell, a Lieutenant in the Royal Navy, the Burgh Conservative Association eventually resolved not to contest the seat. The *Advertiser* applauded this decision, remarking that Fraser Mackintosh had given every satisfaction as a member:

> His attention to the interests of the constituency has been unremitting, his votes have been consistent and his political views are approved of generally by the large majority of the electors.

Referring to an old controversy which had cropped up once again, the

Advertiser felt that the attempt to bring forward a 'full fledged Tory to oppose him' and the support which this had elicited in the Burghs, was good evidence of the 'hollowness and absurdity' of the accusation that Fraser Mackintosh was a Tory.[82] This, of course, was an accusation which would not be rebutted so easily, as would be demonstrated clearly in 1885. Even the *Courier,* which had been critical of him in the past, praised his commitment to the constituency and the solidity of his Liberal voting record in the House of Commons, although, as we have seen, they would be highly critical of him later in 1880.[83]

Conclusion

The period from Fraser Mackintosh's election in 1874 to the early 1880s was an important one in his career. It can be described as a period of consolidation and gives us a clue to Fraser Mackintosh the politician, and how he may have developed if the Crofter issue had not arisen in the following decade. He appears in this period as a solid enough constituency MP, a Liberal, but one who tried to ruffle as few feathers as possible. His biggest contribution in this period was to the Gaelic movement: he had been one of the founding members of the Gaelic Society of Inverness in 1871, and he had continued to publish antiquarian material.[84] In political terms he had been active on behalf of Gaelic in schools, acting as the parliamentary face of the campaign to gain a foothold for that language in Highland schools. These were respectable and uncontroversial activities. Some of his views were not entirely to the liking of his constituency, as we have seen they upbraided him for his lack of radicalism on the game laws. His conservatism on this issue, however, was nothing new and can be traced back through his entire political career. Examining his political views with an eye on how they would develop in the 1880s we can emphasise that his Unionism in 1886 was not a sudden *volte face*, he had long been suspicious of Irish nationalism, both in a fundamental sense, expressed as a worry over the unity of the three Kingdoms, and at a more basic level, expressed in the form of distaste over the parliamentary obstruction which increasingly became an important tactic for the Irish members in the House of Commons in the late 1870s.

This brief examination of the period prior to the 1870s reminds us that the political agenda in the Highlands was not so distinctive from that in Scotland, or even the United Kingdom as a whole. With the exception of the corpus of issues surrounding Gaelic, the questions at stake in elections in the Highlands were broadly similar to those which excited rural constituencies elsewhere, especially the grievances of tenant farmers. The fact that it was Conservative foreign policy which politicised a figure such as Kenneth Mackenzie of Gairloch confirms that political debate in the Highlands was neither geographically nor culturally circumscribed. The profound nature of the challenges presented to, and the responses by, the Westminster political system occasioned by Irish nationalism can be seen in the remarks made by Fraser Mackintosh in the late 1870s.

In the late 1870s Fraser Mackintosh began to dip his toe into more controversial waters. His involvement in the campaign to publicise the Leckmelm evictions was the first hint of the direction his career would take in the 1880s. It is to his involvement in the Crofters' War, a series of events which would catapult him to a wider prominence that we must now turn our attention.

---

[1] E.A. Cameron, 'Embracing the Past: The Highlands in Nineteenth Century Scotland', in D. Broun, R. J. Finlay & M. Lynch, eds, *Image and Identity: The Making and Re-making of Scotland Through the Ages* (Edinburgh, 1998), pp. 203-7.

[2] K. D. Macdonald, 'Life of the Author', in Charles Fraser Mackintosh, *Antiquarian Notes: A series of papers regarding families, and places in the Highland,* (2nd edition, Stirling, 1913), p. xxii.

[3] *TGSI,* 2 (1872-73), pp. 53-54, Speech by Charles Fraser Mackintosh to the Annual Supper.

[4] C. Kidd, 'Teutonist Ethnology and Scottish Nationalist Inhibition, 1780-1880', *SHR,* 73 (1995), p.64.

[5] R. D .Anderson, *Education and the Scottish People, 1750-1918* (Oxford, 1995), p.215.

[6] *TGSI,* 1 (1871-72), p. xi, 'Introduction'.

[7] W. Chambers, ' The Gaelic Nuisance', *Chambers Journal,* no 723, 3 Nov 1877, p. 690; see also, W. Chambers, 'The Gaelic Nuisance', *Chambers Journal,* no 740, 2 Mar 1878, pp. 129-132; *Highland Echo,* 2, 16 Jun, 1 Dec 1877.

[8] 'Gaelic in Highland Schools', *TGSI,* 7 (1877-78), pp. 11-18.

[9] 'Great Celtic Demonstration', *TGSI,* 7 (1877-78), pp. 225-26.

[10] *Inverness Advertiser,* 19 Oct 1877.

[11] M. K. MacLeod, 'The interaction of Scottish educational developments and socio-economic factors on Gaelic education in Gaelic speaking areas, with particular reference to the period 1872-1918', unpublished PhD thesis,

University of Edinburgh, 1981, pp.170-96; V. E. Durkacz, *The Decline of the Celtic Languages: A Study of Linguistic and Cultural Conflict in Scotland, Wales and Ireland from the Reformation to the Twentieth Century* (Edinburgh, 1983), pp. 178-9; V. E. Durkacz, 'Gaelic Education in the Nineteenth Century', *Scottish Educational Studies,* 9 (1977), pp. 23, 27; Anderson, *Education and the Scottish People,* 215-17.

[12] 'Great Celtic Demonstration', p. 229.
[13] 'Great Celtic Demonstration', p. 244.
[14] *PD,* 3rd Ser[ies], vol[ume] 223, col[umn]s 223-4; vol 237, col 1925.
[15] MacLeod, 'Gaelic education', p.205; Durkacz, *Celtic Languages,* p.179; Anderson, *Education and the Scottish people,* p.217, dates this development to 1886.
[16] W. Gillies, 'A Century of Gaelic Scholarship', in W. Gillies (ed), *Gaelic and Scotland, Alba agus a' Ghaidhlig* (Edinburgh, 1989), p.11.
[17] Durkacz, 'Gaelic Education in the Nineteenth Century', p.27.
[18] *Inverness Advertiser,* 13 Oct 1876.
[19] 'Great Celtic Demonstration', pp. 223-4.
[20] I. M. M. Macphail, *The Crofters' War* (Stornoway, 1989), p. 10
[21] *Highlander,* 12 Jan, 9, 23 Mar, 27 Apr, 4 May 1878.
[22] *Highlander,* 9, 16 Nov 1878, 14 Feb 1879.
[23] *PD,* 3rd Ser, vol 254, cols 2073-74.
[24] 'The Gaelic Census', *TGSI,* 10 (1881-83), pp.51-2.
[25] *PD,* 3rd Ser, vol 257, col 329.
[26] *Inverness Courier,* 24 Mar 1881; C. Fraser Mackintosh, 'The Gaelic Census of the Counties of Inverness, Ross and Sutherland', *Celtic Magazine,* 6, no 71, Sept 1881, pp. 438-41; C. W. J. Withers, *Gaelic in Scotland, 1698 -1981: The Geographical History of a Language* (Edinburgh, 1984), p. 210.
[27] *PD,* 3rd Ser, vol 260, col 1536.
[28] *Inverness Courier,* 16 Apr 1881, letter from CFM to Lord Archibald Campbell.
[29] C. W. J. Withers, ' On the geography and social history of Gaelic', in Gillies (ed), *Gaelic and Scotland,,* p. 111.
[30] *Select Committee on the Amendment of the Game Laws of the United Kingdom,* PP. 1872 (337) XI; PP. 1873 (285) XIII.1.
[31] I. G. C. Hutchison, *A Political History of Scotland, 1832-1924: Parties, Elections and Issues* (Edinburgh, 1986), pp.105-6; I. Carter, *Farm Life in Northeast Scotland, 1840-1914* (Edinburgh, 1979), 165-6.
[32] *Inverness Courier,* 27 Jun 1865.
[33] *PD,* 3rd Ser, vol 227, cols 1634-35.
[34] *Inverness Advertiser,* 13 Oct 1874, 8 Oct 1875.
[35] *PD,* 3rd Ser, vol 218, cols 1377-81; see also, A. H. Beesly, 'The Game Laws

and the Committee of 1872', *Fortnightly Review,* 19 (1873), pp. 352-72; A. H. Beesly, 'Deer Forests and Culpable Luxury', *Fortnightly Review,* 19 (1873), pp. 732-53.

[36] G.Hartley, 'Moors and Forests of the North', *Cornhill Magazine*, 46 (1882), p. 349.

[37] W. Orr, *Deer Forests, Crofters and Landlords* (Edinburgh, 1982), pp. 90-115.

[38] Orr, *Deer Forests,* p. 101.

[39] *Inverness Advertiser*, 14 Oct 1881.

[40] T. M. Devine, 'Scottish Farm Labour in the Era of Agricultural Depression, 1875-1900', in T. M. Devine (ed), *Farm Servants and Labour in Lowland Scotland, 1770-1914,* (Edinburgh, 1984), pp. 248-53.

[41] E. Richards, *A History of the Highland Clearances: Agrarian Transformation and the Evictions, 1746-1886,* (London, 1982), pp. 479-80.

[42] See the Agricultural Reports in the *Inverness Courier,* 9 Aug - 6 Dec 1877.

[43] *Inverness Courier,* 8 Aug - 12 Dec 1878.

[44] *Inverness Courier,* 5, 12, Dec 1878.

[45] *Inverness Courier,* 7 Aug 1879; R. Saville, *Bank of Scotland: A History, 1695-1995* (Edinburgh, 1996), p. 423; D. Ross, 'Inverness Bank even had Gaelic on notes!', *Inverness Courier,* 10 Sept 1891.

[46] F. Capie and G. Wood, 'Money in the economy, 1870-1939', in D. Floud and D. McCloskey (eds), *The Economic History of Britain since 1700, second edition, volume 2, 1860-1939* (Cambridge, 1994), p. 228; M. Collins, 'The banking crisis of 1878', *Economic History Review,* 42 (1989), pp. 504-27.

[47] 'The Caledonian Bank Disaster', *Celtic Magazine,* Feb 1879, p.148.

[48] Restiveness among tenant farmers is an important theme in the history of the north of Scotland in this period, see: *Inverness Courier,* 1, 7, 15, Jul 1880, 24 Feb, 10 Mar 1881.

[49] *Inverness Courier,* 21 Aug 1879.

[50] *Inverness Courier,* 10 Jun, 1, 8, 15 Jul, 26 Aug 1880; *Invernessian,* 25 Dec 1880.

[51] *Inverness Courier,* 19 Oct 1880.

[52] D. A. Thornley, *Isaac Butt and Home Rule* (London, 1964), pp. 176-204; L. J. McCaffrey, 'Home rule and the general election of 1874 in Ireland', *Irish Historical Studies,* 9 (1954-55), pp. 190-212.

[53] Thornley, *Isaac Butt,* pp. 300-29; D. A. Thornley, 'The Irish Home Rule Party and Parliamentary Obstruction, 1874-87', *Irish Historical Studies,* 12 (1960-61), pp. 44-5; A. O'Day, 'Defining Ireland's Place in Parliamentary Institutions: Isaac Butt and Parnell in the 1870s', in A. O'Day (ed), *Government and Institutions in the post - 1832 United Kingdom,* (Lewiston, N.Y., 1995), pp. 155-190.

[54] Thornley, *Isaac Butt,* p.300.
[55] *Inverness Advertiser,* 13 Oct 1876.
[56] *Inverness Advertiser,* 19 Oct 1877, *Highland Echo,* 20 Oct 1877.
[57] *Inverness Advertiser,* 21 Dec 1880.
[58] *Inverness Advertiser,* 14 Oct 1881, 15 Oct 1880.
[59] *Inverness Advertiser,* 20 Oct 1882.
[60] *Inverness Courier,* 8 Aug 1878.
[61] *Highlander,* 24 Aug, 7 Sept 1878; *Inverness Courier,* 22 Aug 1878.
[62] *Inverness Courier,* 30 Sept 1880.
[63] NAS, Mackintosh Muniments, GD176/2393/3, L. Davidson to the Mackintosh, 5 Feb 1880; *Inverness Courier,* 29 Jan 1880.
[64] *Highlander,* 15 Jun, 20 Jul, 5 Oct 1878.
[65] *Highlander,* 14 Sept 1879.
[66] *Highlander,* 22 Aug 1879.
[67] NAS, Mackintosh Muniments, GD176/2393/1, Charles Innes to the Mackintosh, 3 Feb 1880.
[68] NAS, Mackintosh Muniments, GD176/1995, Printed Circular Promoting Candidacy of Kenneth Mackenzie of Gairloch as Liberal Candidate for Inverness-shire, 17 January 1880; GD176/2804/13, Charles Innes to Allan Macdonald, 5 Feb 1880; 2804/35, J. MacBean, Kincraig to Allan Macdonald, 12 Feb 1880; *Inverness Courier,* 15, 29 Jan, 19 Feb 1880, 13 Feb 1900; for a profile of Mackenzie, see, *Celtic Magazine,* Nov 1880.
[69] NAS, GD176/2393/1, Charles Innes to the Mackintosh, 4 Feb 1880.
[70] *Inverness Courier,* 19 Feb 1880.
[71] Craig, *Election Results, 1832-1885,* p.588; for a speculative analysis of the electoral changes see, *Highlander,* 6 Feb 1880.
[72] *Highlander,* 27 Feb 1880.
[73] *Inverness Courier,* 11 Mar 1880.
[74] T.O. Lloyd, *The General Election of 1880* (Oxford, 1968), pp. 2, 14-15, 28, 38; H.C.G. Matthew, *Gladstone, 1875-1898* (Oxford, 1995), pp. 41-60; D. Brooks, 'Gladstone and Midlothian: the background to the first campaign', *SHR,* 64 (1985), pp. 42-67; R. Kelley, 'Midlothian: a study in politics and ideas', *Victorian Studies,* 4 (1960-61), pp. 118-40.
[75] *Inverness Courier,* 26 Feb 1880; Lloyd, *General Election of 1880,* pp. 59-60.
[76] *Inverness Courier,* 8 Apr 1880.
[77] *Inverness Courier,* 15 Apr 1880.
[78] *Inverness Courier,* 11 Mar 1880; NAS, Mackintosh Muniments, GD176/2804/67, R.Macgregor, Kincraig to Allan Macdonald, 19 Feb.
[79] Lloyd, *General Election of 1880,* pp. 120-1; NAS, Mackintosh Muniments, GD176/1995, Printed Circular Promoting Candidacy of Sir Kenneth Mackenzie of Gairloch as Liberal Candidate for Inverness-shire, 17 Jan 1880.

[80] *Inverness Courier*, 30 Sept 1880.
[81] Craig, *Election Results, 1832-1885*, p.588; *Inverness Courier*, 22, 29 Apr 1880.
[82] *Inverness Advertiser*, 26 Mar 1880.
[83] *Inverness Courier*, 25 Mar 1880.
[84] To the first volume of *Antiquarian Notes,* which had been published in 1865, and *Dunachton Past and Present: Episodes in the History of the Mackintoshe,* in 1865, Fraser Mackintosh added *Invernessiana: contributions toward a history of the town and parish of Inverness, from 1160 to 1599,* (Inverness, 1875).

Chapter Four

Charles Fraser Mackintosh and the Crofters' Wars

Introduction
This chapter will consider the events from the late 1870s to the appointment of the Royal Commission in early 1883. The growth of the Crofters' movement will be charted and Fraser Mackintosh's role in it will be scrutinised. It will be noted that in this phase of the land agitation and the associated politics in urban Scotland and London, Fraser Mackintosh was not at the centre of events. Indeed, it can be argued the Crofters' movement was originated by individuals whose views were well in advance of those held by the MP for the Inverness Burghs. It was only with the parliamentary calls for the establishment of a Royal Commission in August 1882, that Fraser Mackintosh emerges as an important figure in the Crofters' movement. In his statements on the land question in this period we can see that he had no real strategic appreciation of the kind of political measures which might be required to deal with the grievances of the crofters. He tended to confine himself to rather generalised statements and the most important theme in his rhetoric was his oft repeated calls for the agitation to stay within constitutional and legal bounds. It is almost as if Fraser Mackintosh was frightened by the development of the land agitation. Such strident protests as those in Skye in 1882 and 1883 conflicted with his cherished view of the Highlanders and he was often at pains to counsel caution lest they become perceived as similar to the Irish, whose own land agitation had been ongoing since 1879. Mention of the Irish issue leads us to a second prevalent theme in Fraser Mackintosh's rhetoric of this period, his distaste at the tactics of the Irish MPs in the House of Commons and his frustration at the amount of Parliamentary time taken up by Irish business. In the course of a speech to an audience of farmers in Inverness in 1881 he remarked:

> I am sure that you in Inverness did not send me to Parliament, nor did I go there myself with the intention that I was to do nothing during six or seven months of the year but sit and listen to stories about alleged grievances in only one part of the country.[1]

Some comments will be directed towards the question of why the Crofters' War began when it did and what the relationship of the Crofters' movement to the protests was? Did the protests stimulate the political events, or *vice versa?* In particular, attention will be paid to events of protest prior to 1882, and some of the reasons why they did not spark off a general revolt will be discussed. Further, the relationship between the run of bad seasons and the origins of protest will be tentatively explored. Close examination of the nature of the crises at the start of the 1880s and the chronological fit with the events of protest are revealing and suggest that notions of a simple relationship between sudden poverty and protest are not sustainable.

The Battle of the Braes in 1882 is generally considered to be the opening shot of the Crofters' War. Some attention has been paid to the events of the late 1870s, but not enough. There were two protests in the 1870s which are worthy of attention; the Bernera Riot and subsequent trial in 1874, and the Leckmelm evictions in 1879-1880. The former event has received more scrutiny than the latter; one historian has described it as 'the first resistance by crofters to the domination of their landlords and factors . . . in the post clearance period'; another writer has asserted that it was 'undoubtedly a turning point in the whole saga of Highland landlordism and the responses to it' and a third is emphatic that 'it marked the real beginning of the resurgence'.[2] The first two parts of this chapter will examine these events and will discuss both the changing atmosphere surrounding the land issue in the 1870s and to chart Fraser Mackintosh's changing views on such matters. The campaign to publicise the Leckmelm evictions was his first real outing as a land agitator, although he would certainly have deprecated this description. The latter sections of the chapter will describe his activities during the Crofters' War proper; that is, after the Battle of the Braes in 1882.

The Bernera Riot
The series of events in the west of Lewis in 1874 had a number of key elements. The dispute surrounded the attempt by the estate, owned by Sir James Matheson, to reclaim summer grazings from crofters. A seven mile long dyke had been built by the crofters to enclose the grazing lands; thus, they were not only losing the use of the land but were also being forced to sacrifice their investment in the improvements they had made to it. The Sheriff Officer attempting to serve the summonses of removal was deforced. Further trouble ensued a fortnight later in

Stornoway when one of the alleged deforcers was spotted in the town and attempted to resist arrest. A trial ensued when the accused were defended by Charles Innes, the Inverness solicitor, Conservative agent, and associate of Charles Fraser Mackintosh. His brilliant defence not only secured the acquittal of the crofters but also manipulated the trial so that it appeared as if the factor on the estate, Donald Munro, was the accused, rather than those who had deforced the Sheriff Officers.

This event exposed a number of the classic grievances of the crofters: their susceptibility to summary eviction, the fact that they were not entitled to any compensation for improvements, and the way in which estate managers exploited this tenurial vulnerability to effectively terrorise whole communities. In addition, there may have been a political element in the way in which the defence of the crofters was conducted: Innes, as one of the leading Tories in the Highlands, may have seen an opportunity to embarrass Sir James Matheson, former Liberal MP for Ross-shire. One recent account has argued that this possibility was 'quite untenable' and goes on to argue that it may even have been the case that Sir James paid Innes to defend the crofters in an attempt to 'buy himself out of the difficulty' by deflecting the attention onto Munro.[3] John Murdoch remarked, cryptically: 'It is a fact, although, from what we know of Mr Innes we are not disposed to make much of it, that the Bernera men were fortunate to secure the services of the political agent in Inverness of the Conservatives'.[4] In the absence of firm evidence there is no way of knowing the precise circumstances. What can be said is that Innes was a political animal, as his conduct towards Fraser Mackintosh during the 1885 election would demonstrate.

For our purposes the important point to note is that compared to later events the Bernera riot, important though it was in a local context, did not have the resonance of later events, such as the Leckmelm evictions or the protests after 1882. It was not widely reported in the newspapers and, although a pamphlet giving the proceedings at the trial was published, the event did not capture the imagination of lowland opinion in the way in which the later protests did.[5] Innes seems to have been extraordinarily successful in shifting the focus away from Matheson; even the *Highlander* was hesitant to blame Matheson personally, although it did argue that the controversy was evidence of the way in which, on large estates, the landowner had to devolve considerable power over day-to-day activities to the factor, and the harmful consequences which could result. Murdoch went on to make a typically wide ranging point:

If Sir James, and all the other trustees of God's land in this country are unscrupulous enough to retain the power and the profits of an office after they have ceased to discharge the duties, what right have they to expect that the man to whom they have entrusted the duties will be no more faithful to them than they have been to the great landlord who entrusted them with the administration?[6]

It could be argued that Murdoch's polemics represented a solitary voice. The politicisation of the Gael had not proceeded far enough in 1874 to make the Bernera riot a *cause celebre*. In particular, the coalition of urban interests, which would do much to push the Highland land issue up the political agenda, was not yet in place. It should be noted, however, that there was a range of Gaelic poetry on the Bernera riot. Mhairi Mhor nan Oran composed a song which it is said was 'known even in Lews Castle itself'.[7] This was not the sum of poetry on this important incident; a notable poem was John Smith's 'The Spirit of Kindliness/Spiorad a' Chartannais', which has an essence of assertiveness, but can be read more convincingly as a lament for a more considerate age from a Christian point of view.[8] A more specific comment on the riot is Murdo MacLeod's 'Song to the People of Bernera/Oran Muinntir Bhearnaraidh'. Significantly, this poem seems most likely to have been composed in Glasgow, which in itself is good evidence of the impact of the events in Lewis, and the importance of that city in the development of Highland protest. Interestingly, this poem concentrates its fire on Donald Munro and emphasises the positive role of Sir James Matheson in giving the Bernera crofters a sympathetic hearing.[9] Thus, praise of the actions of the protesters and criticisms of the factor are more important themes in the poetry commenting on this event, rather than outright anti-landlordism. Further, Gaelic poetry tended to be a reaction to events and a means of communicating the news of events of protest from their origin to centres of emigre Gaeldom in the cities, rather than as a direct incitement to further protest. Despite the Gaelic comment on Bernera it does not remove the fact that there were no significant events of protest until the controversy over the Leckmelm evictions five years later. Indeed, from the point of view of someone like John Murdoch, the events at Bernera in 1874 provided good evidence of the need for the urgent politicisation and greater assertiveness of the Gael: this process would be taken further by the Leckmelm evictions.

The Leckmelm Evictions

The newly elected member for the Inverness burghs does not seem to have made any comment on the events in Bernera: indeed, at this point in his career he took very little interest in the land issue. By the time of the controversy over the Leckmelm evictions in 1879 both Fraser Mackintosh's outlook and political conditions in the Highlands had changed markedly. The response to these evictions is testimony to the extent of the changes described in outline in chapter three. Although much of the political activity had related to less profound and challenging agitations, such as those on various linguistic issues, the activity did help to initiate a political network which, although it could not yet be described as a 'movement', was capable of sustaining a much more powerful response to this particular example of the vulnerability and insecurity of the crofting community. Fraser Mackintosh was very much part of this network and it is in this context that we can see the crofter activist in him begin to emerge.

The Leckmelm evictions took place in 1879 when an Aberdeen paper mill owner, Alexander Pirie, purchased the estate of that name in Wester Ross.[10] He was only the latest of a substantial influx of new proprietors, whose wealth was generated by non-Highland activities, to purchase land in the Highlands. Like many, although by no means all, of these individuals - Lord Leverhulme in Lewis in the early 1920s is the best (or worst) example - he had no sympathy with crofting as a rational method of estate management. He attempted to evict the crofters, divest them of their stock and improvements, and transform them into estate employees.[11] As MacPhail points out: 'it was symptomatic of the new atmosphere in the Highlands in the late 1870s that almost immediately a public outcry was raised'.[12] Hunter presents a more downbeat assessment of the same events:

> In 1880 John Murdoch, Angus Sutherland and several kindred spirits had hailed as a glorious opportunity to launch a Highland land reform movement an attempt to evict a number of crofters from Leckmelm . . . On that particular occasion, however, little had come of their endeavours.[13]

This is slightly unfair in that the Leckmelm evictions did stimulate great interest in the Highland press and among the politically active classes, especially in Inverness and Glasgow. At a meeting of the Glasgow Highland Association in November 1880, Henry Whyte remarked that 'the evictions at Leckmelm caused the land question to be considered and discussed by many who would have disregarded it'.[14] Further, it ignores the major gladiator on behalf of the evicted of Leckmelm, the local Free Church minister, John Macmillan. Macmillan was a tireless advocate of the cause, writing endless letters to the press and giving a major speech on the subject at a meeting in the Music Hall in Inverness in 1880.[15] Alexander Mackenzie described this meeting as 'the real beginning in earnest of the present movement throughout the Highlands in favour of Land reform, and the curtailment of landlord power over their unfortunate tenants'.[16] Indeed, Macmillan was only one of a number of clergymen who became involved in the campaign on behalf of the Leckmelm crofters; others included the Rev John Mactavish of the Free East Church in Inverness and the Rev Charles MacEchern of the Gaelic charge of the Church of Scotland in Inverness.[17]

The discussion of the Leckmelm evictions will attempt to explore Fraser Mackintosh's role but also to assess the importance of the event to the growth of the network which would become the Crofters' movement in the 1880s.

Fraser Mackintosh's first involvement in the controversy over the Leckmelm evictions came in August 1880 when he put down a Parliamentary Question to the Home Secretary on the subject. He asked Harcourt whether he was aware of the Leckmelm evictions and whether:

> . . . steps will be taken by government to prevent the eviction of the Leckmelm crofters, none of whom are in arrear of rent, without granting adequate compensation or providing them with other houses.

Harcourt replied that he regretted the course of events in Ross-shire but that it was his view that 'the government had no right to interfere in the matter'.[18] This was a classic statement of the government's view at the time and it was the central achievement of the developing Crofters movement that it managed to change this view.[19]

He also made a speech in February 1880 to the *Glasgow Inverness-shire Association* in which he referred to the Leckmelm evictions, asking:

> Is there not a landholder in the Highlands with plenty of acres useless at present, but fit for cultivation, noblehearted enough to step forward and welcome these our threatened and unhappy brethren, and give them homes and opportunities for honourable industry and livelihood.

This was scarcely a very radical proposition as he was not even asking for the restitution of the evicted. He seemed to have accepted the fact of the eviction and was appealing to other landlords to come forward to rescue the reputation of the class by their benevolence towards the evicted.

Indeed, the remainder of his remarks on the land question on this occasion demonstrate just how far short of genuine, challenging, radicalism Fraser Mackintosh's views were at this point in his career. He went on to argue:

> Much as I love the Highlands, and desire to see it peopled by Highlanders, yet it would be absurd to suppose that the country is capable of supporting a large population, and if it were capable it would not be right that people should always remain at home.

In a classic statement of his view that Highlanders had a duty to the British nation and to the Empire as well as to their own race and country he argued that to avoid falling into 'the narrowest views and become unwilling, if not incapable, of rising in the social scale, or keeping abreast of the times' Highlanders should not necessarily be tied to their native homes:

> Therefore, while I desire to see the fire always alight in the Highland home, and some one or more of the family, according to circumstances, remaining, I wish that others should go out into the world, into the army or navy, into the professions, or engage in commerce, and after a life of industry, return to their native place, and become a source of wealth and happiness to the locality.[20]

This statement was in direct contradiction to the views of the Crofters' movement as they developed in the 1880s; they were utterly unwilling to concede the point that there was insufficient land for all the Highland people: to concede such a point, they felt, would be to admit that the current land system in the Highlands was valid. In advancing this argument Fraser Mackintosh was arguing a very similar point to that advanced by landowners, most notably Lady Gordon Cathcart, the proprietor of Benbecula, South Uist and Barra.[21]

Fraser Mackintosh, at this point, was certainly not as radical on the land issue as the man who led the controversy over the Leckmelm evictions, John Macmillan, the local Free Church minister. At a meeting in Inverness in 1880 Macmillan denounced Pirie in no uncertain terms:

> . . . no Englishman or Scotchman worthy of the name would ever do what Mr Pirie has done and every good proprietor in Ross-shire and throughout the world disapproves of what he has done.

Macmillan went on to argue that he hoped the grievances of the Leckmelm crofters would have a wider significance:

> . . . whatever became of Leckmelm and its interests, whose fate, so far as I can apprehend, is nearly already sealed (I must say through the supineness and the indifference of our representatives in Parliament), I can confidently hope that a campaign has been inaugurated which shall not be abandoned until the cruel and ravaging foe is routed for ever off the field and a yoke of iron which neither we nor our forefathers were able to bear, will be wrenched and snapped asunder and removed from the neck of our peasantry, never more to be replaced until the civilisation of the nineteenth century will give place to the barbarianism of the original Britons.[22]

Macmillan, unlike Fraser Mackintosh, was able to see the wider lessons and the broader significance of the local controversy and his vision extended to the notion of a more general Crofters' movement. By late 1880 there were signs that Macmillan's hopes would come to fruition, a meeting of the Glasgow Branch of the *Irish Land League* passed a resolution and a meeting was held in London, chaired by Dr Roderick Macdonald (the future Crofter MP for Ross-shire), at which Pirie's actions were denounced.[23] An exchange of correspondence between Macmillan and Pirie ensued in the early weeks of 1881, but it soon became a rather bland point-scoring exercise and very little was achieved. The fact that this was still a transitional phase can be seen by the fact that Lochiel could be cheered at a meeting of the Skye Gathering in Glasgow when remarking that 'there is an astonishing amount of contentment to be found among many of the most lowly habitations of the West Highlands'.[24] John Murdoch recognised the importance of the moment, as he argued in December 1880:

> It would be wise in our Highland lairds and MPs, to recognise the growing public voice in Scotland on the land question, and to act in sympathy with it, while it only takes the form of anti-land-law. A very

little more resistance on the part of the lairds and Lords, and a little more apathy on the part of legislating Commons, may force the movement into the Irish shape of anti-land-lord. Much easier terms will satisfy people today than will suffice a few years hence.[25]

A noteworthy aspect of the Leckmelm controversy was the way in which Pirie was excoriated as an outsider. This can be contrasted with the way in which Matheson, the landlord in the Bernera dispute, escaped largely unscathed despite the actions of his factor. As we have noted, this may have had something to do with Matheson's own careful tactics at the time. It was also related to the attention Matheson paid to the cultivation of his own reputation which resulted in the position of respect which he enjoyed. He was lauded, for example, for his perceived humanity and generosity during the famine of the 1840s. A further factor in his favour was that he was not seen as an outsider; although he and his nephew were recent purchasers of land in the Highlands, their family was perceived to have a long Highland pedigree.[26] None of these factors were present to protect Pirie from the obloquy of Macmillan and other advocates of the Leckmelm crofters. Macmillan described Pirie as 'a paper manufacturer in the granite city of Aberdeen, where they say there are hard heads, and, where, I believe, there are hard hearts'.[27]

By December 1880 it had become clear that the controversy over the Leckmelm evictions was not going to go away and a further meeting was held in Inverness, this time not on the specific subject of events at Leckmelm, but on the 'Land Laws' in general. Fraser Mackintosh presided at this meeting and his speech deserves some scrutiny as it was his first lengthy statement on the land question. We might speculate that Fraser Mackintosh, who saw himself as 'member for the Highlands', had realised that he would have to become involved in the movement in a more obvious manner if his popular appellation was to have any substance. Prior to 1880 his views on the crofter issue were not made public and it was certainly not the case that he did very much to drive the issue onto the political agenda; rather, as we have seen, this role fell to others, while Fraser Mackintosh rather tagged along once the issue became prominent. Nevertheless, his speech in Inverness contains some important evidence of the way his rhetoric was developing. Part of his objective here was to rebut the allegation made by Pirie that he, Fraser Mackintosh, was only involved in the Leckmelm agitation in order to ingratiate himself with his constituents who had disapproved of his actions over the recent *Hares and Rabbits Bill.*

Fraser Mackintosh made it clear that he did not support evictions and compulsory emigration, nor did he agree with Lochiel, who had stated in his speech in Glasgow earlier in the year that crofters should merely be 'left alone', and have assurances that they would not be removed or be subjected to undue increases in rent. There is nothing in Fraser Mackintosh's rhetoric, however, which could be described as anti-landlord. He made it clear that he saw the role of the landlord as crucial in establishing the security of the crofter. He pressed landlords to:

> Encourage him (the crofter) by wood from the estate, which costs the landlord next to nothing: countenance him by kindly words of approval; give substantial prizes for the best kept house, neatest garden, tidiest fields, and so evoke emulation, and I am convinced that wonders will be worked, and large tracts of improvable land will yet be reclaimed, and the wealth of the country added to besides the comfort of the possessors.

Emphasising the theme of respectability and restraint which we have noted in earlier speeches on Highland issues, Fraser Mackintosh rounded off his remarks by saying:

> We want nothing illegal. We want nothing unconstitutional. But we are to consider resolutions which are moderate and fair, and which breathe a determination which nothing but fulfilment will satisfy.[28]

This speech can be said to inaugurate a new stage in Fraser Mackintosh's career, a stage which would be dominated by the land question. Along with Charles Cameron and Donald MacFarlane, he would pursue the issue in parliament, serve on the Royal Commission which they pressed for and, in 1885, come forward as a Crofter candidate for the County of Inverness. It is in this period that Fraser Mackintosh has received the greatest amount of attention from historians. The examination of his career and his rhetoric prior to the Crofters' War permits this stage of his career to be contextualised to a greater extent than before; it also aids understanding of the way his career and his views developed after 1886.

The Crofters' War

During the early 1880s Fraser Mackintosh was one of a small number of MPs who acted to kept the grievances of crofters in the public eye. His position as a member of this small group was recognised by Gaelic commentators in this period.[29] After he had questioned the Home Secretary, Sir William Harcourt, about the Leckmelm evictions in 1880, he remarked: 'I am glad that I have had the privilege of setting a movement in foot in Parliament which must lead to the amelioration of the poor Highland crofter'.[30] Two other prominent supporters of the crofters in parliament were Charles Cameron, one of the three MPs for Glasgow, and Donald H. MacFarlane, the Caithness-born member for the Irish county of Carlow. Cameron was noted as a newspaper proprietor as well as a Liberal politician; the *North British Daily Mail,* of which he had been the editor and sole proprietor since the mid - 1860s, was a prominent voice for radical Liberalism. He has been described as a 'faddist' and it is certainly the case that he had a remarkable record in single issue campaigns, being successful in having private member's bills passed on a variety of subjects, from temperance and the imprisonment of debtors to the conferring of the municipal franchise upon women. There were, however, two issues in which Cameron took a deeper and more abiding interest: Disestablishment of the Church of Scotland and the grievances of the crofters.[31]

MacFarlane had been born in Caithness in 1830, but had spent most of his younger days in Australia and India where he had built up a substantial fortune as the senior partner in the firm of Begg, Dunlop and Co., Calcutta merchants. His politics were orthodox radical Liberal and when he came forward for Carlow in 1880 he had little track record, or even interest, in Irish issues. He cannot accurately be described as a Parnellite, or even as an Irish Nationalist; indeed, he became increasingly disaffected with the direction in which Parnell was taking the party in the late 1870s and 1880s. O'Day has argued that by 1882 he was a 'marginal member of the party' and that by 1885 he was a 'renegade Parnellite'. He attracted some suspicion from his more strident Irish colleagues on the grounds of his Scottish descent and the perceived convenience of his conversion, on the occasion of his marriage, to Roman Catholicism.[32] Like Fraser Mackintosh, MacFarlane was something of an outsider in politics; indeed, despite the apparent contrast over Irish issues, MacFarlane was the Crofter MP with whom Fraser Mackintosh can be most readily compared. Meek notes the irony that as a merchant trading in the empire MacFarlane was 'a product of those very forces that were transforming the Highlands'.[33]

The main tactic pursued by this small group was to establish that the crofters did have grievances worthy of the attention of the government.

As we have seen, in 1880, at the time of the Leckmelm evictions, this was denied by the government. In 1881 there was an attempt to exploit the debate on the Irish Land Bill to draw attention to the crofter issue. Fraser Mackintosh put down a motion as the Bill was moving towards its Committee stage that its provisions regarding evictions should apply to all tenancies in Scotland worth less than £20.[34] This tactic had no prospect of success, but it did serve to draw attention to the fact that Irish small tenants were receiving the attention of the legislature while Scottish crofters were being ignored. Fraser Mackintosh seems to have thought better of pressing this motion and chose not to do so when called upon in the House of Commons[35]. He attracted some criticism in his constituency for his attitude on this question. The *Courier* commented that the crofters 'have not experienced, or at least have not complained, of the grievances which agitate the Irish peasantry'.[36] In many ways Fraser Mackintosh was the least active of this group of MPs, especially on the land issue. While he kept up the pressure on linguistic questions, Cameron and MacFarlane were more vocal on the land question in 1880 and 1881. Cameron, in particular, seemed to be the most keen to link localised grievances to more general political questions. In the course of asking the Home Secretary a question about evictions in Skye he enquired:

> ... whether, taking into account the recent frequency of such evictions in the Highlands of Scotland, Government will consider the propriety of extending to the Highland crofter population protection against arbitrary dispossession similar to that which the law affords in the case of copyholders in England and small tenant farmers in Ireland.[37]

It would be MacFarlane, supported by Cameron, J. Dick Peddie (the radical Liberal member for Kilmarnock), and Sir George Campbell (Kirkcaldy), who would press hardest in Parliament for a Royal Commission in 1882.

While 1881 had seen some skirmishing, over Leckmelm and at Kilmuir, the following year would see the Crofters' War moving onto different levels of intensity and of publicity. There were a number of reasons for this, partly relating to the momentum which had been built up by the Leckmelm and Kilmuir agitations, but the catalyst for further developments was a severe down turn in economic and social conditions in late 1881. Just as Charles Fraser Mackintosh was inaugurating the *London Inverness-shire Association* a fearsome storm was brewing on the west coast of Scotland. The destruction which this storm wrought, especially to fishing boats and gear, can scarcely be exaggerated.[38] The distress caused and the need to provide relief to those stricken by it, resulted in a number of meetings in the main towns of the Highlands and beyond in late 1881 and early 1882. This put the Highlands on the wider agenda of public life in Scotland, but in a rather submissive manner. Not since the 1840s had there been such widespread appeals for money to support destitute Highlanders. These meetings did not link the social and economic condition of the stricken crofters to wider grievances relating to their tenurial condition. The statements on these occasions concerned the need to relieve a suffering, but respectable population. Those who were involved in the land agitation were notable by their absence, as ministers, and other members of the Highland and expatriate middle classes, enunciated appeals on behalf of those who had suffered losses in the winter storms. The Rev Mackinnon of Strath, Skye, for example, stated that the object 'was to give men - frugal, law abiding, brave and industrious - rendered destitute by an appalling and sudden calamity, the means of earning a livelihood'. The Rev Dr Mackay of the Free North Church in Inverness rounded off his appeal with some hyperbole, stating:

> In religion, in morals, in frugal industry, in bravery and in all those good qualities that go to make up good men and women, he believed the fishing population of the West Coast were unsurpassed by any other class in the country.[39]

Most studies of the Crofters' War have paid greater attention to the strife of the following winter, and this is surely sensible.[40] The relationship between poverty and agitation is by no means clear. These issues have also been debated with reference to the outbreak of land agitation in Ireland in 1879; both parallels and contrasts can be drawn with the Highland case. In both societies periods of extreme destitution had been experienced before, most notably during the famines of the 1840s, but also in the early 1860s, without protests such as occurred in the 1880s.[41] It has been suggested that during the intervening period of relative prosperity a 'revolution of rising expectations' had occurred which had produced a generation which 'would not take kindly to any threat of a return to the conditions which had prevailed in the first half of the nineteenth century'.[42] To more recent writers on the Irish case this has seemed an overly simplistic explanation for the outbreak of protest. The period of prosperity between the end of the depression of the early 1860s and the outbreak of the Land War in 1879, does not seem to be long enough to bear the weight of explanation for such a profound event.[43] There do seem to be a number of factors, present in the Irish case but absent in the Highland one, which are relevant here. The first is the fact that Irish rural society was distinctive in a European context for the depth and longevity of traditions of protest. While recent studies have sought to dispel the myth of the passive Highlander it should be emphasised that the Irish comparison is an overly exacting one in this regard.[44] The second point relates to the existence of powerful and politically sophisticated emigre communities. The Irish community in North America, composed as it was of famine emigrants and their descendants, was a fertile breeding ground for a powerful nationalist critique of Anglo-Irish relations. The political and financial links between the Irish-American community and the Land League were crucial in the early years of the Land League. In the Scottish case such links only served to cause tension and controversy, as John Murdoch discovered.[45] Scottish communities in emigrant destinations lacked the politicisation of their Irish counterparts. The link between the land issue and the wider political demands of Irish nationalism gave the Irish Land War an extra level of threat for the Government.

These points go some way towards explaining why the Irish Land War was a more challenging event for the establishment than the Crofters' War. Even in Scotland the relationship between agitation and destitution is by no means clear. There had been agitation, most notably over the Leckmelm evictions, prior to the storms of 1881, and the key early events of the Crofters' War, at Glendale and Braes, took place before the worst of the conditions occasioned by the storms of late 1882. Two points can be made here; firstly, the publicity given to the Braes dispute helped to generalise the Crofters' War and give a spur to the organisation of the movement; secondly, the government saw the growing protests in the light of what had occurred in Ireland over the previous three years and may have unconsciously contributed to the spread of protest by an exaggerated reaction.

By the end of 1882 there had been several important further developments in the course of the agitation in the Highlands which made the political consequences of the severe conditions of late 1882 and early 1883 so much more potent.[46] The Leckmelm agitation had rather petered out in 1881, as it became evident that Pirie was utterly obdurate and was not going to alter his plans for the way he wished to manage his estate.

The focus of the agitation in 1881 and 1882 moved to the island of Skye and, initially at least, to the estate of another landowner who could be described as an outsider, William Fraser of Kilmuir. Fraser's home was at Newton House just outside Nairn, and he was well known as a prominent Liberal, having been active in persuading Kenneth Mackenzie of Gairloch to stand in the election of 1880. Fraser had purchased the large Kilmuir estate from Lord Macdonald in 1855 and was determined to make sweeping changes in the way in which it was run. While many landlords across the Highlands were willing to accept the fact that crofters paid very low rents, Fraser was determined to raise those on the Kilmuir estate. For these actions he attracted a great deal of criticism, rapidly becoming one of the hate figures of the emerging Highland land movement.[47] This was seen most clearly in 1877 when the *Highlander* published a report of the great flood in Uig which swept away a burial ground and resulted in the bodies being washed up among the ruins of his factor's residence, which had also been destroyed by the flood waters. The offending paragraph remarked:

> . . . it is strange that nearly all the dead buried in Uig during the last five hundred years should be brought up, as it were, against the house, as if the dead in their graves arose to perform the vengeance which the living had not the spirit to execute.[48]

Fraser sued and substantial damages were awarded in his favour, a course of action which was injurious to the financially struggling newspaper.[49] The article is usually interpreted as evidence of the growth of anti-landlord feeling in the Highlands in the late 1870s; this, however, is not the whole story. The paragraph went on to comment:

> . . . although the living would not put forth a hand themselves against the laird, they do not hesitate to express their regret that the proprietor was not in the place of the manager when he was swept away. It is sadder than the destruction itself, that such feelings should be kindled under the land laws of Great Britain.[50]

There are two interesting themes here; firstly, the notion that the people of the estate were not assertive enough to grasp the nettle of anti-landlordism and, secondly, that there was something to be regretted in the way that good feeling between landlord and tenant had given way to such tension. This can be interpreted as a desire to return to the halcyon days of satisfactory tenurial relations rather than a willingness to countenance the root and branch destruction of landlordism. Such feelings would be a crucial theme in the Crofters' War.

The living began to emulate the deceased as the Kilmuir estate became the centre of agitation in the early 1880s. Protest over rent began in a sporadic manner in 1877, and by 1880 and 1881 it had become more organised and resulted in the estate offering rent abatements. This was one of the first examples of agitation achieving a result.[51] Part of the reason for this was the growth of agitation elsewhere on the island, most notably at Braes, near Portree from April 1882, and at Glendale in the west of the island, after the Whitsun rent collection in 1882. A landlord like Pirie in Leckmelm could hold out as long as the agitation did not spread beyond his estate, but in Fraser's correspondence with his factor there is a palpable sense of a siege mentality as crofters elsewhere on the island began to get restive.[52] The Kilmuir agitation was novel in that it was mostly about rent levels: at Braes and Glendale, and in most other cases throughout the Crofters' War, the agitation would centre on disputes over grazing lands.

In this period of rising agitation one further development must be noted, namely the decline and failure of Murdoch's *Highlander*. It had always been a delicate financial operation, heavily dependant on Murdoch's extraordinary energy, to keep the newspaper going. The basic cause of the problem had been the persistent under-capitalisation of the venture from its inception. In April 1878 Murdoch appealed for an extra £700 of capital, 'at once', although he admitted that he needed £1400 to put the paper on a secure footing. This money was not forthcoming and in November 1878 the *Highlander* was auctioned twice without a buyer being found, and for a time the paper was in the hands of liquidators; by early December, however, Murdoch had regained control. This crisis had passed over without any solution being found to the underlying problem of lack of capital.[53] Whilst in public Murdoch declared that the paper had added to 'the moral stature of its constituents' and 'developed elements of character which are better than land and houses, and which no gold could buy' in his autobiography he took a more critical line. He remarked that the survival of the paper had been 'more due to our creditors patience and good sense than to the zeal and munificence of our Highland clients over the world'.[54]

As Murdoch later recalled, the parlous financial condition of the *Highlander* necessitated his going out among the people of the

Highlands to collect subscriptions, and he made use of these opportunities to address the people. The nature of Murdoch's addresses reveals a great deal about his perspective on the condition of the Highlanders.

> I may add that I did not always address them exclusively on the land. I often spoke to them on "The stuff we're made of" and told them of the constituents of the body and how to keep it in vigour. Sometimes on temperance and in the larger townships and villages, on some Gaelic literary subject, so as to encourage the people to set a high value on things pertaining to their country and position - lastly to their race, lore and language.

Above all, Murdoch declared his objective to be, not only the material improvement of the Highlanders, but 'developing their own capabilities and stirring them up to work out their own elevation'.[55]

In July 1881 the *Highlander* ceased to be a weekly newspaper and struggled on until early 1882 as a monthly review. Although Murdoch declared that the principles and objectives of the paper would remain the same, the new format did not allow any scope for the distinctive zeal which had characterised the paper at its prime and it soon ceased publication.[56] Some evidence of the personal bitterness and disappointment which this occasioned on John Murdoch's behalf can be gauged from a letter he wrote to the *Irish World* in May 1882:

> I had just to give up everything - plant, stock, private furniture, my books - everything, in short, towards paying the debts which I incurred in trying to keep an organ through which the oppressed Celts in this country could express themselves; and I am houseless while they are paperless and under the necessity of accepting such space as the organs of the enemy give them.[57]

Although other newspapers, such as the *Oban Times* under the editorship of Duncan Cameron, and Alexander Mackenzie's *Scottish Highlander,* which was published weekly until 1898, espoused the cause of the crofters, they lacked the idealistic and holistic approach to the problems of the Highlands which had characterised the *Highlander*. It is ironic that the *Highlander* faded from the scene just at the moment when the simmering protests of the crofters reached a new level.

Protest and Politics

The Battle of the Braes was the event which put the grievances of the crofters on the wider political agenda. In many ways it was the classic dispute of the Crofters War: the crofters of Braes and the Macdonald estate management disputed the rights to grazing on Ben Lee. The crofters continually grazed their animals on land which the estate wished to lease as a sheep farm. Attempts to serve notices on the crofters resulted in deforcement of the Sheriff Officers and ultimately a large body of police had to be drafted from outside the Highlands to force their way into the township, running the gauntlet as they did so, in order to make the necessary arrests.[58] The events themselves were dramatic enough, but what really made the Battle of the Braes significant was the publicity which it received; the events were widely reported in the press of London, of Lowland Scotland and, significantly, of Ireland. It has been suggested that in addition to these factors the Battle of the Braes received wider prominence than, say, the Leckmelm evictions, because the events in Ireland and the paranoia of the Sheriff of Inverness, William Ivory, made 'a movement out of a very minor land dispute'.[59]

While these points are pertinent they do not tell the whole story. The Irish land agitation was up and running, and probably at a more intense level, than a year earlier when the controversy over the Leckmelm evictions was at its height. Further, while Ivory's gargantuan ego, a direct contrast with his physical stature, should not be discounted as a factor, it was not a significant one. Ivory's paranoia grated as much with the government as it did with the crofters. In fact, the Sheriff was an ideal propaganda weapon for the crofters' movement; his presence ensured that they had no need to draw caricatures of insensitive and overweaning representatives of authority.

A further development in 1882, which in many ways can be seen as the key year in the development of protest in the Highlands, was the institutionalisation and organisation of the Crofters' movement. The core of the movement was already in existence in the form of the *Federation of Celtic Societies*, which had been in existence since 1878, and the *Skye Vigilance Committee*, which had been formed in mid-1881 in response to the difficulties of crofters on the Kilmuir estate. The reaction to the agitation on Skye replicated in an expanded form the reaction to the Leckmelm evictions a year earlier. Meetings were held in Glasgow in May 1882, and in London in February 1883. Thus the importance of linking up events in the Highlands with the politically active urban Gaels was established at an early stage in the crofters' agitation. The urban agitation brought people like Gavin B. Clark, Angus Sutherland and Roderick Macdonald, all to become Crofter MPs, to prominence. Three organisations established in late 1882 or early 1883 formed the core of the Crofters' movement: the *Highland Land Law Reform Associations* of London and Edinburgh, and the *Sutherland Association*.[60] The first use of the term *Highland Land Law Reform Association* had come in March 1882, before the establishment of the organisations in either Edinburgh, London or Sutherland, even before the Battle of the Braes, and it was associated with a group in Inverness. Alexander Mackenzie was at the forefront of this new association and its Council included such local luminaries as the Town Clerk, Kenneth Macdonald, later Fraser Mackintosh's political agent; Colin Chisolm who had been involved in the *Gaelic Society of Inverness*; John Whyte, the local librarian and brother of Henry Whyte of Glasgow ('Fionn'); and the Rev John Mactavish of the Free East Church in the town. The objects of the new association were as follows:

> ... by constitutional means, and irrespective of party politics, to effect such changes in the Land Laws as shall prevent the waste of large tracts of productive lands in the North, shall provide security of tenure, increased protection to the tillers of the soil, and promote the general welfare of the people, particularly throughout the Highlands of Scotland.[61]

At this stage in the crofters agitation, Inverness was an important centre of activity. In November 1882 this was made clear when the leading Irish nationalist and land campaigner Michael Davitt made a speech in the town on 'Land Nationalisation and Highland depopulation'.[62]

The Braes controversy did not end with the arrest of the crofters who had deforced the Sheriff officer in April, it continued when it emerged that they were to be tried by summary process rather than by jury. Indeed, this was the occasion of Fraser Mackintosh's only foray into the controversy when he signed a letter to the *Times* protesting about the lack of a jury.[63]

In September 1882 Fraser Mackintosh received a deputation from the Inverness *HLLRA* in the Royal Hotel in Inverness. In response to statements by the Rev John Mactavish and Alexander Mackenzie, Fraser Mackintosh said that he concurred with the objects of their Association and that he believed that changes in the land laws in the Highlands 'must be brought about in a quiet orderly and constitutional manner', and he concluded that he supported the call for a Royal Commission to be appointed to examine the grievances of the Crofters.[64] This episode demonstrates, yet again, the limitations of Fraser Mackintosh's view of the developing crofter agitation. He had distanced himself, or at least remained aloof from, the protests. This is seen quite clearly in mid-1882 when the *Federation of Celtic Societies* was debating the land question and proposing to lobby the government in an attempt to promote land reform. While Charles Cameron wrote a long letter to the Federation stating that it was 'the imperative duty' of the government to deal 'with the land question in Scotland in a broad and statesmanlike spirit while it is still within manageable compass', Fraser Mackintosh communicated with the Federation in a very different spirit; he trusted that they would be 'moderate, though determined, and that no language should be used which might prejudice matters'. He does not seem to have been involved in the establishment of either the Edinburgh or London *HLLRA*, events which involved expressions of much greater radicalism than anything which Fraser Mackintosh would have adhered to. He was, however, one of a long list of Vice Presidents of the London *HLLRA*; this was not particularly significant as this was a largely honorary position which indicated only general support for the objectives of the Association. He does not seem to have been on the Executive of the Association.[65] His support for the Royal Commission can be seen as a respectable demand which would decrease the justification for agitation and produce an official response to the grievances of the crofters.

In November 1882 he expressed similar sentiments in the course of an address to the *London Inverness-shire Association*. In this speech he demonstrated that his thinking on deer forests had advanced somewhat; declaring that due to the 'great demand for deer forests and sport generally the population was diminishing on a most alarming scale'. Later in the speech, however, he returned to two of his familiar themes, the preferential treatment given to Ireland and the need to keep the agitation within recognised boundaries. On Ireland he complained 'whenever there was the least trouble or excitement the government and everybody else immediately gave attention to it' and he concluded by remarking that 'he had no violent object in view, desiring only that the population should not come to be regarded in the future as discontented and disaffected'.[66]

Indeed, at this point in his career Fraser Mackintosh was in receipt of the firm support of the *Inverness Courier* which remarked that he had 'supported the government with more heartiness than at any previous point in his career'. With reference to the crofters' agitation they approved of the member's emollient approach, pointing out that:

> It is to be hoped that the hon. member will at least be prudent and neither stir up elements of strife, nor fan the embers of a decaying fire. No man knows better than Mr Fraser Mackintosh that an injudicious crusade on the land question would be injurious to the best interests of the Highland people.[67]

As we have seen, Fraser Mackintosh was in no danger of stirring strife or fanning embers, far less flames, as far as the land agitation was concerned. It is hardly likely that he would have received such an endorsement if he had been in the forefront of the crofter agitation and this provides further evidence that his role was strictly limited at this point.

The previous winter had seen much social and economic chaos caused by the sudden storms of November 1881 which destroyed a potentially prosperous year. The winter of 1882 - 83 was difficult for the crofters and cottars of the west coast and the islands, but in a different way. In late September it became clear that the potato disease, which had struck periodically since 1846, was 'virulent throughout the west coast'.[68] This was a serious problem because it was likely to have such long lasting effects, not only in terms of the immediate food shortage but also the likelihood that there would be a shortage of seed and, therefore, a light crop in the following year. This pattern had been established in the 1840s, and the relief operation in 1883 paid a great deal of attention to trying to deal with the likely shortage of seed potatoes.[69] At the beginning of the following month violent storms once more visited the west coast and the islands. The *Inverness Courier's* correspondent from the north end of Skye reported that:

> Fields are almost cleared of their fine crops of oats and hay, scattered in all directions, and some driven into the sea. Scarcely a single stook was seen standing. Houses were unroofed, deserted by their inhabitants.[70]

In addition to the difficulties caused by the potato disease and the violent storms there was also the added blow of a dramatic failure of earnings from the fishing industry which was such a vital prop to the crofting communities of the west and the islands.[71] The geographical concentration of the crisis was notable, the worst conditions were in the Hebrides and particularly Skye and Lewis, the two islands which relied to the greatest extent on earnings from the east coast fishing. Evidence from other areas, where the economy was more mixed, suggest that the impact of the crisis was variable. It is notable, however, that the agitation in 1883 was at its peak in Skye and Lewis, the very areas where the potato failures and collapse of earnings from fishing were most keenly felt.[72] Thus, the crisis was the same kind of multifaceted event as had struck the Highlands in the late 1840s (indeed, local observers in Lewis reckoned conditions to be worse than in 1846): being the second bad winter in succession and coming after the events at Kilmuir, Braes, and Glendale and after the beginnings of the organisation of the Crofters' movement, it had much more profound effects politically and in augmenting the protests which had already occurred. [73] It added great weight to the demands for a Royal Commission to examine the causes of the crofters' grievances. Further, 1883 saw more widespread, organised and politicised protest than either of the previous two years. The main event of 1883, however, was the appointment and work of the Napier Commission. This would bring Fraser Mackintosh into much closer communion with the crofting community.

---

[1] *Inverness Courier,* 23 Aug 1881.
[2] I. M. M. MacPhail, *The Crofters' War* (Stornoway, 1989), p. 15; J. Buchanan, *The Lewis Land Struggle: Na Gaisgich* (Stornoway, 1996), p.25; D. E. Meek, 'Gaelic Poets of the Land Agitation', *TGSI,* 49 (1974-76), p. 320; see also, I. F. Grigor, 'Crofters and the Land Question, (1870-1920)', unpublished PhD thesis, two volumes, University of Glasgow, 1989, i, pp 116-20.
[3] J. S. Grant, *A shilling for your scowl: The history of a Scottish legal mafia* (Stornoway, 1992), p. 151.
[4] *Highlander,* 26 Sept 1874.
[5] *Highlander,* 25 Apr, 9 May 1874; *Inverness Advertiser,* 21, 24 Apr 1874; only the *Highlander* provided any extended commentary on the implications of the event; *Report of the so-called Bernera Rioters at Stornoway, on the 17 and 18th July 1874* (n.p. 1874; reprinted facsimile edition, Edinburgh, 1985).
[6] *Highlander,* 26 Sept 1874.
[7] D. E. Meek, 'The Role of Song in the Highland Land Agitation', *Scottish Gaelic Studies,* 16 (1990), p.10.
[8] For the text of the poem see D. E. Meek (ed), *Tuath is Tighearna: Tenants*

and Landlords, An Anthology of Gaelic Poetry of Social and Political Protest from the Clearances to the Land Agitation (1800-1890) (Edinburgh, Scottish Gaelic Texts Society, 1995), pp. 90-97, 213-20; see also Meek, 'Gaelic Poets', p.321.
[9] Meek, *Tuath is Tighearna,* pp.86-9, 210-212.
[10] J. N. Bartlett, 'Investment for survival: Culter Mills Paper Company Limited, 1865-1914', *Northern Scotland,* 5 (1982-83), pp. 31-56.
[11] For accounts of the Leckmelm evictions, see: MacPhail, *Crofters' War,* pp.20-1; E. Richards, *A History of the Highland Clearances: Agrarian Transformation and the Evictions, 1746-1886,* (London, 1982), pp.140-1; T. M. Devine, *Clanship to Crofters' War: The social transformation of the Scottish Highlands* (Manchester, 1993), pp. 223-4; I. F. Grigor, *Mightier than a lord: the Highland crofters' struggle for the land,* (Stornoway, 1979), pp. 36-8.
[12] MacPhail, *Crofters' War,* p.20.
[13] J. Hunter, *The Making of the Crofting Community* (Edinburgh, 1976), p.141.
[14] *Highlander,* 17 Nov 1880.
[15] *Inverness Courier,* 18, 30 Nov 1880; *Invernessian,* 27 Nov 1880; J. D. Wood, 'Land Reform in the Atlantic Community, 1879-90: towards a comparative approach', unpublished M.Litt thesis, University of Edinburgh, 1981, p.317.
[16] A. Mackenzie, *A History of the Highland Clearances* (Inverness, 1883, reprinted Edinburgh, 1994), p. 317.
[17] E. A. Cameron, 'Minister was a blunt instrument of God', *Inverness Courier,* 5 Jan 1999.
[18] *PD,* 3rd Series, volume 254, columns 1937-8.
[19] E. A. Cameron, *Land for the People? The British Government and the Scottish Highlands, c.1880-1925* (East Linton, 1996), pp. 16-19.
[20] *Inverness Courier,* 26 Feb 1880.
[21] Cameron, *Land for the People?,* pp. 25, 92.
[22] *Inverness Courier,* 18 Nov 1880; see also *Highlander,* 24 Nov 1880.
[23] *Inverness Courier,* 23, 25 Nov 1880.
[24] *Inverness Courier,* 4 Dec 1880; *Highlander,* 8 Dec 1880; the connections between Highland landowners and the various Highland societies of urban Scotland has been usefully explored by; J. Mackenzie, 'The Highland community in Glasgow in the nineteenth century: a study of non assimilation', unpublished PhD thesis, University of Stirling, 1987, pp. 334-6; see also, C. W. J. Withers, *Urban Highlanders: Highland-Lowland Migration and Urban Gaelic Culture, 1700-1900* (East Linton, 1998), pp. 190-3.
[25] *Highlander,* 8 Dec 1880.
[26] A. Mackenzie, *History of the Mathesons with genealogies of the various families,* (2nd ed, Stirling and London, 1900), A. Macbain (ed), p.142. Matheson's reputation has been rather uncritically accepted by historians, see; T. C. Smout, *A Century of the Scottish People, 1830-1950* (London, 1986),

p.69; Richards, *Agrarian Transformation,* pp. 236, 416; for a different perspective, see; T. M. Devine, *The Great Highland Famine: Hunger, Emigration and the Scottish Highlands in the Nineteenth Century* (Edinburgh, 1988), pp. 212-23.

[27] *Inverness Courier,* 18 Nov 1880.

[28] *Inverness Courier,* 23 Dec 1880; *Highlander,* 22, 29 Dec 1880.

[29] Meek, *Tuath is Tighearna,* pp. 131-2, 242-3.

[30] *Inverness Courier,* 23 Dec 1880.

[31] *Who Was Who,* vol ii, *1916-28* (5th ed, London, 1992), pp. 127;*Glasgow Herald,* 4 Oct 1924; I. G. C. Hutchison, *A Political History of Scotland, 1832-1924: Parties, Elections and Issues* (Edinburgh, 1986), pp. 103, 134, 157. 185; I. G. C. Hutchison, 'Politics and Society in mid-Victorian Glasgow, 1846-1886', unpublished PhD thesis, University of Edinburgh, 1974, pp. 199-215; J. G. Kellas, 'The Liberal Party and the Scottish Church Disestablishment Crisis', *English Historical Review,* 79 (1964), pp. 31-46.

[32] A. O'Day, *The English Face of Irish Nationalism: Parnellite Involvement in British Politics, 1880-1886* (Dublin, 1977), pp. 140, 159-60; D.E. Meek, 'The Catholic Knight of Crofting: Sir Donald Horne MacFarlane, M.P. for Argyll, 1885-86, 1892-95', *TGSI,* 59 (1992-94), pp. 70-122.

[33] Meek, 'Catholic Knight', pp.75-6.

[34] *Inverness Courier,* 10, 14 May 1881.

[35] *Invernessian,* June 1881.

[36] *Inverness Courier,* 28 May 1881.

[37] *PD,* 3rd Ser, vol. 262, col. 355.

[38] *Inverness Courier,* 24, 29 Nov 1881.

[39] *Inverness Courier,* 16 Feb 1882.

[40] Hunter, *Crofting Community,* p.131.

[41] J.S. Donnelly, 'The Irish Agricultural Depression of 1859-64', *Irish Economic and Social History,* 3 (1976), pp. 33-54;G. Moran, 'Near Famine: The Crisis in the West of Ireland, 1879-82', *Irish Studies Review,* No 18 (Spring 1997), pp.14-21.

[42] Hunter, *Crofting Community,* p. 128-9; J.S. Donnelly, *The Land and the People of Nineteenth-Century Cork: The Rural Economy and the Land Question* (London, 1975), pp. 249-50.

[43] W. E. Vaughan, *Landlords and Tenants in Mid-Victorian Ireland* (Oxford, 1994), p. 211.

[44] Devine, *Clanship to Crofters' War,* p. 210.

[45] J.D. Wood, 'Transatlantic Land Reform: America and the Crofters Revolt, 1878-1888', *SHR,* 63, (1984), pp. 79-104.

[46] D. W. Crowley, 'The "Crofters' Party", 1885-1892', *SHR,* 35 (1956), p.112.

[47] MacPhail, *Crofters' War,* p.19; Hunter, *Crofting Community,* p.133.

[48] *Highlander,* 3 Nov 1877.

[49] *Highlander,* 1 Dec 1877, 13 Apr 1878.
[50] *Highlander,* 3 Nov 1877.
[51] MacPhail, *Crofters' War,* pp. 27-36; Hunter, *Crofting Community,* p.133.
[52] HRA, Kilmuir Estate Papers, AG/Inv/10/28, Fraser to Alexander Macdonald, 5 Apr, 2 May 1882; AG/Inv/10/29, Fraser to Macdonald, 7 Feb 1883.
[53] *Highlander,* 13 Apr, 16, 23, 30 Nov 1878.
[54] *Highlander,* 7 Dec 1878; MLG, John Murdoch Autobiography, volume iv, p. 204.
[55] MLG, John Murdoch Autobiography, volume iv, pp. 183-4.
[56] *Highlander,* July 1881.
[57] Quoted by Wood, 'Land Reform in the Atlantic Community', pp.204-5.
[58] MacPhail, *Crofters War,* pp.36-45; Hunter, *Crofting Community,* pp. 133-37; Cameron, *Land for the People?,* p.17.
[59] H. J. Hanham, 'The Problem of Highland Discontent, 1880-85', *Transactions of the Royal Historical Society,* 5th Series, 19 (1969), pp. 64-5.
[60] Macphail, *Crofters' War,* pp. 88-93; Hunter, *Crofting Community,* p.143.
[61] *Inverness Courier,* 2 Mar 1882; Fionn, 'The Late Colin Chisholm, Inverness', *Celtic Monthly,* 4 (1896), p. 73.
[62] *Inverness Courier,* 7 Nov 1882.
[63] MacPhail, *Crofters' War,* pp.45-6; *Inverness Courier,* 11 May 1882.
[64] *Inverness Courier,* 12 Sept 1882.
[65] MacPhail, *Crofters' War,* p.230, Appendix E.
[66] *Inverness Courier,* 25 Nov 1882.
[67] *Inverness Courier,* 19 Oct 1882.
[68] *Inverness Courier,* 28 Sept 1882.
[69] *Reports as to the Alleged Destitution in the Western Highlands and Islands,* PP 1883 LIX.
[70] *Inverness Courier,* 5 Oct 1882. There are reports from across the Highlands on the damage done by the storms in this issue of the *Courier.*
[71] Hunter, Crofting Community, p.131; MacPhail, *Crofters' War,* p.229, Appendix D.
[72] 'Copy of Minute of Parochial Board of Gairloch', *Alleged Destitution*; see report of 'Meeting of the Natives of Lochaber in Inverness', *Inverness Courier,* 19 Dec 1882.
[73] *Alleged Destitution.*

Chapter Five

The Napier Commission

Introduction
The appointment of the *Napier Commission* was the crucial turning point in the Crofters' Wars. It indicated that the government was prepared to take account of the fact that the Highland land issue deserved consideration as a special issue. It also gave the crofting community the opportunity to voice their own version of the grievances which they faced, rather than having others, whether Free Church ministers, or Members of Parliament, speak for them.[1]

The appointment of the Napier Commission was the most important result of the activities of the small group of MPs who had drawn attention to the grievances of the Crofters prior to 1883.[2] In November 1882 Fraser Mackintosh requested a Royal Commission to look into the matter. In early 1883 he wrote to Sir William Harcourt, the Home Secretary, pointing out that a wide constituency of opinion was in favour of an enquiry and forwarding a motion signed by 21 MPs.[3] The government were reluctant to grant such a request as they did not want to create the impression that the crofter problem required special treatment. Harcourt, however, did not want to refuse on this occasion only to give in later, something which might be interpreted as a sign of weakness. He was well aware of the political damage which would result from such vacillation. Harcourt announced to parliament in March 1883 that a Commission would be appointed, his objective being to take the heat out of the developing crofter agitation.[4]

Membership of the Commission
Before considering the impact of the Commission and the way in which the leaders of the Crofters' movement, such as Alexander Mackenzie or John Murdoch, reacted to it, we must consider the personnel of the Commission. The Chairman, Lord Napier and Ettrick, was a Border landowner who had been a career diplomat, serving in Vienna, Constantinople, St Petersburg, the USA, the Hague, and Berlin, before being appointed Governor of Madras in January 1866. Following the assassination of the Earl of Mayo in 1872, he acted as temporary

Governor General of India, but was passed over for the permanent appointment and retired to Scotland.[5] His experience in India in the 1860s, where much attention was paid to land tenure in the aftermath of the rebellion of 1857, gave him an obvious background on the land question. More interesting, however, in the light of his subsequent ideas on the Highlands, were his experiences in Russia in the early 1860s. In the course of a revealing address to the annual meeting of the *National Association for the Promotion of Social Science* in Plymouth in 1872, he touched on some interesting themes. He noted the tendency towards the consolidation of land in great estates and the proliferation of tenancies-at-will. He went on to note that, while serving in St Petersburg, he had

> the good fortune to be a witness . . . of the promulgation of the Act of Emancipation and Endowment, and, notwithstanding the disenchantments which are ever ready to follow in the track of philanthropy, the scene still remains the greatest recollection of my life, an impression that can never be repeated and can never be forgotten . .

Whilst he did not underestimate the limitations of the emancipation of the Russian peasantry, especially the continuing authority of the village (through which the peasants held their land in a collective manner), he was clear that the granting of 'a legal and lasting interest in the land of Russia to 50 million of its inhabitants' must 'inevitably conduct them to the full exercise of individual liberty, and to the full enjoyment of individual property'. It is striking that when Napier came to compose the section on land in the report of the Royal Commission he adapted the idea of the township as the central feature of the new order which he proposed. He recorded a similar impression of the people of India in that their 'dignity and self respect' was augmented by the firm possession of property rights.[6] Some regarded Lord Napier's thoughts on land reform as being unduly radical for translation to the United Kingdom; the *Times* remarked that 'we see no particular reason for setting to work to imitate either Russia or Germany or India in the matter of our land laws'.[7] Nevertheless, it is notable that in both India and Russia, although on a much larger scale, he had acquired experience of land reform in the aftermath of protest. In the Indian case an extra dimension was added by the fact that reforms were based on the regularisation of historical and traditional forms of land tenure. In one of his earliest speeches in the House of Lords Napier sought to draw attention to some aspects of the Scottish land question. He asked whether it would be possible to have a return of statistics showing the amount of land under cultivation and capable of improvement and the extent of land used for sport but capable of cultivation. His motivation for this interest, he declared, was the increasing price of food, the extent to which the nation was becoming dependant on foreign sources for food supply, and the importance of ascertaining 'in what degree the productive powers of our own kingdom could be developed.' In particular, he was worried about the amount of land which was 'purposely retained in an unproductive state, simply for the sport and entertainment of the upper classes.'[8] In an early indication of the debate which would occur over the contents of the *Royal Commission Report* in 1883, the Duke of Argyll rose to pour scorn on Lord Napier's request for information. Argyll felt that the information requested could not be supplied without the exercise of highly subjective opinions as to the use and the potential capabilities of land.[9] This was the first in a series of clashes between the two men; it should be noted that while Napier was Governor of Madras (1866-72) and temporary Viceroy of India (1872), Argyll was Secretary of State for India. There is no evidence that they clashed over policy matters during this period.[10] It can be seen, then, that Napier had an interest in the land question from an international, imperial and domestic perspective.

The other members of the Commission, alongside Fraser Mackintosh, can be placed into two groups, with Fraser Mackintosh and Napier having a foot in either camp. The first group were the Celtic Scholars, namely Mackinnon and Nicolson; the second group were the politicians, namely Lochiel and Mackenzie of Gairloch. Professor Donald Mackinnon was the first holder of the Chair of Celtic at the University of Edinburgh. Mackinnon was a native of Colonsay and had trained as a teacher in Edinburgh. His first post was at Lochinver in Ross-shire. In 1869 he graduated in Mental Philosophy from the University of Edinburgh and was involved in educational administration, firstly with the Church of Scotland and subsequently with the Edinburgh School Board. He was a surprise appointment to the Chair of Celtic, which many expected to go to one of the eminent Celtic scholars of the time, such as Thomas Maclauchlan or John Francis Campbell. He had participated in the SSPCK's revised translation of the Bible, and had edited a *Catalogue of Gaelic Manuscripts in Scotland* as well as editing the *Celtic Review*. His lasting contribution to scholarship, however, was primarily that of an educator, although his attitude to the preservation of Gaelic was more uncompromising than many of his generation.[11]

Mackinnon had been recommended to the government as a potential member of the Royal Commission by Lady Gordon Cathcart who was impressed with his knowledge of the Highlands and its people and felt that he would be a 'very popular appointment as far as the Crofters themselves are concerned'.[12]

Sheriff Alexander Nicolson, Sheriff of Kirkcudbright, but a native of Skye, was a colleague of Mackinnon in scriptural translation and a noted scholar in his own right. His main publication was a volume of Gaelic Proverbs. He was also a famous mountaineer, pioneering several new routes in the Cuillins.[13] Interestingly, Nicolson had reacted to the news of the outbreak of the Battle of the Braes by issuing a 'little leaflet', with an address to the crofters of Skye, in which he lamented the fact that 'Skyemen are now imitating the Irish, and making themselves objects of derision and dread'.[14] This was a typical response among those who thought they had claims to be leaders of opinion in the Highlands. Indeed, in these early days of the Crofters' War there was suspicion and deprecation of contemporary events in Ireland, this would change over time. Nicolson also felt, based on a reading of Alexander Mackenzie's *History of the Highland Clearances,* that earlier anti-clearance protests were just as serious as those of 1882 and if this were more widely known hysterical reactions to the Crofters' protests would have been less likely.[15]

The politicians on the Commission were Donald Cameron of Lochiel, Fraser Mackintosh's predecessor as MP for Inverness-shire, and Sir Kenneth Mackenzie of Gairloch, a Liberal in politics who had unsuccessfully challenged Lochiel for Inverness-shire in 1880, and was well known as a liberal landowner. Many thought this to be a landlord dominated body: even Fraser Mackintosh, by virtue of his ownership of small suburban estates near Inverness, was held to be a landowner.[16] Perhaps not a great deal can be read into the political weighting of the Commission, Napier was a Liberal, although a Unionist one after 1886, as was Fraser Mackintosh of course; Lochiel was a Tory, but his fellow landowner, Mackenzie was a Liberal, as were Mackinnon and Nicolson. The most noticeable feature of the membership of the Napier Commission was the antiquarian and philological bent of many of its members: Fraser Mackintosh, Nicolson and Mackinnon were scholars of the Celtic past, with Napier having an academic interest in land tenure based on his experiences in Russia and India, as we have seen.[17]

The Work of the Commission

The appointment of the Commission was greeted with enthusiasm by Gaelic commentators, in contrast to supporters of the Crofters' movement, who condemned it as being dominated by landlords. Charles Mackinnon's 'Failte a' Choimisein/ Welcome to the Commission' and John MacLean's 'Teachdairean na Banrighinn/ The Queen's Commissioners', both express such optimism and expectation that the Commission would bring direct and tangible benefits to the crofters.[18]

Fraser Mackintosh has been described as the member of the Commission most favourably disposed towards the Crofters.[19] This is a difficult claim to substantiate, but what can be discerned from Fraser Mackintosh's line of questioning is that he was particularly hard on the factors who appeared before the Commission, perhaps in an effort to put as much distance between the political image he was currently trying to develop as the Member for the Highlands and his own factorial past. His questioning of William Gunn, factor on the Cromartie estate; George Malcolm, factor for Ellice of Invergarry and advocate of Deer Forests; John Peter, factor for Lord Lovat; or James Mollison, factor for Baillie of Dochfour demonstrates this; one can detect, even in the printed proceedings of the Commission, a more critical tone than his fellow Commissioners.[20]

Another interesting feature of Fraser Mackintosh's membership of the Commission was that it entailed investigation into the estate management of his former colleague on the Union Street project, George G. Mackay. Mackay had gone on to be a minor landowner, with estates in Raasay, Sutherland and Lochaber. He had also published his own thoughts on estate management and the Highland land laws. In the late 1850s he argued that wholesale clearances had been immensely damaging to the Highlands but he did not advocate a multiplicity of small crofts as an alternative. He felt that a graduated system of small farms with tenants on strict leases and paying moderate rents would produce a 'class more contented and happy - more independent and free from care'.[21] By the 1880s he was arguing that traditional 'kindly' landlordism was the answer to the Crofters' problems: he wrote of the crofter

> I propose simply to let him alone, so far as agitation and the foolish speaking and writing of assuming patriots are concerned, and commend him to the sympathy and kindly feeling of his landlord - and there is usually no want of it.[22]

During the Napier Commission, however, a different tale emerged as to the nature of his estate management. The Free Church minister on the island of Raasay, which Mackay had purchased in 1872, argued that Mackay's 'chief aim appears to have been to make pecuniary gain by the purchase, accordingly he set immediately about increasing the rents'.[23] We should necessarily be wary of evidence of this nature, as most witnesses to the Napier Commission were keen to put the worst possible construction on the activities of landowners. Nevertheless, interesting corroboration comes from evidence to the Commission from another estate owned by Mackay, Rosehall in Sutherland. The events on this estate, according to the statement of the crofters, sounded remarkably similar to later events in Leckmelm. Mackay purchased the estate from Sir James Matheson in 1870 and immediately set about changing the terms of the crofters' tenure; removing pasture land and restricting their right to arable land. The response of the crofters of Rosehall in 1870 was in dramatic contrast to their counterparts at Leckmelm, perhaps because they lacked the leadership of someone like John Macmillan. As one of them recounted to the Napier Commission:

> ... no one at first thought of submitting to Mr Mackay's terms, but as the fatal day approached, and no provision had been made for it, men's hearts began to fail them, and gradually one after another succumbed to the threatening storm till nearly all agreed to give the new scheme a trial.[24]

Fraser Mackintosh does not seem to have pursued the issue of the nature of his former colleague's methods of estate management despite their divergence from his printed views. Nevertheless, it is interesting that two men who had such similar concerns in the 1860s should turn up on apparently opposite sides of the debate on the land question two decades later.

An interesting issue which came up in the course of questioning by the Napier Commissioners was the extent to which the crofter evidence was stimulated by activists such as John Murdoch and Alexander Mackenzie. Neither Murdoch nor Mackenzie sought to deny that they had helped the Crofters prepare their evidence prior to the visit of the Commission: indeed, Murdoch published a pamphlet in Gaelic and English in 1883 which, it has been argued, was an attempt to 'provide crofters with a selective but systematic Biblical basis for their claims against their landlords'.[25] Major Fraser of Kilmuir, predictably enough, felt that the evidence given by the crofters 'generally was that of malcontents urged on by agitators'.[26] The Mackintosh informed his factor that he should give detailed evidence about the use of club farms on the estate and noted that 'there has been too much from the popular view and it was now quite time for the "crotchetmongers" to see that there are two sides'.[27] Ranald MacDonald, the factor on the Gordon Cathcart estates actually went as far as to try and discredit the witnesses who came forward to give evidence on conditions on the island of Barra. William Gunn, factor on the estates of the Earl of Cromartie, later deprecated the 'abuse and statements grossly untrue' which characterised the evidence of the 'ungrateful people'.[28] Clearly, Highland landlords and their employees were discomfited by the prospect of their tenantry speaking out. Such outspokenness was a novelty, partly because of the extent of landlord coercion which engendered such fear on the part of the crofting community. This runs through the evidence of the crofters to the Commission and lies behind the frequent accusations of crofters being threatened with eviction if they gave evidence to the Commissioners. This touched such a raw nerve among landlords that the duke of Argyll led a deputation to the Home Office to present a vigorous denial that such heavy handed tactics were used.[29] The Secretary to the Commission, Malcolm McNeill, would later argue that the Commission had a negative effect on the Crofters and on tenurial relations in the Highlands:

> The crofters entertained the belief that the Commission possessed executive and administrative powers, that their enquiry would issue in immediate action at their instance, and, therefore, that the more they could be induced to receive as evidence the more signal would be the overthrow of the landlords. The whole matter, and still more the tone, of the crofters' evidence before that Commission indicates a deep hostility to landlords with whom, but two years before, they had lived on terms of mutual regard, . . . and they made the most of their case - not always (or often) by fair statement - before it.[30]

These issues were explored by the Commissioners with John Murdoch and Alexander Mackenzie.

Murdoch, in his prepared statement to the Commission, emphasised that the landlord side had considerable resources and information at their disposal in the preparation of their case and that the crofters had few such resources to call upon. With this mismatch in mind, he played down the activity of the Crofters' movement in assisting crofters with the preparation of evidence. He noted that

> the weightiest part of the work of these pioneers was mitigating the adverse influences of men who had for so long kept the crofters in a state of unworthy fear . . . the height of my desire was to have them speak out their own minds in their own native way. I went out in the sincere desire to help the Commission to as full a knowledge of the crofters' case as possible.[31]

Alexander Mackenzie informed the Commissioners that he had toured Skye, North and South Uist and the North West seaboard in advance of the Commissioners in an effort to encourage crofters and cottars to tell the truth about their tenurial relations. He agreed with John Murdoch in finding a community in fear: 'those who, in many cases, had the worst grievances to tell, would not muster courage enough to present them, unless they were questioned regarding them in detail by the Commissioners'.[32] Later in the session Fraser Mackintosh returned to this theme with Mackenzie, and the discussion centred on the need to prepare the crofters, unused as they were to proceedings conducted in English.[33] Further on in his evidence Fraser Mackintosh pressed Mackenzie on the question of the nature of the agitation: Mackenzie confirmed that it was his opinion that education and the depth of grievances had produced the agitation as it stood in 1883. He went on to argue that the Napier Commission was crucial in that it had the capacity to recommend reforms which would quell the agitation. Indeed, it seems that Mackenzie, as opposed to Murdoch, was desirous of controlling the agitation. Mackenzie went as far as to say that he felt that 'if no steps are taken almost immediately you will have a social revolution in the Highlands'.[34] He went on to argue, despite his earlier references to the fear inherent in the crofting community, that the consequences of inadequate reform would be damaging:

> I know we had to keep it back instead of encouraging agitation since this Commission commenced, - I and others of my friends who were forcing on public meetings and a regular propaganda throughout the Highlands in connection with this question, and we had to put our foot down pretty firmly to keep the people from the south from coming here, and carrying on an agitation, independently of us, in the north, into every corner of the Highlands. We thought it only respectful to

this Commission that no such agitation should be permitted till this Commission was at an end;[35]

It is possible that Mackenzie was trying to emphasise to the Commission the importance of their task, he had, after all, referred to it as the 'most important event for the Highlanders since the battle of Culloden'.[36] Further, given that the Commission had been appointed, partly at least, in an attempt to quell agitation, Mackenzie may have been trying to direct the Commissioners to the best manner of fulfilling their remit. Nevertheless, there was a genuine worry in the Highlands about the baleful effects of 'outside agitators': mostly, these worries concerned the Irish influence. This theme arose when Murdoch appeared before the Commission and he had the opportunity to defend himself over the question of whether he had received money for the *Highlander* from Irish American sources in 1879.[37] Indeed, Murdoch regarded the questioning before the Napier Commission on this subject as 'the only approach to a vindication which I ever got'.[38] In questioning these leaders of the Crofters' movement, the Commissioners were deeply interested in the precise nature of their influence over crofters and their contribution to the agitation. We have already noted that Fraser Mackintosh's statements in the early part of the Crofters' War concentrated on the need to keep the agitation within the bounds of respectability and this comes through clearly from Mackenzie's evidence to the Commission and the suspicion with which the Commissioners treated Murdoch. Clearly, the fundamentalism of Murdoch's position attracted the ire of Commissioners, such as Mackenzie of Gairloch, who were concerned about his desire to 'do away with landlordism'. In some senses this was unfair, as Murdoch had a coherent, if somewhat idealistic vision, which did not involve 'any definite scheme', but which rested on 'the revival of the spirit of the people . . . the calling forth of their intelligence, common sense, and enterprise'.[39] This was bound to be a challenging message in a society which had been dominated by landowners whose energies had long been concentrated against such a revival of spirit.

The Report of the Commission
Most studies of the recommendations of the Napier Commission have concentrated on the ideas put forward in relation to the land issue. It should be recognised, however, that the report contained

recommendations on a wide variety of subjects.[40] Indeed, in retrospect, the Report can be seen as the start of a new approach by the Government to the Highlands. As has been argued:

> The Napier Commission was to represent a landmark in the modern history of the Highlands. It marked a watershed between decades of Government repression or, at best, inactivity, and a century . . . of more positive responses to the Highland problem in the form of various enquiries and ensuing development initiatives amongst which the Congested Districts Board takes a prominent place.[41]

This claim can only be measured if the recommendations of the Napier Commission are considered in a comprehensive fashion, including an analysis of its ideas on education, emigration, fisheries and sporting estates, alongside a brief restatement of the well known ideas on the land issue.

The Report began with a consideration of the validity of the oral evidence put forward by the Crofters: the conclusion which was reached was that, although it may not have been factually correct in every detail, it effectively conveyed the moral force generated by the grievances of the crofters; and it was held to corroborate what was 'written in indelible characters on the surface of the soil'. Nevertheless, the Report considered the salient point when it noted that the evidence, although not deliberately manipulated, was a product of the agitated political circumstances of the Highlands in 1883.[42] Indeed, as A. D. Cameron has argued: 'many of the statements must have been written by local people soon after hearing a speech by [Alexander Mackenzie] or John Murdoch'.[43] Such activity can be viewed either as the factor which gave the crofters the confidence to come forward to give evidence, or as the factor which produced evidence which merely reflected the political rhetoric which was washing round the Highlands at the time. Eric Richards has argued that the evidence given to the Commission was 'the climax of a century of seething ill-will in many parts of the Highlands'.[44] Fraser Mackintosh, himself felt that it would be the evidence given to the Commission, rather than the report which would have the greater impact.[45]

The essence of Napier's ideas on land involved giving security of tenure and thirty year improving leases to crofters who held land worth more than £6. Crofters with land worth less than £6 were not to be given such concessions but were to be encouraged to emigrate. The 'township' was to be responsible for the management of the common pasture and all settlements with three or more holdings with common pasture, or a history of such within a forty year period, were to be constituted as townships. Napier felt that the township had a 'distinct existence in the sentiments and traditions of its component members'.[46] It is interesting to note that he had regarded the 'village', the key element in the emancipation of the Russian serfs in 1861, much more negatively. The distinction between the two cases lay in Napier's varying perceptions of the Russian peasant and of the Highland crofter. Of the former he had remarked in 1873:

> Immersed in ignorance, subject to the prescriptions of a venerable superstition, encompassed by the hardships of nature and the seduction of a predominant vice, the mass of the Russian people will emerge laboriously from the second thraldom of the village and the State . . .[47]

The tone of his comments on the Scottish crofters was much more positive, although somewhat condescending:

> . . . it is right to add that even among the poorest and least educated class who came before us there were many examples of candour, kindness, and native intelligence, testifying to the unaltered worth of the Highland people.[48]

As well as recommendations on the land question the *Napier Commission* also reported in detail on the potential of the fishing industry to the crofting community. The proposals in this area would be oft repeated in the 1890s and early 1900s: the construction of harbours; assistance to crofters to buy boats and tackle; and improvements in communications. The Commission drew the contrast between the part-time crofter fishermen of the west coast and the full-time fishermen of the east coast. Even in this area land was identified as the key issue; as the Report concluded:

> If by emigration and the operation of other remedial measures, the bulk of the future population of the Highlands and Islands can be put in possession of larger holdings of land, such as they themselves wish for, a smaller number will engage in the fishing industry than at present is the case. A substantial croft demands the undivided energies of the crofter. But while fewer will probably devote themselves to fishing in

the future, these may be expected to prosecute their calling with greater energy and persistence than is commonly the case at present in many districts of the North West Highlands and Islands.[49]

The development of the fishing industry had been a constant theme of those interested in the development of the Highlands since the eighteenth century and possibly before, and would continue to be so in the period after the publication of the *Napier Commission Report*. Organisations such as the *Congested Districts Board*, the *Fishery Board for Scotland* and the *Board of Agriculture for Scotland*, would not depart meaningfully from the ideas put forward by Napier in 1884.[50]

The Report of the Commission also commented on education in the Highlands; indeed, this was one of the most controversial areas of the report. Alexander Nicolson had been responsible for the report on the Hebrides in an earlier Royal Commission on the Education question, chaired by the Duke of Argyll in the 1860s.[51] Lochiel had also been interested in the education question during his parliamentary career; in 1872 he had been responsible for an amendment to the Education (Scotland) Bill which permitted the State to subsidise education in parishes where rate income was inadequate.[52] Three aspects of the education question were considered: revenue, provision and Gaelic education. The Report noted that the 1872 Act had imposed a 'new pecuniary burden on the people'. The 1872 Act had also necessitated an extensive programme of school building; to meet SED Regulations, and thereby to qualify for further grants, these buildings had to be built to a certain standard. It was widely felt that these standards were not appropriate to the Highlands, where less sophisticated buildings would have sufficed. Although it was emphasised that levels of attendance, regularity of payment of fees and teachers' pay had all improved since the passage of the 1872 Act, there were still problems with operating a national education system in the Highlands.[53] The Report stated this in dramatic terms:

> The conditions of life from a family in the island of Heisker, in the Outer Hebrides, or Foula in the Shetland Islands, are almost as different from those of a family in Midlothian or Middlesex, as if they lived in another Hemisphere. The application to such places of the same rules, to entitle them to benefit from the national provision for education, as are suitable for densely peopled localities of smaller area, would be unjust and absurd, and in point of fact it is not done but

further modification of these rules for the benefit of such places is still required, and more consideration of geographical facts.[54]

Although these were extreme examples, consideration would have to involve the realisation of the scattered nature of the population, the difficulty of the terrain, both of which were held to affect school attendance, as well as the linguistic aspect of education in the Highlands. There was a 'Catch 22' problem for Highland schools in that poor attendance affected not only fee income, but also eligibility for extra money from the SED, the lack of which depressed the standard of school buildings and other facilities and thereby diminished an incentive to attend.

It was the question of Gaelic which occasioned the most debate, however. It would be fair to say that the SED were not well disposed to Gaelic as an element of the school curriculum; it was recognised as a necessary evil in the early years of the curriculum as a means of inculcating basic literacy, skills which could then be applied to the acquisition of English. There was nothing new in this attitude, as we have seen. Despite the fact that the *Napier Commission* argued that 'Educational use of Gaelic should be not only permitted but enjoined' and that it should be made a 'Specific Subject' eligible for grants, this deeply held contemporary attitude was present in their thoughts on this aspect of Highland life:

> The first object of all the educational machinery set agoing in the Highlands at the public expense is to enable every Highland child as soon as possible to speak, read and write the English language correctly; and the question is, can that be done efficiently, in the case of a child who hears and speaks nothing but Gaelic at home, without making any use of the only language the child understands.[55]

The SED consulted its Inspectorate over the proposals in the *Napier Commission* and the response was hostile to the tone of the recommendations. The ideas on education were held to be rather partisan, written as they were by Sheriff Nicolson, although this would not have been widely known at the time. Inspectors noted that the evidence presented to the Commission on educational matters was limited, a point admitted in the Report itself. One Inspector went as far as to argue that the inclusion of education in the report was the result of the personal interests of Fraser Mackintosh and Sheriff Nicolson, and that the conclusions ran counter to the evidence given by schoolmasters and 'men of business', as opposed to that of John Murdoch and Professor Blackie, 'who may both be left out of account'.[56] It was the suggestion that the Highlands deserved special treatment which roused the ire of the Inspectors who communicated with the SED on the subject, and the lengthiest comment devoted considerable space to denying that the Highlands were particularly ill-served by educational facilities or disadvantaged by the attendance requirements imposed by the SED. On the question of Gaelic the Inspector agreed that Gaelic should be utilised as a means of furthering English literacy, but denied that there was any significant demand for its inclusion in the curriculum as a 'Specific Subject'. The argument here was on the grounds that the tide of social progress was operating steadily and positively, through the media of trade, migration and contact with the lowlands, to move the Highlander out of a Gaelic speaking world, both mentally and physically. He concluded:

> That the Education Act is to be, what may be called the voluntary eviction Act of the future is a belief firmly held by all intelligent residents in the North and many of the present unfortunate complications would probably have been avoided had the Education Act been passed ten years sooner.[57]

This is an interesting opinion in that many people thought that the more extensive educational provision in the Highlands was one of the reasons for the outbreak of the crofters' agitation in the early 1880s, presumably what the Inspector meant by 'unfortunate complications'. The exchange of views certainly indicates that education was still very much a contested political issue, if not at a mass level, then at least among those who aspired to lead opinion in the Highlands. Anderson argues that the SED's view was that 'Gaelic . . . reflected a parochial and backward looking patriotism which stood in the way of wider loyalties'.[58] This certainly seems to have been the view of the Secretary of the SED, Henry Craik, who was stridently opposed to Gaelic education. In his book, *A Century of Scottish History,* Craik remarked that 'one essential condition' for the onset of progress in the Highlands was 'the spread of the English language - an opinion which the sentimentalists of our own day have vainly tried to controvert'.[59] Nevertheless, it should be noted that both Fraser Mackintosh and Nicolson, who seemed to be instrumental in putting education on the agenda of the *Napier*

Commission, were scarcely suspicious of 'wider loyalties'.

Emigration was a key element of the *Napier Commission Report*, and one which is often underplayed in accounts of the Commission. Indeed, it could be argued that it was the key element, as none of the other proposals, on land tenure or fishing, for example, were coherent without it. In this area the Commissioners, went against much of the evidence they had heard, which had 'repeatedly stated that there is no need for emigration'. Nevertheless, this section of the report went on to argue that 'the prevailing land agitation has not been without considerable influence in prompting the expressed dislike to emigration' and looked forward to a time when 'overpopulation is clearly shown under any distribution of the land' and the people's 'aversion to emigration will disappear'.[60] This was tantamount to a direct challenge to the Crofters' movement which had argued that emigration should not be contemplated when considerable acreages were still being used for sport and other exclusive forms of land use. The report noted that few crofters had the facilities to finance their own emigration; nor 'can much direct assistance be expected from the proprietors of these impoverished parts'; state assistance was objected to on the grounds that it weakened the self reliance of the recipient of such aid. The conclusion was that emigration from the Highlands was as necessitous as it had been in 1851, when the *Emigration Advances Act* was passed, and that the organisation of such an exercise should be 'placed under the immediate direction of the officers of the Imperial Government rather than under the control of the local authorities'.[61] This was also reminiscent of the 1850s, when government officials such as Sir John MacNeill and Charles Trevelyan, played a prominent role in the organisation of Highland emigration. The comparison with Ireland is also relevant here: after the extreme destitution in Ireland in 1879-80 two Royal Commissions had suggested emigration as a solution to the problems of the west of Ireland and the Quaker philanthropist, James Hack Tuke, had undertaken a private scheme. Tuke's operation, which oversaw the emigration of 1,300 people in 1882, encouraged the government to act. Money was duly advanced under the provisions of the 1882 *Arrears of Rent Act* and the *Tramways and Public Companies Act* of 1883. Under these arrangements around 25,000 people, carefully chosen and deemed to be suitably deserving, were assisted to emigrate from Ireland to Canada.[62]

The final controversial area of the Napier Report which requires consideration here is that concerning Deer Forests. This was one of the most contentious aspects of the Crofters' War: the use of large tracts of land for sport alongside a prevailing perception that crofters were starved of land seemed to encapsulate the essential injustice of the Highland land system. No matter how hard advocates of the Deer Forests, such as George Malcolm, Factor for the Ellices of Invergarry, who owned vast deer forests in Glengarry and Glenquoich, argued that very little of the land so used could be profitably occupied, the issue remained potent.[63] Cameron of Lochiel, owner of substantial deer forests himself, composed the section of the Report which referred to this question and presented a conventional defence of the deer forest system. Lochiel has also been a member of the *Select Committee of the Game Laws* in the early 1870s and was an ardent defender of sporting estates, of which he owned a substantial example.[64] He emphasised that few evictions took place in the creation of deer forests, as most were carved out of former sheep farms no longer considered profitable; it was also noted that most deer forest land was at high altitude and thereby unsuitable for crofter occupancy; and it was concluded that the economic loss to the nation in terms of food supply was minimal, such was the reliance on imported food:

> The soil of a whole county, even of a whole region here, might be laid waste, and the deficit would be promptly covered by the despatch of grain from Manitoba or California, and of meat from Texas or Australia. The extinction of production in Scotland would involve no appreciable scarcity in Lancashire or London, except in reference to the highest quality of live meat; it would only furnish a stimulus to industry in some foreign state or colonial dependency.[65]

It was clear, however, even to Lochiel, that this kind of economic calculation was not the main source of opposition to deer forests. Although the Commission would not go as far as to recommend legislative restrictions on the extent of deer forests, the Report did recommend that sporting estates should not encroach any further on the pasture or arable land of crofters and should not descend below a stipulated line of elevation, perhaps around 1000 feet, or a little lower in disadvantaged western areas. Finally, it was noted that sporting estates represented 'valuable interests . . . which could not be set aside without imposing on the proprietor greater sacrifices than he could be justly required to undergo'.[66]

When the report of the *Napier Commission* was issued in the summer of 1884 Fraser Mackintosh appended a note of dissent to it. Lochiel and Mackenzie of Gairloch also did so, but, arguably, Fraser Mackintosh's short note struck at the most fundamental aspect of the Report. The substance of his dissent concerned Napier's core idea that only crofters with land worth more than £6 per anum should benefit from security of tenure. Fraser Mackintosh felt that would 'cut out . . . many deserving crofters'. He was also opposed to the state assisting individuals to emigrate, he preferred family emigration, but his opposition to emigration ran deeper:

> re-occupation by, and distribution among, crofters and cottars of much land now used as large farms will be beneficial to the state, to the owner and to the occupier. Until this is done, much as I deplore the present position of the congested districts, I must view with jealousy state aided emigration.[67]

This is in direct contrast to his earlier views, such as those which he expressed in his speech to the *Glasgow Inverness-shire Association* in February 1880. This new statement, however, put Fraser Mackintosh in a position much closer to that eventually adopted by the government in 1885-86, after they had rejected Napier's ideas on the land issue as impractical.

Conclusion

The *Napier Commission Report* is a much more wide ranging document than is often recognised, containing proposals on education, the administration of justice and communications; in the latter areas Fraser Mackintosh was responsible for drafting the final report.[68] Fraser Mackintosh was in no doubt as to the value of the evidence given by crofters to the *Napier Commission*; at the Dingwall Conference of the HLLRA, in September 1884, he remarked that the evidence showed 'that in the whole history of Europe there has never been a people who have been so ill-used as the people of the North of Scotland had during the last 150 years'.[69] The precise nature of this claim may be questionable but the statement does graphically illustrate the point that despite the political marginalisation of the *Napier Commission Report* the evidence given by the crofters had a considerable impact, and was used for political propaganda by the HLLRA in their campaigns after 1884.

Overall, the *Napier Commission Report* failed to meet the expectations of the Crofters and it did not reduce the level of agitation in the Highlands. The conclusion of the Report, which referred to the need for 'tranquillity' if the 'benefits' of the scheme were to be felt, as well as the circumstances in which the Commission was established, suggest that this was the aspiration.[70] G. B. Clark, of the London, HLLRA, and soon to be the Crofter MP for Caithness, predicted that 'the great majority of the crofters and cottars will consider it as unsatisfactory as they considered the composition of the Commission. The recommendations of the Commission will not remedy the admitted evils that exist'.[71] Alexander Mackenzie also condemned the report as inadequate; especially so in offering only some crofters security of tenure and he particularly attacked the notion of emigration.[72]

The Report was also the occasion of a lengthy exchange of views, in print and in debate in the House of Lords, between Lord Napier and the Duke of Argyll. Argyll attacked the report as flawed because it did not recognise the fact that the crofter was not merely a small farmer but a labourer who had an attachment to the land, and it was too much land, rather than too little, which was the obstacle to progress in the crofting community.[73] Lord Napier, it seems, was not intimidated by such ducal opinions, which he felt would 'popularize us'.[74] The Report was also subjected to criticism by J. S. Nicholson, Professor of Political Economy at the University of Edinburgh: Nicholson argued that the recommendations were so unrealistic that they would only serve to worsen the agitation once it was evident that they could not be realised.[75] The Crofters' movement were not slow to come to this realisation, as they formally recorded their disappointment with the *Napier Commission's* proposals at the Annual Conference of the HLLRA at Dingwall in September 1884, and intimated their intention to campaign for a more complete and radical overhaul of the Highland land system.[76]

In the background to these exchanges of views, and at the centre of the expectations of the Crofters, was the *Irish Land Act of 1881*. This legislation had conferred security of tenure on all tenants-at-will in Ireland and ultimately became the model for the *Crofters' Act of 1886*. Napier had given specific consideration to the model provided by the *Irish Land Act* in the course of composing the recommendations concerning land in his Report: he noted that 'all that has been said and done in regard to Ireland and the *Irish Act* has been impressed upon the imagination and aspirations of the people'.[77] Nevertheless, he was determined not to let the *Irish Land Act* influence the substance of his ideas on the land question. He did not think a general review of the levels of rents, comprehensive fixity of tenure, 'far less the power of free sale', was required in the Highlands. He went on to make what was, in the light of subsequent events in the Highlands, a very salient point when he suggested that legislation on the model of the *Irish Act* would not 'give the people any extension of area, the thing they most want'.[78] Fraser Mackintosh noted Napier's opposition to copying the *Irish Land Act*, but remarked 'that is no reason why others should not advocate its application'.[79] Indeed, the application of the Irish Act to Highland conditions became the substance of the government's position in 1885 and 1886 as they moved to legislate on the crofter question.

Napier's report did not receive a positive reception in government circles: in particular, his ideas on the constitution of townships attracted particular derision. The *Napier Report* had limited impact on the *Crofters' Act* as it emerged in 1885 and 1886. A conference of landowners met in Inverness in early 1885 to consider the extent of voluntary concessions which might be granted in an attempt to obviate the unwanted interference of legislation. The proposals which emerged from this meeting were inadequate for the purpose and the government proceeded to attempt to legislate, unsuccessfully in 1885 and successfully in 1886, using the *Irish Land Act of 1881* as their model.[80]

---

[1] *Quiz,* 1 Jun 1883, p. 12; 'Men You Know - No 575', *The Bailie,* 24 October 1883.

[2] *PD,* 3rd Ser, vol 274, col 1927.

[3] CFM to Sir William Harcourt, 23 Feb 1883, *Inverness Advertiser,* 2 Mar 1883.

[4] Cameron, *Land for the People,* pp. 18-19.

[5] S. Lee (ed), *Dictionary of National Biography, xxii, Supplement,* (London, 1909), pp. 1090-93; *Scotsman,* 20 Dec 1898; *Times,* 20 Dec 1898; *Longman's Magazine,* February 1899, p.378.

[6] *Times,* 12 Sept 1872.

[7] *Times,* 13 Sept 1872.

[8] *PD,* 3S, 216, 1478-9; *Highlander,* 5 Jul 1873.

[9] *PD,* 3S, 216, 1482-5.

[10] G. Douglas Campbell, 8th Duke of Argyll, *Autobiography and Memoirs* (2 vols, London, 1906), ii, pp. 269-92.

[11] L. Mackinnon, (ed), *Prose Writings of Donald Mackinnon, 1839-1914* (Edinburgh, Scottish Gaelic Texts Society, 1956), pp. xiii-xxvi; *Testimonials in Favour of Donald Mackinnon, MA, (formerly Hamilton Fellow of the University of Edinburgh) Candidate for the Chair of Celtic Languages, History, Literature*

and Antiquities in the University of Edinburgh; D. Mackinnon, *University of Edinburgh, Celtic Chair, Inaugural Address* (Edinburgh, 1883); D. Mackinnon (ed), *A Descriptive Catalogue of Gaelic Manuscripts in the Advocate's Library, Edinburgh, and elsewhere in Scotland,* (Edinburgh, 1912);*Oban Times,* 20 Jun 1914.

[12] Bodleian Library Oxford, MS Harcourt Dep 114, ff.104-5, Lady Gordon Cathcart, to Harcourt, 14 Mar 1883.

[13] Fionn, 'Sheriff Nicolson', *Celtic Monthly,* 1 (1892-3), p. 85; 'Sheriff Nicolson', *Highland Monthly,* 4 (1892-3), pp. 701-2; I. Macdonald, 'Alexander Nicolson and His Collection', in A. Nicolson, *A Collection of Gaelic Proverbs and Familiar Phrases* (Edinburgh, 1996); MacPhail, *Crofters War,* pp. 70-1.

[14] *Inverness Courier,* 25 Apr 1882.

[15] BLO, MS Harcourt Dep 114, ff. 101, Alexander Nicolson, to Harcourt, 14 Mar 1883.

[16] Hunter, 'Politics of Highland Land Law Reform', p.50.

[17] Cameron, *Land for the People,* p.20; E. Richards, *A History of the Highland Clearances: Emigration, Protest, Reasons* (London, 1985), p. 84; for a description of the Commissioners during their visit to Glasgow, see *Quiz,* 26 October 1883, pp. 6-7.

[18] Meek, *Tuath is Tighearna,* pp. 124-7, 237-9.

[19] C. Byam Shaw (ed), *Pigeon Holes of Memory: the life of Dr John Mackenzie, 1803-86* (London, 1988), p. 278.

[20] *Report of the Commission of Inquiry into the Condition of the Crofters and Cottars in the Highlands and Islands of Scotland,* PP. 1884, XXXVI, Qs 40617-28, 42270-342, 42668-729, 42841-875.

[21] G. G. Mackay, *On the Management of Landed Property in the Highlands of Scotland* (Edinburgh, 1858), pp. 18-19.

[22] G. G. Mackay, *The Land and the Land Laws* (Inverness, 1882), pp. 8-9.

[23] *Commission,* Appendix A, no xvii, Statement of Rev Angus Galbraith, p.62; R. Sharpe, *Raasay: A Study in Island History,* (London, 1982), p. 69.

[24] *Commission,* Q. 39730, p. 2569.

[25] D. E. Meek, 'The Land Question Answered for the Bible; The Land Question and the Development of a Highland Theology of Liberation', *SGM,* 103 (1987), p. 87.

[26] HRA, KEP, AG/INV/10/29, Fraser to Alexander MacDonald, 4 Nov 1883.

[27] NAS, GD176/2633/31, The Mackintosh to Allan Macdonald, 15 Oct 1883.

[28] J. L. Campbell, 'The Crofter's Commission in Barra, 1883', in J. L. Campbell (ed), *The Book of Barra* (Reprinted, Stornoway, 1998), pp. 198-204; E. Richards & M. Clough, *Cromartie: Highland Life, 1650-1914* (Aberdeen, 1989), p.323.

[29] Cameron, *Land for the People,* p. 21.

[30] NAS, Crofting Files, AF67/401, Confidential Reports to the Secretary for

Scotland on the condition of the Western Highlands and Islands, by Malcolm McNeill, Edinburgh, October 1886, pp. 3-4.

[31] *Commission,* Q. 44463, p. 3073-4; the inflammatory nature of Murdoch's remarks during his statement caused Lochiel, MacKenzie and Fraser Mackintosh to leave the room and, ultimately, Napier had to suspend proceedings to restore order, see I. M. M. MacPhail, 'The Napier Commission', *TGSI,* 48 (1972-4), pp. 454.

[32] *Commission,* Q. 41058, p. 2688.
[33] *Commission,* Q. 41106-7, p.2697.
[34] *Commission,* Q. 41150, pp.2700-1.
[35] *Commission,* Q. 41152, p. 2701.
[36] *Commission,* Q. 41107, p. 2697.
[37] *Commission,* Q. 44494-500, p.3092-3; Wood, 'Land Reform in the Atlantic Community', p.202.
[38] MLG, John Murdoch Autobiography, volume v, pp. 24-5.
[39] *Commission,* Q. 44463, p.3088; Q. 44501, p.3093.
[40] A. D. Cameron, *Go Listen to the Crofters: The Napier Commission and Crofting a Century Ago* (Stornoway, 1986), pp. 122-3; Cameron, *Land for the People,* pp.22-27; Hunter, *Crofting Community,* p.146; Macphail, *Crofters' War,* pp.84-5; Richards, *Emigration, Protest, Reasons,* 86-89; Fraser Grigor, 'Crofters and the Land Question', pp. 139-62.
[41] A. M. McCleery, 'The Role of the Highland Development Agency: with particular reference to the work of the Congested Districts Board, 1897-1912', unpublished PhD thesis, University of Glasgow, 1984, p.125.
[42] *Commission,* p.2; this issue is discussed in Richards, *Emigration, Protests, Reasons,* pp. 85-8.
[43] Cameron, *Go Listen to the Crofters,* p. 6.
[44] Richards & Clough, *Cromartie,* p. 313.
[45] *Inverness Courier,* 19 June 1883, the occasion of these remarks was the opening of the Inverness Free Library. Fraser Mackintosh may, or may not, have been affected by the fact that the Commissioners had recently escaped death by drowning when their ship, *The Lively* was wrecked off Stornoway; see also N. Newton, *The Life and Times of Inverness* (Edinburgh, 1996), p. 145.
[46] *Commission,* p.17.
[47] *Times,* 12 Sept 1872.
[48] *Commission,* pp. 2-3.
[49] *Commission,* p. 59.
[50] Cameron, *Land for the People,* pp.72-4.
[51] *Report on the State of Education in the Hebrides,* PP 1867, XXV.
[52] MacPhail, *Crofters' War,* p.70.
[53] *Commission,* pp.66, 69-73; for a discussion of these questions, see R. D. Anderson, *Education and the Scottish People, 1750-1918,* (Oxford, 1995), pp.

183-4, 216-7.
[54] *Commission*, p. 69.
[55] *Commission*, p. 78.
[56] NAS, ED7/1/1, Memorandum on the Education Chapter in the Royal Commission's Report on the Condition of the Crofters and Cottars in the Highlands and Islands of Scotland; Notes on the Education Section of the report issued by the Highlands and Islands Commissioners; *Commission*, p.66.
[57] NAS, ED7/1/1, Memorandum on the Education Chapter.
[58] Anderson, *Education and the Scottish People*, p. 217.
[59] H. Craik, *A Century of Scottish History: From the Days Before the '45 to Those Within Living Memory* (Edinburgh & London, 1901), p. 23.
[60] *Commission*, p.103.
[61] *Commission*, pp. 103-108.
[62] G. Moran, 'Escape from Hunger: The Trials and Tribulations of the Irish State Aided Emigrants in North America in the 1880s', *Studia Hibernica*, 29 (1995-97), pp. 99-103; the Napier Commissioners were aware of this activity, see *Commission*, p.104.
[63] *Commission*, Qs 42269-42478, pp. 2822 - 2867; Malcolm published a slightly revised version of his statement to the Commission in pamphlet form, G. Malcolm, *The Population, Crofts, Sheep-Walks, and Deer Forests of the Highlands and Islands* (Edinburgh, 1883).
[64] D. Cameron of Lochiel, 'A Defence of Deer Forests', *Nineteenth Century*, 18 (1885), pp. 197-208.
[65] *Commission*, p. 93-4.
[66] *Commission*, pp. 95-6.
[67] *Commission*, p.137, Memorandum by Mr Fraser Mackintosh of Drummond, M.P.
[68] NAS, AF50/1, Minute Book of the Royal Commission on the Condition of the Crofters and Cottars of the West Highlands of Scotland. The section on emigration was written by Sir Kenneth Mackenzie, fisheries by Professor Mackinnon, education by Sheriff Nicolson, deer forests by Lochiel and the conclusion by Lord Napier.
[69] *Inverness Courier*, 4 Sept 1884.
[70] *Commission*, p. 111.
[71] G. B. Clark, *The Highland Land Question*, (London, 1885), p. 3.
[72] A. Mackenzie, 'Report of the Royal Commission: an analysis', *Celtic Magazine*, no 104, Jun 1884, pp. 359-82.
[73] Duke of Argyll, 'A corrected picture of the Highlands', *Nineteenth Century*, 26 (1884); Lord Napier, 'The Highland crofters: a vindication of the report of the crofters' Commission', *Nineteenth Century*, 27 (1885), pp. 437-63; *PD*, 3rd Ser., vol. 294, col., 106-18; Cameron, *Land for the People?*, pp. 24-28.
[74] NLS, MS 2635, Blackie MS, CFM to John Stuart Blackie, 4 Jul 1884.

[75] J. S. Nicholson, *Examination of the Crofters' Commission Report*, (Edinburgh, 1884), pp.7-8.
[76] Hunter, *Crofting Community*, p. 147.
[77] BLO, MS Harcourt Dep 114, f. 159, Napier to Harcourt, 1 Nov 1883.
[78] BLO, MS Harcourt Dep 115, f.10, Napier to Harcourt, 3 Apr 1884; similar views were expressed by Ranald MacDonald, who acted as Lady Gordon Cathcart's factor in South Uist, Benbecula and Barra, see; R. MacDonald, *The Crofters' Bill, With an anlysis of its Provisions: and the Crofters Commissioners' Report, With Copious Index* (Aberdeen, 1885), pp. xvii - xx.
[79] NLS, MS 2635, Blackie MS, CFM to John Stuart Blackie, 23 Oct 1884.
[80] Cameron, *Land for the People,* pp. 25-39, considers these events in detail.

Chapter Six

Charles Fraser Mackintosh and Political Re-alignment, 1885-86

Introduction
This chapter will examine two crucial years in Fraser Mackintosh's political career, in the political history of the Highlands and of the United Kingdom. The electorate was extended from 3.04 million to 5.7 million in the United Kingdom; from 293,000 to 560,000 in Scotland; and from 1,851 to 9,330 (a far larger proportional increase than in the UK or Scotland) in Inverness-shire, with the concession of the household franchise in both counties and burghs in the electoral reforms of 1884 and 1885.[1] The passage of these reforms had brought the country to the brink of a constitutional crisis and, to a greater extent than was the case in either 1832 or 1867-8, these reforms revolutionised politics in Britain. The scale of the increase in the electorate was only part of a series of reforms which comprehensively altered the machinery of politics across the United Kingdom. Legislation on Corrupt Practices in 1883 had attacked a long-standing problem, although one which was not at its worst in Scotland; redistribution of seats had improved the representation of urban areas in a way which was generally thought to have benefited the Tories; the extension of the hours of polling made it much easier for the new working class voters to record their votes; and the effect of the whole package was the creation of a more uniform and modern, although not necessarily democratic, electoral system across the United Kingdom.[2] With a small number of exceptions, single member constituencies were now the norm; the number of MPs was increased from 652 to 670 but the increase in the number of constituencies was more marked, from 416 to 643.[3] The single election which produced three members for the city of Glasgow, for example, was replaced with a division of the city into seven discrete constituencies.[4] By the early 1890s around 56 per cent of the Scottish adult male population had the vote.[5] Both the requirement to possess the franchise qualification for up to twelve months in some cases, and the efforts of the party agents in the registration courts, meant that the system was not truly democratic. Mobile populations, such as the

Irish community in urban Scotland, were particularly badly affected by the residence qualification.[6] This was less of a problem in rural areas, although the infrequency and inaccessibility of registration courts was a potentially serious problem. This was something to which Fraser Mackintosh drew attention during the 1885 election campaign when he argued that the failure to hold registration courts in the Outer Hebrides had effectively disenfranchised precisely the class of 'capable citizens' which the reforms were designed to benefit. During the campaign the *Scottish Highlander* accused the Liberal and Conservative agents of attempting to oppose the registration of crofters. This was standard practice, the Registration Courts were an important party political battlefield as agents sought to maximise the potential vote for their candidate and minimise that of their opponents.[7]

Fraser Mackintosh had hosted what the *Inverness Courier* called a 'Great Reform Demonstration' at Lochardil in September 1884, where he was joined by Sir Kenneth Mackenzie of Gairloch, Ronald Munro Ferguson, the MP for Ross-shire, and Sir Charles Cameron. In his speech on this occasion Fraser Mackintosh emphasised that he had long supported the idea of the county householder franchise (indeed, his election address for 1874 bears this point out), and that he was in favour of redistribution. He concluded:

> . . . in regard to Scotland especially whether you take her in point of population, or in reference to her proportion of taxation yielded to the nation, we are entitled to considerably more members that we have at present.[8]

At this point, it should be recalled, Fraser Mackintosh was still the member for the Inverness Burghs and had not yet indicated his intention to stand for Inverness-shire at the next general election. He was still keen to emphasise his credentials as an independent Liberal and a prominent figure in the town of Inverness; the holding of a reform rally on his land should be seen in this light rather than as the beginning of his pitch for county votes.

Events were enlivened even more by further constitutional debate, this time over Ireland, and this had an impact on the crofter issue. The Liberal government which had been elected in 1880 began the process of legislating on the crofter issue in early 1885 and by the middle of May the first Crofters' Bill was read in Parliament. The Bill was not to reach the statute book, however, as the government fell rather unexpectedly in

June, when the Irish MPs supported the Conservatives on an amendment to the Budget.[9] Due to the recent electoral reforms, however, the electoral registers were not ready and an election could not begin until mid-November; Lord Salisbury was persuaded to head a 'caretaker administration' to govern the country until the election could be held. The balance of the parties after the election placed the Irish party in a position of great power as they held the balance between the Liberals and the Tories. They could have conspired to wreck any Tory administration, or they could put the Liberals in power with a solid majority. The Irish had let it be known during the campaign that they might support a Conservative government and Parnell had issued a 'manifesto' instructing the Irish community in Britain to vote Conservative. Once it became known, in December 1885, that Gladstone had become convinced of the need for Irish Home Rule, the way was clear for the Irish to support the Liberals and eject the Salisbury administration; this event took place on an amendment to the Queen's Speech in late January 1886.[10] This government, and the short 1886 parliament, was dominated by the issue of Irish Home Rule, which, ultimately, was to split the Liberal party and bring the government down. All other legislation, including the second attempt to pass a *Crofters' Bill* was handled in such a manner as to ensure that the maximum amount of time could be devoted to the Irish bill. In the case of the Crofters' Bill the result was that it was forced through its parliamentary stages with the government showing a resolute unwillingness to accept any of the amendments put forward by the Crofter M.P.s and their supporters who were generally disappointed with its contents. The Act received Royal Assent just before the government fell in June 1886.[11]

This chapter will seek to examine these events from Fraser Mackintosh's point of view. He was involved in them to the extent that he was elected for one of the newly enlarged and politically energised rural constituencies in 1885. In this capacity he was at the centre of a political revolution in the Scottish Highlands.[12] We have noted in earlier chapters the way in which Highland politics became increasingly contested over the period from 1874 to 1884 but the extension of the franchise opened a new vista for the Crofters' movement, allowing them to move into parliamentary politics. The successes at the elections of 1885 and 1886 are the important point to note here, rather than any achievements which flowed from such parliamentary representation. It could be argued that with his work as a member of the Napier

Commission, which greatly enhanced his reputation among the crofters and gave him credibility as a crofter candidate in 1885, Fraser Mackintosh had entered the mainstream of the Crofters' movement to a greater extent than before. This position was not to last for very long, however. It was the Irish Home Rule Issue, which was at the heart of the second great crisis in British politics in this crucial period, which was the occasion of his renewed marginalisation. As we have noted in earlier chapters Fraser Mackintosh was not well disposed towards the Irish members and their tactics in parliament, nor was he very understanding of Irish grievances, either agrarian or constitutional. Thus, Fraser Mackintosh was the only one of the Crofter MPs to vote against the Irish Home Rule Bill and to come forward as a Liberal Unionist in 1886. This did not have any immediately damaging political consequences for him as he was returned unopposed in 1886, but over the 1886 to 1892 parliament he became steadily more detached from his crofter constituents, and they from him, culminating in his defeat by another Crofter candidate at the General Election of 1892.

This chapter will cover three areas; the circumstances of Fraser Mackintosh's crofter candidature for Inverness-shire in 1885; the three cornered election contest in Inverness-shire; an exploration of the background and some of the motivations for Fraser Mackintosh's vote against Irish Home Rule will complete the chapter. Throughout the discussion the extent to which Fraser Mackintosh's rhetoric on the land issue had become radicalised will be an important theme.

The principal reason for this advancement in his views may have been the change in the constituency to which he was appealing; the radical and newly enfranchised crofters of the county rather than the citizens of the Burghs. Perhaps a less cynical view would be that he had undergone a genuine conversion based on his experience on the Napier Commission and his involvement with the HLLRA.

Political Realignment, 1885-1886
The 1885 general election was a long drawn out affair, there was almost five months for campaigning and three candidates in the field in Inverness-shire, including Fraser Mackintosh. Reginald MacLeod was the Conservative candidate: a former agent for the party in Glasgow, he was the heir to what was left of the MacLeod of MacLeod estates in Skye. After the election he went on to be a civil servant, eventually resigning his post as Under Secretary for Scotland to fight Inverness

once again for the Conservatives in January 1910.[13] Kenneth Mackenzie of Gairloch was standing for the Liberals, he was a former colleague of Fraser Mackintosh on the Napier Commission and a landlord with a reputation for sympathy towards the crofters on his estate. He had fought the seat for the Liberals in 1880, losing to Lochiel.

The first issue to be considered in this context are the circumstances and the motivations surrounding Fraser Mackintosh's abandonment of the representation of the Inverness Burghs seat in favour of entering a contest for the county seat. There was thorough condemnation of Fraser Mackintosh for switching seats and for potentially dividing the Liberal interest in the county. The *Ross-shire Journal* called his actions 'shabby in the extreme', the *Courier,* and even his traditional ally the *Advertiser,* also deprecated his actions.[14] In this campaign, however, Fraser Mackintosh had a new supporter: Alexander Mackenzie, a close associate of Fraser Mackintosh, had begun his pro-crofter newspaper, the *Scottish Highlander,* in time for the beginning of the campaign. Mackenzie was assiduous in his defence of Fraser Mackintosh from the attacks of other newspapers.[15] Most of the comment on Fraser Mackintosh's actions in this period have been rather bland, merely recording his change of seat without going into the reasons for it or the controversy which it aroused.[16] MacPhail merely remarks that 'the shire constituency, with its larger number of crofter electors, would be a safer seat for him'.[17] There may well be an important point behind this statement. Fraser Mackintosh's political agenda was now dominated by the land issue, the Inverness burghs election of 1885 was dominated by the Church issue with the Free Church Constitutionalist and future Lord Chancellor, R. B. Finlay, winning the seat. Fraser Mackintosh was an opponent of disestablishment, but from a straightforward *Established Church* point of view. He had never made much of the Church issue and the strength of the *Free Church* in Inverness may have told against him in the burgh election. Dis-establishment was the main issue in the country as a whole in the 1885 election.[18]

There were two aspects of the controversy over his move to the county seat; first his decision to leave the burghs enraged his supporters there. Secondly, Duncan Cameron of the *Oban Times* was already in the field as a Crofter candidate; Cameron had come forward in late 1884 to challenge Mackenzie and MacLeod, "landlords men" according to the *Oban Times*.[19] Late 1884 was a propitious moment for a Crofter candidate to come forward: Sheriff Ivory was leading a military expedition to Skye in the aftermath of serious disorder on the Kilmuir estate in the north of the island, and the whole island was in a state of agitation. Cameron actually met Ivory and attempted to convince him that the intervention of the military would be counter-productive. Cameron addressed a series of meetings in Skye culminating in a 'huge gathering' in Uig where he was named as the prospective candidate for the county.[20] The *Oban Times* declared that his name would 'henceforth represent the people's cause in the contest for this county' and described him as a 'Land Law Reform candidate'.[21] Sir William Harcourt, the Home Secretary, felt that the candidature of Duncan Cameron and the reception which he received in Skye was an indication that the crofters had 'thrown overboard Fraser Mackintosh as not sufficiently advanced.' This view can only come from a determination to put the worst possible construction on events and a desire to find a candidate 'who has the authority to represent the crofters'.[22] At this point, although it was clear that Cameron of Lochiel would not contest the seat at the next election, Fraser Mackintosh's own intentions were unclear; MacPhail has argued that the possibility, under the redistribution proposals then under consideration, of the creation of a Western Isles seat, which would include Skye, was a factor in his thinking. This would leave room for two Crofter candidates, one for the insular seat and one for the seat on the mainland. Opponents of the crofters also felt there might be a tactical advantage in separating the Western Isles from the mainland. The duke of Argyll reported to Gladstone that he had been in contact with Ronald Munro Ferguson, the Liberal MP for Ross-shire, who had argued that the resulting mainland county constituencies would return 'such members as himself with tolerable security'.[23] The final redistribution proposals were published in December and they did not include the creation of a new seat in the Western Isles.[24] In these circumstances it was clear that there was not room for two Crofter candidates; indeed, one newspaper published a lengthy psephological article purporting to demonstrate that neither Fraser Mackintosh nor Cameron could win if both contested the seat. The conclusion was that if either Fraser Mackintosh or Cameron withdrew 'the crofters can undoubtedly carry their man'.[25] Cameron had to be persuaded to withdraw, and this was eventually achieved through the offices of Donald Murray of the London HLLRA[26] Thus, from July 1885 Fraser Mackintosh had the field to himself as a Crofter candidate against Mackenzie and Macleod.

Some indication of the surprise which Fraser Mackintosh's decision caused can be gained from the fact that as late as October 1884 he informed his burgh constituents 'I do intend to claim your suffrages in the future'.[27] It seems that there was some preliminary correspondence between Fraser MacKintosh and his agent, Donald Reid, in early 1884 over the prospect of Fraser Mackintosh coming forward as a Liberal candidate in the County. The seat was thought to be up for grabs due to the impending retirement of Lochiel, the sitting Conservative MP. The correspondence was published in August 1885, once the election campaign was underway, and was open to several different interpretations. The *Courier* concluded that it demonstrated that Fraser Mackintosh was not asked to come forward and was only now doing so out of spite towards Mackenzie of Gairloch, who seemed to have usurped him as the favoured Liberal candidate.[28] The *Scottish Highlander* argued that Mackenzie's acceptance of the Inverness Liberal candidature after seeming to rule himself out of politics by declining the candidature for Ross-shire on the grounds of age, was an act of discourtesy to Fraser Mackintosh. Under the old franchise Fraser Mackintosh, according to the *Scottish Highlander,* would not have contested the election: under the extended franchise after the 1885 Act he did not feel so constrained.[29] Thus, it can be concluded that the extension of the franchise presented a political opportunity to Fraser Mackintosh and he saw himself as a more sympathetic candidate for the crofters than Mackenzie, who had failed to beat Lochiel, under the old franchise, in 1880. What is certainly clear is that Fraser Mackintosh was not trusted by many prominent Liberals in the constituency: the rapid advance of his views on the land question raised their suspicions and he was criticised for dividing the Liberal interest.[30] In Nairn, there was some disquiet over the member's decision to contest the County seat, but the more dominant feeling was a fear that he was putting his place in the House of Commons at risk by so doing. One of Fraser Mackintosh's supporters in Nairn expressed himself to be 'astonished that Mr Fraser Mackintosh, holding as he did a secure seat and a respectable position should throw up that position and offer to blow a horn among the crofters in the West'.[31]

Even in the national press Fraser Mackintosh's actions attracted criticism. The *Scotsman* ran a lengthy editorial in January 1885 excoriating his actions. His abandonment of the Inverness Burghs was, it was held, merely 'an opportunity to gratify his own vanity'. The article also raised the spectre of his Tory past and cast severe doubt on his credentials as a 'friend of the Crofters': Fraser Mackintosh was described as 'the man who, until the crofter was made the tool of agitation, never gave the slightest indication of any special interest in him or his welfare'. The ultimate insult which the *Scotsman* could muster was to condemn the member for the Inverness Burghs as 'sort of Highland Parnell'.[32] This was not a reference to his views on Ireland, but can be explained by the perception of Parnell as an arch manipulator of the political process and chief bogeyman of the day. The contempt towards Fraser Mackintosh evident in this article is extraordinary and is evidence of the extent to which the sincerity of his tortuous path towards espousal of the cause of the crofters was regarded with scepticism. There were two other factors which should also be borne in mind when considering this article. Firstly, the *Scotsman* was aware of the damage which Fraser Mackintosh could do to the prospects of Kenneth Mackenzie of Gairloch in the election. Mackenzie was just the kind of orthodox Liberal landowner of whom the *Scotsman* approved, a candidate who was scarcely likely to disturb the equilibrium of Highland politics should he be elected. Secondly, it is vital to appreciate the horror with which the *Scotsman* viewed the Crofters' War and all its consequences. According to the paper the grievances of the crofters were manufactured by agitators from furth of the Highlands who had undue influence over the politically unsophisticated and gullible crofters. The Whig orthodoxy peddled by the *Scotsman* could only deprecate the challenge to authority which the Crofters' War seemed to represent.

During the campaign this issue cropped up a number of times. In the course of a speech in Raasay in October 1885, Fraser Mackintosh brought the issue up himself and used it in an attempt to demonstrate the longevity of his commitment to the cause of the crofters, something on which he may have felt himself to be vulnerable. He remarked that as a Burgh member he had frequently been 'taunted' when discussing the crofter issue and he now wished to come forward as a candidate for the county, especially so as the crofters had been enfranchised, because he felt that 'the proper man' to speak on behalf of the 'smaller holders of the soil' was the 'member for the county'.[33] This view was echoed by the newspaper of the London HLLRA, the *Crofter,* which argued that in order for Fraser Mackintosh to campaign properly on behalf of the crofters 'there was nothing left for him but to retire from the burgh contest . . . and to submit his conduct as Crofter Commissioner and Land Law Reformer to the verdict of a great crofter and agricultural constituency, such as his native county of Inverness . . . '.[34] After having made so much in 1874 of the necessity of the electorate playing a prominent part in the selection of parliamentary candidates, it is ironic that historians and contemporary political opponents have argued that Fraser Mackintosh had no real popular mandate to come forward as a Crofter candidate in 1885. MacPhail argues that Fraser Mackintosh's candidature was promoted by an 'Inverness clique' composed of Alexander Mackenzie, the Dean of Guild, and Kenneth MacDonald, the Town Clerk.[35] The *Chronicle* also tried to make something out of this: in an article entitled 'Mr Fraser Mackintosh's Inconsistencies' they noted that he had supported the 'duty of constituencies to select candidates' in 1873 but that he had 'no mandate' in Inverness-shire in 1885.[36] There is some substance in this point in that Fraser Mackintosh was not called forth as a candidate by crofters' meetings in the same way as Duncan Cameron. His credentials as a Crofter candidate, membership of the Napier Commission and activity in parliament were established through his own rhetoric.

There was yet another dimension to the array of newspapers, and hence the political scene, in Inverness by 1885: the Conservative interest had raised money for their own title, the *Northern Chronicle,* which began publication in 1881. Interestingly, it was Fraser Mackintosh's former associate and future tormentor, and the erstwhile defender of the Bernera crofters, Charles Innes, who took the leading part in this enterprise. The starting point of this scheme was the apathy of the Conservative interest in the county and the fact that the press in the North were overwhelmingly Liberal (something which was true of the Scottish press as a whole in this period). The leading newspaper in the North of Scotland was the staunchly Liberal *Aberdeen Free Press* and both of the long established newspapers in Inverness, the *Advertiser* and the *Courier*, were Liberal. There was also the *Highlander* of course, and although its party political stance was unorthodox, it did not extend to general support for the Conservative Party. Murdoch's financially struggling newspaper was part of this story, however. Innes and Lochiel attempted to prey on the *Highlander* in an effort to buy it over and re-launch it as a Conservative organ for the Highlands. This scheme did not come to fruition and the Conservatives were left with no option but to raise sufficient funds to start their own newspaper. This they duly did and the *Northern Chronicle* began publication in 1881.[37] The publication of the *Chronicle,* along with Lochiel's victory over Kenneth Mackenzie of Gairloch in 1880, can be noticed as evidence of a small rearguard action by the Conservatives in Inverness-shire in the last years of unreformed politics. For our purposes it is important to note that Innes used the *Chronicle* to take a leading part in raising a series of allegations about Fraser Mackintosh.

The 1885 election campaign represented a great opportunity for the newly enfranchised crofters: across the Highland counties Crofter candidates presented themselves to the enlarged electorate. Sometimes, as in the case of Fraser Mackintosh, Donald MacFarlane in Argyll, or the Marquis of Stafford in Sutherland, these were well known, but repackaged, products. In other cases, such as the appearance of Gavin Clark, Angus Sutherland, and Roderick MacDonald in Caithness, Sutherland, and Ross-shire respectively, or the forgotten Crofter MP, John MacDonald Cameron, in the Northern Burghs, these were men making their first appearance before a Highland electorate.[38] The *Crofter* was adamant as to the duty of the new electors:

> The first duty of the newly enfranchised people is to unite together as one man, and send into parliament men who are known to be in full sympathy with the popular cause, and who are pledged to carry out the needed legislative reforms . . . if with the representation of the Northern Constituencies now virtually in their hands, the people of the Highlands still continue to send landlords into parliament it requires but few words to show that their cause will at once become more hopeless than it ever was before.[39]

This kind of advice demonstrates just how unpredictable political conditions actually were in mid-1885: no-one really knew how the new electorate would behave. Would the fear, to which the evidence to the Napier Commission so frequently referred, manifest itself in the elections? Would the secrecy of the ballot be trusted by the unaccustomed voters? Would the Crofter candidates, especially those labelled as 'carpet baggers', prove to be attractive to the Highland electorate? These questions would be resolved over the next five months as the lengthy election campaign unfolded.

Fraser Mackintosh made his opening remarks in the 1885 election campaign on his own lands at Drummond, near Inverness, to an audience of the feuars. These were interesting circumstances for Fraser Mackintosh to fire his opening salvoes in the election campaign. The fact that he made this speech on his own property and to an audience of people who had taken out feus on that property served to emphasise one of his roles in Highland society: that of landowner. While feuars were not in exactly the same position as tenants, they were in something of a subordinate position to the candidate. They were, of course, county electors, the Drummond estate being outside the boundaries of the Burgh of Inverness. The content of his speech is also interesting and can be usefully compared to his speeches at the beginning of the Crofters' Wars which were analysed in chapter four. In this opening address of the 1885 campaign he was at pains to stress that he had long-standing credentials on the land issue, arguing that he had always taken a 'deep and active interest' in 'the reform of the land laws in the Highlands'. He condemned the *1885 Crofters' Bill* as 'entirely inadequate' and went on to say;

> It did not recognise the expansion and enlargement of holdings; it did not give any compulsory powers to break up the large farms or deer forests to provide room for the people who were overcrowded ... as a legislative measure for the material improvement of the Highland people, it was not worth the paper it was written on.

He demonstrated that he was well aware of the prevailing political conditions in the constituency, which is not something which could be said of either of his opponents, he told the people of Drummond that:

> The people in the islands had nearly all become members of the HLLRA and they had determined that they would return no one to parliament who would not advocate the breaking up of these large farms and Deer Forests and insist that justice was done to the people.

He rounded off the speech by showing that he had every intention of fulfilling these criteria, saying that he 'believed in the Highlands for the Highlanders, not for sheep or deer'.[40] This speech demonstrates the extent to which politics in the county had altered in their priorities. As has been noted in earlier chapters, prior to electoral reform the bulk of the electors were in the wealthier eastern portion of the county and the west and the islands had very little political power. To this extent, there had been a revolution in the composition of the constituency, as Fraser Mackintosh was well aware, it was the crofters of the west who dictated the terms of post 1885 politics in the Highlands. Indeed, the new circumstances of politics had thrown down a challenge to the crofters - rather than continue to send landlords or their representatives to parliament the London HLLRA urged the crofters to:

. . . unite together as one man, and send into parliament men who are known to be in full sympathy with the popular cause, and who are pledged to carry out the needed legislative reforms.[41]

This was the first contested election Fraser Mackintosh had faced since 1874 and many of the old allegations cropped up once again. His Tory background in Inverness in the 1850s, and his alleged membership of the Junior Carlton Club from 1864 to 1873, for example. This Club was closely associated with the Conservative Party, having been set up in 1864 for those who were unable to get into either of the other clubs associated with the party, the Carlton itself, or the Conservative, due to the long waiting lists. Membership definitely signified a measure of allegiance to Conservative views and Hanham has described it as 'aristocratic'.[42] There were, however, a new and more dangerous group of allegations focusing on his activities as a factor. The *Chronicle* raised allegations about evictions at Alvie in Strathspey; about aggressive estate management at Lochend, outside Inverness; and about the removal of tenants without compensation on the Mackintosh estates in Lochaber. Further attacks centred on what was perceived to be his general political inconsistency and the apparent contradiction of a former factor standing as a Crofter candidate.[43] The *Courier* regarded his candidature as highly opportunistic, deprecated his attempt to 'set class against class and to pose as the candidate for the working men, downtrodden by tyrannical superiors' and rounded off a hostile article by declaring Fraser Mackintosh's speech to be 'cant'.[44] The *Aberdeen Daily Free Press*, one of the leading Liberal newspapers in the North also deprecated the idea of Crofter candidates standing against Liberals.[45] The *Highland News*, at this stage a newspaper generally supportive of Fraser Mackintosh, printed a poem entitled 'An Epistle to the Crofters' by "Robert Burns Jnr"(and later apologised for doing so):

> A Tory first and then a Whig
> He always was a wretched prig -
> Land Leaguer he's become;
> He'll preach all day about the land,
> His words are like a rope of sand,
> Or smoke flying up the lum.
> He shouts "three acres and a coo"
> He'll give you all the land,
> With sheep and stirks and steadings new,

Charles Fraser Mackintosh and Political Re-alignment, 1885-86   153

> From Chamberlain's rash band.
> O crofters! Your softers! To listen to such bosh,
> Or vote for that doater C. Fraser Mackintosh.[46]

This poem reflected a number of themes about the career and character of Fraser Mackintosh, points which had emerged in other forms of electoral material: the notion that he had travelled a long and insincere political journey from Tory to Crofter; his willingness to promise virtually anything in return for votes; and the shallowness of his views on the land question and, in particular, the idea that he was influenced by Joseph Chamberlain and Jesse Collings whose advocacy of small holdings under the slogan 'three acres and a cow', was part of Chamberlain's so-called 'Unauthorised Programme'.

This welter of allegation, fuelled by a large body of anonymous correspondence in the newspapers, gave the campaign a keen edge.[47] The other candidates soon got in on the act, Kenneth Mackenzie, who had most to lose from Fraser Mackintosh's presence, often accused him of conning the voters with lavish promises, vague generalities and an impractical policy on the land question. He attempted to discredit the notion of Fraser Mackintosh as a sincere friend of the crofters, remarking in the early stages of the campaign;

> Mr Fraser Mackintosh as a factor, and I as a proprietor, have both had to do with crofters; but so far as I can learn, his management was not of a type which could entitle him to be called a crofters' friend.[48]

Mackenzie constantly accused Fraser Mackintosh of doing no more than dividing the Liberal interest in the constituency. This was not the only echo of the 1874 contest; as in the earlier contest doubts were raised about Fraser Mackintosh's commitment to the label he was campaigning under, and accusations were levelled that he was willing to promise anything, regardless of practicalities, just to get elected.

The *Northern Chronicle* and the Tories in the county sought, with some success, to polarise the contest between Reginald MacLeod and Fraser Mackintosh, while retaining support for Macleod who was preferable as the candidate of the party likely to form the next government. The *Chronicle* asked, in November 1885:

> What will Sir Kenneth be if sent to the House of Commons? A mere cypher in a chaotic opposition. What will Mr Fraser Mackintosh be?

> The obscurest man of an obscure coterie, powerless for either good or ill, or one of the last joints in the draggled tail of the Irish Party. Electors, return Mr MacLeod, who will not only be an honour to you, but as one of the dominant party, a member who can look after your interests.[49]

These tactical considerations should not blind us to the fact that the election was fought on the land issue and Fraser Mackintosh and his opponents fought energetic campaigns throughout the vast constituency. Colonel William Fraser, the proprietor of Kilmuir in the north of Skye, noted that the Land League were putting in a 'tremendous effort on behalf of Fraser Mackintosh': Fraser concluded that there would be a 'decided majority' for Fraser Mackintosh on his estate.[50] Fraser Mackintosh used a yacht to visit the coastal and insular areas of the constituency during the election campaign. Many of the meetings he held in the Hebrides were conducted in Gaelic. On occasion, however, Fraser Mackintosh could be hesitant in his use of the language at political meetings. Although he gave many speeches in Gaelic, when asked a question in that language he frequently answered in English after making a self deprecating remark about his facility in Gaelic.[51] During this election campaign Fraser Mackintosh was accompanied on part of his tour of the island of Skye by Mhairi Mhor, the poetess who had supported him in Inverness in 1874.[52] By 1885 there was a substantial amount of Gaelic poetry commenting on the election, and much of it was imbued with a greater sense of optimism than had been evident at earlier stages of the crofters' struggle. This can be seen very clearly in a poem by Donald MacDonald of Greenock, published in the *Oban Times* October 1885. Entitled 'Bratach nan Croitearan/ The Crofters' Banner' it expressed a belief in the efficacy of parliamentary representation to deal with the grievances of the crofters:

> The unfaithful landlords have stolen
> our ancestors' rights from us,
> and they have left us bare, with nothing -
> we had no way of rising up.
>
> But we will get a strong leader
> who will go to parliament very soon;
> the good MacFarlane will carry our banner,
> and no enemy will overcome it.

> And now he will not be alone
> standing up for the people's rights;
> Mackintosh will be at his shoulder,
> and, along with him, will tackle the enemy.[53]

Again, it is significant that such an assertive poem came not from the Highlands but from an urban area, in this case Greenock. It is also significant that the poem clearly identifies Donald MacFarlane and Charles Fraser Mackintosh as the key parliamentary defenders of the crofters. A poem such as this, published in an obviously pro - crofter organ as the *Oban Times,* would have had quite a wide circulation. Donald Mackinnon of Glasgow's 'Oran mu Chor nan Croitearan/ Song on the Crofter's Plight' expressed similar sentiments, although, as it was published in January 1885, it did not have the optimism induced by the election in November and December of that year:

> Although the Gaels have few friends in the struggle
> there is a small but significant number in Parliament itself;
> although the sky is overcast, and the weather foul,
> the clouds will be dispersed, and the sun will shine through.[54]

This Gaelic material supports the view that the extension of the franchise and the prominence of Crofter candidates at the General Election of 1885 was a major watershed in the confidence and optimism of the crofters. Along with the evidence from newspapers and other commentaries it also confirms that the election in the Highland counties took place in what was, in part at least, a Gaelic context.

Fraser Mackintosh published his election address in November: his policy was largely that of the HLLRA. He regarded the Liberals first *Crofters' Bill* as 'valueless' and advocated 'security of tenure, fair rents, and compensation for improvements... free sale ... and the compulsory breaking up of deer forests and large farms'. He recommended government loans to help crofters stock their enlarged lands, and an 'Independent Land Court' to implement these proposals. In the prevailing political atmosphere this was the only sensible programme with which a Crofter candidate could approach the newly enlarged electorate of the county of Inverness. The enthusiasm with which Fraser Mackintosh espoused these proposals is in marked contrast to his views on such questions at earlier points in his career. His advocacy of the destruction of deer forests and the wholesale amendment of the game laws are two notable examples of this tendency. His ideas on rural freedom even extended to the notion that salmon found in 'navigable waters' should be regarded as the 'inalienable right of the people'. There were two other issues which Fraser Mackintosh highlighted; the administration of justice in the Highlands, and further reform of the electoral system. The former issue was one which had been investigated by the *Napier Commission* and in which Fraser Mackintosh was particularly interested in the light of a long running feud in which he was engaged with Sheriff Ivory, the acerbic and egotistical Sheriff Principal of Inverness. Ivory was a dedicated opponent of the Crofters and, in a particularly high handed fashion, had one of his Sheriff Clerk Deputes at Portree, Dugald Maclachlan, dismissed for his more favourable attitude towards them.[55] It was, no doubt, Ivory who Fraser Mackintosh had in mind when he pointed out in his election address that Sheriffs in the Highlands should be 'free of local influences'. We have already noted the controversy over the operation of the registration courts; Fraser Mackintosh believed that voters should not have to prove their right to vote through the courts. He also advocated manhood suffrage and granting the vote to female householders. The latter idea was one which had appeared in his 1874 election address in the Inverness Burghs. A final theme worth noticing is Fraser Mackintosh's customary declaration of his political independence; he argued that the 'claims of my fellow Highlanders' were more important than 'party ties'. [56]

Fraser Mackintosh's staunchest supporter, Alexander Mackenzie in the *Scottish Highlander*, argued that 'Land Law Reform' was the 'one important question before the constituency', although dis-establishment and other traditional issues also figured in the campaign; a review of the press coverage of the election reveals the substance behind Mackenzie's assertion. Mackenzie, perhaps sensitive to the charge that Fraser Mackintosh was a late convert to the cause, argued that what marked him out from the other two candidates was his participation in the HLLRA. conference at Portree. [57] Fraser Mackintosh used this as a base to begin a tour of the Outer Hebridean portion of the constituency; although there were attempts, such as at a meeting at Sleat in September, by Tory supporters to raise awkward issues, such as his Conservative and factorial past, the Crofter candidate made serene progress and was received enthusiastically by the newly enfranchised crofters.[58]

There was a palpable sense of fear among the organs of Whig and Tory opinion concerning the prospects of the Crofter candidates. The

Scotsman devoted space to talking down their prospects of and describing them as 'carpet baggers', and talking up the prospects of orthodox Liberal candidates, such as Clarence Sinclair of Ulbster in Caithness; Ronald Munro Ferguson in Ross-shire; and Sir Kenneth Mackenzie in Inverness-shire. The *Northern Chronicle* urged 'Skyemen to rally round the son of Dunvegan, who reflects credit on your island already, and who, if sent to Parliament, will be your ablest and best friend, and do you and your island credit. The *Inverness Courier* called Fraser Mackintosh's election proposals 'little better than bribes dangled before the eyes of crofters, whose poverty it is supposed will make them susceptible'.[59] William Fraser of Kilmuir, nominally a Liberal, could find little of comfort in the views of any of the candidates: he found Kenneth Mackenzie's address to be 'very advanced' and he was worried by the prospect of the Conservatives bringing forward the idea of 'peasant proprietorship', although he noted that Reginald Macleod had made little mention of the idea during his campaign.[60] This feeling of insecurity among the proprietorial community was perhaps the explanation behind one of the more bizarre events during the election campaign: the refusal of Lord Dunmore, proprietor in Harris, to give Fraser Mackintosh permission to visit St Clement's Chapel at Rodel in South Harris whilst he was visiting the island to hold election meetings.[61]

The result of the election was an emphatic victory for Fraser Mackintosh, who received 3555 votes, Reginald MacLeod was second with 2031 and Sir Kenneth Mackenzie third with 1897.[62] The novelty of the extended franchise produced a high turnout and massive enthusiasm for the political process. The result was greeted with jubilation in the crofting districts: copies of the *Courier* and the *Advertiser* were burnt in Skye, and bonfires were lit, including one above Fasach in Glendale which would have been in full view of Dunvegan Castle.[63] Colonel Fraser of Kilmuir remarked in the aftermath of the election result that he 'feared we shall have to face unsettled times'.[64] Fraser Mackintosh was joined in parliament by three other Crofter MPs, Roderick MacDonald for Ross-shire, Gavin Clark for Caithness and Donald MacFarlane for Argyll. The *Courier* predicted that they would achieve 'infinitely little' in parliament.[65] The electors of Sutherland, who preferred the Marquis of Stafford to Angus Sutherland, the crofter candidate, were condemned as a disgrace by Alexander Mackenzie in the *Scottish Highlander,* echoing the words of the Mulbuie poet, John MacLean.[66] MacLean's poem,

'Cho-dhiu Thogainn Fonn nan Gaisgeach/ I would sing the Heroes' Praise', was composed in honour of the victory of Roderick MacDonald in Ross-shire but contained comments on the other Crofter M.P.s, including the controversial Dr Clark who was praised as 'Truly fine gentleman'; the poem concluded:

> How proud we can be -
> with Dr MacDonald and MacFarlane,
> and Fraser Mackintosh, the hero;
> the people of Sutherland are a disgrace.[67]

In addition, the members elected for Orkney and Shetland, and the Northern Burghs, Leonard Lyell and John Macdonald Cameron, also gave broad support to the Crofter MPs in parliament.[68] The *Scotsman,* as might be expected, was less than delighted with these results, describing them as 'much to be regretted' and going to great lengths to argue that the fact that the inability of many voters in the crofting areas to read English meant that they were not exposed to 'influences, which are elsewhere great . . .'. The fact that Fraser Mackintosh and the other crofter candidates 'had the help of many Gaelic speakers' meant that they were 'able to put their own case in their own way'. In fact, the Highland counties were held by the *Scotsman* to be the exception to the fact that 'moderate' candidates had triumphed over 'advanced' candidates throughout Scotland. The lavish promises which the Crofter candidates made were held to be another important reason for their victories; the *Scotsman* remarked that the 'crofters, unfortunately have been deluded with promises of nearly everything they desire, from "three acres and a cow" to the right to catch the best salmon that swim in river or sea'.[69]

The Crofters' Act and Irish Home Rule, 1886
The wider political situation placed Fraser Mackintosh in an awkward position. The Irish issue dominated politics and Parnell had issued a manifesto encouraging the Irish community in Britain to vote Conservative, as the best hope of progress on Irish Home Rule seemed to come from that direction.[70] The result of the election gave the Liberals a majority over the Conservatives of 86, a lead which was exactly balanced by the Irish nationalists. As knowledge of Gladstone's support for Home Rule emerged in late 1885, the Irish switched allegiance and he formed his third administration in January 1886. The two main issues which absorbed the legislative energy of the government were the *Crofters' Bill*

and the *Irish Home Rule Bill*. The government rammed the former through the House of Commons and, much to the disappointment of the Crofter MPs, refused to accept any significant amendments. The basic reason for this was that every spare moment of parliamentary time was required for the *Irish Home Rule Bill* and the *Land Purchase Bill* which was to accompany it. This had been used, partly as an excuse, perhaps, to explain inactivity on the question of Scottish Church Disestablishment.[71] It has been noted, however, that the *Crofters' Bill* fared better than some other potential legislation in that parliamentary time was actually found for it. It has even been suggested that Gladstone took a personal interest in this because he wished to keep the Crofter M.P.s on-side with a view to the likelihood of an exceedingly close vote on Irish Home Rule.[72] A more subtle suggestion has been put forward by Matthew, who suggests that one advantage of finding time for the *Crofters' Bill* early in the session, before the Irish legislation began to clog up the parliamentary timetable was that it worked 'the Liberal MPs together on a "Celtic Fringe" question'.[73] The 1886 *Crofters' Bill* was firmly based on the *Irish Land Act of 1881* and differed from the 1885 *Crofters' Bill* only in the appointment of a Land Court and slightly stronger provisions for enlarging crofts.[74] The Crofters' movement reacted with disappointment to the substance of the Bill and to the government's method of forcing it through parliament. Fraser Mackintosh was no exception; in his election address in 1886 he remarked that the act was 'inadequate'.[75] During the parliamentary debates he articulated the view that the Bill was incomplete and made worse by the government's unwillingness to accept sensible amendments. He did admit that the Bill was a great improvement on the Bill of 1885, especially in regard to the clause which created provisions for the enlargement of holdings. Overall, however, he felt that the Bill was 'full of pitfalls, and was certain to give rise to a great deal of litigation'. One important 'pitfall' was the fact that the provisions for extending crofters' holdings was limited to grazing lands. Fraser Mackintosh felt that this went against the intention of the Bill to restore the position of the crofters to what it had been eighty years ago, and would do nothing to help the extremely congested crofting communities, especially those in the Hebrides, who required arable rather than grazing land.[76] This point struck at the central inadequacy of the *Crofters' Bill* and Fraser Mackintosh was only one of many to make this point. The limited provisions to extend crofters' land remained largely a dead letter until 1911 when a new piece of legislation with greater powers was passed. This failing was a source of some concern to the *Crofters' Commission* which had been established to oversee the operation of the crofting legislation and which came under considerable pressure on this point.[77] Fraser Mackintosh made a wider point towards the end of his speech:

> ... the people would not cease agitating until they obtained their just rights. In a word, the Bill would not be complete without some provision for the case of the cottars and, in regard to deer forests.[78]

This was straight out of the manifesto of the HLLRA: cottars, the landless element in the Highlands, had largely been ignored by the Bill and deer forests were scarcely threatened by it either. The latter, of course, were one of the great bugbears of the Crofters' movement and the debate over the extent to which they absorbed land which could have been made available to crofters, would continue until the early 1920s.

Perhaps this is an indication of the way in which the stridency of Fraser Mackintosh's rhetoric had advanced since 1884. After the General Election of 1885, of course, he was no longer able to style himself the 'Member for the Highlands', The other Highland counties were no longer represented by landlords or their associates, but by Crofter MPs whose ideas on the Highland land issue were just as advanced, or in the case of Gavin Clark, the MP for Caithness, more advanced than Fraser Mackintosh's.

It has been suggested that Fraser Mackintosh and MacFarlane were not very active in the campaign, led by Clark and MacDonald, supported by 'other English and Scottish radicals', to try and amend the Bill.[79] Fraser Mackintosh did, however, manage to secure one amendment to the bill; although it was on quite a minor issue it was one which Fraser Mackintosh had a long standing interest in. There had been calls for all the members of the Commission which was to be established to implement the act to be Gaelic speakers. The government would not accept this, but, at Fraser Mackintosh's suggestion, they did demur to accept the view that one member of the Commission should be a Gaelic speaker.[80] Fraser Mackintosh was less successful with amendments proposing that the notion of crofting parishes should be abolished and that the Bill should apply 'wherever there are crofters'.[81] This was never likely to be accepted given that the precise formula of the geographical coverage of the Act had been such a contentious subject of debate within the government during the framing of the Bill.[82] Fraser Mackintosh also raised, without any success, the subject of leaseholders who were excluded from the protections given to crofters on year-to-year arrangements.[83] While it might be justifiable to argue that Fraser Mackintosh was not so active as Gavin Clark or Donald MacFarlane in the Committee stage of the *Crofters' Bill* in 1886, he was certainly more active than Roderick Macdonald in this regard. There were a number of active and vocal Liberal MPs who supported the campaign to have the 1886 Bill amended. These included Duncan MacLaren's son, Charles, who sat for Stafford; John McCulloch, a noted Dumfriesshire farmer, who sat for the St Rollox division of Glasgow; Sir George Campbell, the Liberal MP for Kirkcaldy; and Sir J. W. Ramsden, the proprietor of Ardverikie, an estate on the shores of Loch Laggan, and member for the West Riding of Yorkshire. The members for West and East Aberdeenshire, Dr Robert Farquharson and Peter Esslemont (the latter referred to himself as a Crofter MP), were also active in the debates, especially on the question of the extension of the Bill to cover Aberdeenshire.[84]

As we have noted in earlier chapters, the position of Ireland was in the background of the politics of the 1870s and after the outbreak of the Irish Land War in 1879 and the great electoral advances made by Parnellite nationalists at the General Election of 1880, the issue became almost all consuming. Most debate in the early 1880s concentrated on the twin problems of how to deal with the law and order aspects of the *Irish Land War* and how to legislate on the land issue itself. From 1882 Parnell shifted his attention from rural agitation and turned to a strategy of engagement with the Liberal Party in an effort to advance the cause of Irish Home Rule. Parnell's precise objective was never coherently articulated because he was playing to multiple audiences in Ireland and in Britain. Despite this process of engagement with the Liberal Party there was scarcely any sign that the party leaders were prepared to embrace a scheme of Home Rule which would devolve significant power to a Dublin Parliament. Meanwhile, in a private context, the Liberal leader and Prime Minister, William Gladstone, was also engaging with the Irish issue. In the realm of public politics, policy on Ireland from 1883 concentrated on bringing Ireland into the scheme of Franchise reform currently under consideration and thinking about ways to introduce a more modern system of Irish local government. In other parts of the United Kingdom constitutional restiveness was also becoming evident. There had long been an undercurrent in Scottish politics that specifically Scottish issues, such as education and ecclesiastical politics, were not sensitively dealt with by either the Westminster parliament or the Whitehall administration. This was qualitatively different from Irish concerns: in Scotland the desire was for more and better Union. A campaign which involved such establishment figures as Charles Cooper, the editor of the *Scotsman,* and Lord Rosebery, aimed at the creation of a separate Scottish department of Government headed by a cabinet minister with responsibility for Scottish affairs. An earlier compromise which involved Rosebery acting as a Minister in the Home Office with responsibility for Scottish issues was not a conspicuous success. It was one of the few positive acts of Salisbury's caretaker administration in late 1885 to carry through the plans of the Liberal administration and create the Scottish Office. Its early sphere of responsibility was limited and the Secretary for Scotland was not automatically of cabinet rank. This reform was presented as a means of making the Union work more effectively for Scotland and it was not analogous to contemporary events in Ireland. It is difficult to argue that these events formed a precursor to the big constitutional debates of 1886. Although one can exaggerate the suddenness of Gladstone's movement towards espousal of Home Rule for Ireland, one cannot overemphasise the suddenness of the emergence of the issue into the public arena. There was no hint during the General Election of 1885 that the new Parliament would consider Irish Home Rule, the notion that the country had not been consulted on the matter became an important weapon in the Unionist armoury.[85] These facts go some way towards explaining the extraordinary impact of the Irish Home Rule Issue in 1886. One author has called it 'the deepest and most intense constitutional crisis of the century'.[86]

A further aspect of the Home Rule debate which enlivened proceedings was the way in which politics and personalities interacted with each other. The most detailed and authoritative account of the Home Rule crisis presents it as a classic episode in high politics, with political manoeuvre and tactical considerations taking much greater prominence than ideas and issues.[87] More recently, however, historians have turned to an examination of the wider aspects of the crisis, encapsulating the individuals concerned and the different impact of the crisis in different parts of the country.[88] Another strand of historiography on the Home Rule split concentrates on the motivations of Members of Parliament and analyses the extent to which they were motivated in their voting by party considerations, the influence of class, or intrinsic attitudes to

Ireland.[89] The central point which emerges from the research of these historians is that the influences which acted on individual politicians, inducing them to vote one way or the other on Irish Home Rule, were much more complex than would be suggested by simply looking at the views such politicians had taken up over the years on the Irish question.[90] Hostility or loyalty to leading players such as Chamberlain or Gladstone, men who attracted both hostility and loyalty in almost equal measure, were at least as important as coherent positions on detailed aspects of the Bill.[91]

Before moving on to consider Fraser Mackintosh's position it is worth briefly laying out the chronology of events between the General Elections of 1885 and 1886 as they related to Irish Home Rule. On the 17th of December 1885, based on information from Gladstone's son, Herbert, the press published the news that the Prime Minister was actively considering a scheme of Home Rule for Ireland. This obviously affected the party situation in Parliament and encouraged the Irish Nationalists to look more positively on the Liberals after their dalliance with the Tories during the election. There is very little evidence, however, for the argument that either the substance of Gladstone's views, or the timing of their publication, was primarily based on this consideration. Parliament opened for the new session on 21st January 1886, Salisbury's caretaker administration fell on the 27th of January and Gladstone agreed to form his third administration on the 1st of February.[92] Now that Gladstone was in government his difficulties with Irish Home Rule really began. Gladstone proposed two Bills as part of his Irish settlement: a *Land Purchase Bill,* partly designed to appease Irish landowners, and a *Government of Ireland Bill.* Whilst the appeasement of Irish landowners may have been an important objective, the *Land Purchase Bill* also served to widen the scope of the opposition to Home Rule, as Matthew has pointed out:

> . . . the political formula for mutual self-contradiction was there: the land-owning classes disliked Home Rule: many Home Rulers in England, Wales and Scotland, disliked land purchase.[93]

By March 1886 the two bills were ready for presentation to the Cabinet. Fractious debate ensued and resulted in the resignation of Joseph Chamberlain, President of the *Local Government Board,* and George Otto Trevelyan, the Secretary for Scotland, on the 26th of March. The latter departure from the government marred the passage of the *Crofters'*

Bill, which he had drafted, and would surely have piloted through the House of Commons more sensitively than J. H. A Macdonald, the Lord Advocate, to whom the task fell.[94]

The Government of Ireland Bill contained provisions to establish a single chamber in Dublin which would have responsibility for domestic Irish affairs; power over Imperial, foreign and defence related issues was to be retained by the Westminster Parliament.[95] The Bill was presented to the House of Commons on the 8th of April 1886. This was one of the great parliamentary occasions of the century: one Scottish member recorded in his diary that he had to drive to the House 'at the preposterously early hour of 10.45am' just to secure a place![96] This became the signal for a period of intense politicking by those, led by Gladstone, who supported the principle of Home Rule and those, led by the radical Joseph Chamberlain and the Whig Lord Hartington, who, for a variety of reasons, opposed Gladstone's plans. In May and early June Chamberlain and Hartington attempted to marshal their forces against Home Rule.[97] The crucial vote on the third reading in the House of Commons came on the 8th of June 1886. The Bill was defeated by 341 votes to 311 and the majority included 94 Liberals who had voted against the measure.[98] Fraser Mackintosh was the only one of the Crofter MPs who voted against the Bill.

The Liberal party had divided in a most complex manner over Irish Home Rule. The split was led by the radical Joseph Chamberlain, and the archetypal Whig Lord Hartington. Among the Scottish MPs, there was no real coherence to the group of 23 members who voted against the Bill. Fraser Mackintosh, who had radical pretensions, voted against the Bill, as did the almost communistic MP for East Fife, John Boyd Kinnear.[99] Other radicals who voted against the Bill included J. W. Barclay. Of Northern MPs, Fraser Mackintosh's successor in the Inverness Burghs, R. B. Finlay, and the unpredictable member for Sutherland, the Marquis of Stafford, revealed their colours as Unionists. Stafford had written to Professor Blackie pointing out that Gladstone had 'smashed the Liberal party and it would have been a very miserable and dishonest party if it had not been smashed'.[100] John Ramsay, the Member for Falkirk, and owner of land on Islay, and John Ramsden of Ardverikie, were also among those who opposed the Bill.[101] Although the notion of a revolt of the Whigs is a rather simplistic explanation, there were a large number of Whigs who opposed the Bill; exceptions, however, included Lord Rosebery who had severe doubts about the idea of Irish Home Rule but retained a deep fealty to Gladstone.[102] The complications of the Liberal split of 1886 were compounded by the fact that the party had not been wholly united before 1886, with tensions emerging over disestablishment and labour representation for example.[103]

Whilst many factors influenced the vote on Irish Home Rule, there were specific aspects of the Bill which caused particular controversy. One of the most heated debates surrounded clause 24 of the Bill which proposed the exclusion of the Irish members from Westminster. For Chamberlain, this aspect of the Bill threatened imperial unity.[104] The second problematic area was the proposal in the *Land Purchase Bill* to compensate Irish landowners for the loss of their land. This attracted much radical opposition on the grounds that it seemed anachronistic to compensate the people who seemed to be 'largely responsible for Ireland's agrarian problems' and that the interests of British taxpayers 'were being put at risk in order to finance a rescue operation for an unpopular landed elite'. This was especially relevant in Scotland where the land issue and anti-landlordism were such important features of political debate.[105] In the Highlands, Donald MacFarlane in Argyll, Roderick MacDonald in Ross-shire, and John MacDonald Cameron in the Northern Burghs, all of whom supported Home Rule, opposed land purchase. This was scarcely surprising given the views of the new electors and the fact that the Crofters' Bills were predicated on notions of dual ownership, which had such different ideological roots from land purchase.[106] Curiously and, by his own admission, rather individualistically, Lord Napier supported land purchase but opposed Home Rule![107] Fraser Mackintosh opposed both Home Rule for Ireland and land purchase.[108] We have already examined Fraser Mackintosh's views on Ireland, noting his long-standing hostility towards the Irish MPs and their tactics in the House of Commons. He remarked that the disruption to the business of the House of Commons occasioned by the Irish tactics had a knock on effect in the way in which Scottish business was neglected by the House.[109] He was not, however, an out and out 'Unionist', he was in favour of a scheme of 'Home Rule all round' which would bolster the unity of the 'Three Kingdoms' and the Empire. Fraser Mackintosh's idea involved the MPs for Scotland, England and Ireland sitting separately for a period of three months to consider Scottish, Irish or English questions and then sitting together as the 'Imperial Parliament' for another period of three months.[110] The espousal of 'Home Rule All Round' was for some a tactical ploy to add a veneer of principle to their destructive opposition to Irish Home Rule. It has been argued, for example, that Joseph Chamberlain resorted to advocacy of the idea in 1886 for this reason.[111] It should be noted however, that Chamberlain had sought a number of different alternatives to deal with the constitutional problem posed by Ireland. In 1885 he had put forward a scheme for a legislative body in Dublin composed of representatives of modernised Irish local government institutions and in 1888 he was thinking about a federal solution; although admitting that Scotland had far better claims than Ireland to be thought of as a nation, his thinking was extremely muddy on the question of national identity.[112] A further problem with 'Home Rule All Round', and this became clear during the crisis over the *Irish Home Rule Bill* in 1912, was how to separate English domestic issues from UK issues.[113] 'Home Rule All Round' was not a serious proposition in 1886; Scottish, unlike Irish, opinion was insufficiently clear for the idea to be taken seriously by Gladstone. This does not mean that there was not a Scottish dimension to the crisis of 1886. In fact this operated in two ways: firstly, in thinking about the constitutional details of Irish Home Rule Gladstone drew, not only on Imperial precedents, such as the Canada Act of 1867, but also on a normative notion of what might properly be done for Scotland should the question arise.[114] Further, as we have seen, the idea of Scottish Home Rule as a corollary of Irish Home Rule added an extra dimension to Scottish Liberal Unionism.

In his election address in 1886 Fraser Mackintosh argued that while he 'was in favour of a comprehensive measure of National Government of each part of the United Kingdom . . . which does not interfere with the unity of the Empire. . .', he could not give his support to

> any measures which, like the Government of Ireland Bill recently rejected by the House of Commons, and the other Bill regarding land purchase in Ireland, which was declared to be inseparable from it, tend to disintegrate the United Kingdom, and, while affecting to be final, settle nothing.[115]

This is an extra dimension of the Home Rule debate in Scotland, namely that views on Irish Home Rule were often compounded by the fact that the notion of Home Rule for Scotland was also part of the debate. Not all Scottish Liberal Unionists were of this disposition: Arthur Eliott, the member for Roxburgh, was opposed to the notion; he regarded the idea of a 'Scotch Parliament' as an 'anachronism and an absurdity'.[116] Fraser

Mackintosh, on the other hand, appears as one of a wide range of Vice-Presidents of the *Scottish Home Rule Association*, which had been formed in 1886 and was committed to Home Rule for Scotland within the context of the Union and the empire.[117] Hanham, using Fraser Mackintosh as a specific example, refers to the SHRA as

> desiring to embarrass the Liberal leaders and of backing those Liberal Unionists who were willing to try a measure of devolution in Scotland, where it would be safe to make the experiment, but were opposed to what they considered Gladstone's foolhardy Irish policy.[118]

There was nothing unusual in Fraser Mackintosh's opposition to Irish Home Rule, his support for Scottish Home Rule, 'Home Rule all Round' and belief in the integrity of the empire. Such a set of beliefs were fairly standard among late nineteenth century Liberals, especially the notion that constitutional rearrangement should have as its ultimate objective the bolstering of British and Imperial unity and strength.[119] Neither was Fraser Mackintosh an 'ultra radical', as has been claimed. Although, as we have seen, he expressed advanced views on the land question and was also a supporter of free education, he was opposed to other aspects of the radical agenda, such as Disestablishment. It would be easy, but somewhat misleading, to bracket Fraser Mackintosh with other Radical Unionists, such as J. W. Barclay. His record in parliament prior to 1882 and his subsequent political behaviour from 1886 until his defeat in 1892, mean that this categorisation cannot be sustained. His vote against Irish Home Rule can partly be put down to his long expressed irritation at the special treatment Ireland received in the House of Commons compared to Scotland, and his distaste for the methods of the Irish MPs. Wider issues must also be included in any assessment of his actions in this regard: these would include, possible resentment at the way the Liberals had managed the passage of the Crofters' Bill through parliament; more important was his suspicion that Gladstone's Bill, catering for the Irish alone, would be deeply divisive and could ultimately threaten the Union and the Empire.[120]

Fraser Mackintosh was not in attendance at any of the meetings held by Chamberlain or Hartington in their attempts to establish a Liberal Unionist grouping. He did, however, write to Lord Hartington giving his apologies for being unable to attend a meeting of anti-Home-Rule Liberals which the latter had convened at the beginning of June 1886.[121] Perhaps it is significant that Fraser Mackintosh kept quite a low profile in this regard, as he was well aware that his stance on Irish Home Rule was far from universally popular in his new constituency. By the end of April 1886 Chamberlain had drawn up a list of sixty eight M.Ps whom he regarded as likely to vote against the Irish Home Rule Bill, plus a further fifteen who were more likely to abstain, Fraser Mackintosh's name did not figure on this list. A further undated list of likely Unionists does contain his name annotated with a question mark.[122] It is possible that he may have been reluctant to attach himself to the coat-tails of Joseph Chamberlain, a deeply controversial politician, whose popularity in the Highlands may have been in decline from a high point in mid-1885 when he delivered a famous anti-landlord speech in Inverness.[123] Hartington, on the other hand, was a much more low key figure; it has been argued that he was 'excepted from the general condemnation of Liberal Unionists' and regarded as a much more trustworthy and 'straightforward' figure than Chamberlain.[124] Thus, there may have been an element of political calculation on Fraser Mackintosh's behalf here as he sought to minimise the fallout from the potentially awkward position he had taken up on Irish Home Rule. The primacy of the land question may have been his saviour at the 1886 election and postponed his defeat until 1892. That defeat, of course, had much to do with factors other than Ireland.

The response in the constituency to Fraser Mackintosh's actions was mixed, but nobody can really have been surprised at the course he had taken. Alexander MacKenzie declared that while he disagreed with Fraser Mackintosh over Ireland, the land issue was of paramount importance and he would support him on that basis. This pattern of disagreement between local activists and members of Irish Home Rule was quite a common feature across Scotland. Partly, this was to do with 'personal affection', as has been argued, but also by local circumstance. In many cases there was simply not enough time to organise an alternative candidature, or, as in the case of Fraser Mackintosh in Inverness, there were good local reasons not to attempt to unseat an MP who, although heterodox on Irish Home Rule, had given satisfaction on other important questions.[125] With the actions of Fraser Mackintosh, the defeat of Donald MacFarlane in Argyll by the Tory landlord, Malcolm of Poltalloch, and the hedging of Roderick MacDonald, the *Chronicle* was pleased with the Highland electorate; noting that 'a majority' of Highland constituencies 'declared for the maintenance of the British Empire and the protection under the Union Jack of Irish Protestants and loyal Catholics'.[126]

As the Liberal Unionists and the Conservatives had agreed an electoral pact, the only potential threat to Fraser Mackintosh at the 1886 election was from the Gladstonian Liberals, and they were well aware that although there was some dissatisfaction among crofters on the Irish issue, Fraser Mackintosh retained the confidence of his constituency on the land issue. In the event, Fraser Mackintosh was returned unopposed, one of 11 uncontested elections in Scotland in 1886.[127] *Dod's Parliamentary Companion*, in which MPs submitted their own entries, informs us that Fraser Mackintosh described himself as a crofter/Liberal Unionist.[128]

Conclusion

This short period is crucial to our understanding of Charles Fraser Mackintosh and Highland politics in a wider sense. It is the prime example of the necessity of analysing Highland politics in the widest possible context, and building issues such as electoral reform and constitutional change into the narrative of Highland politics. All the available sources for Highland politics point outwards in this manner: even the most random sample of the local press in the Highlands in 1886 will reveal at least as much comment on Irish Home Rule, the strengths and weaknesses of the leading characters and the significance of the issue for the United Kingdom, Scotland and the Highlands. The Irish Home Rule Bill soaked up a vast amount of parliamentary time in 1886 and had a decisive impact on the shaping of the *Crofters' Bill* and on the power of the Crofter MPs to amend that particular piece of legislation. The 1886 and, as we shall see, the 1892 elections were fought out over the attitude of the candidates to the question of Irish Home Rule; this applied as much to the Highlands as to any other part of the country. These issues also crop up in Gaelic poetry: for example, the verses published by the 'The Lame Tailor'/An Tàillear Crùbach' in the *Northern Chronicle* in 1887 use the Irish question to criticise Donald MacFarlane and to celebrate his defeat at the hands of Colonel Malcolm of Poltalloch at the general election of 1886.

> May success and prosperity for ever attend
> Argyllshire of the [many] heroes;
> they turned their backs on MacFarlane,
> on the Pope and on Gladstone;
> they turned their backs on the wretches -

Parnell's lads - and their habits;
the constituency is now as was customary
raising high the blue banner -
the Union Jack.[129]

The obvious point which emerges from these sources is that Highland politics in this period can only be understood with reference to the wider political agenda: even although the Crofter MPs had narrowly focused objectives revolving around the Highland land question, they were shaped by wider questions.

This is especially true of Charles Fraser Mackintosh. His political behaviour on Highland questions was not noticeably different from that of the other Crofter MPs, it was Ireland that made the difference. His actions on the Irish question marked him out as singular among the Crofter MPs, although, ironically, his views were not so different from Donald MacFarlane, who, as we have just seen, was excoriated as a fellow-traveller of Parnell. At the General Election of 1886, although he was unopposed, Fraser Mackintosh chose to stand as a Crofter/Liberal Unionist, thus explicitly marking himself out as distinctive from the other Crofter MPs. Before we consider Fraser Mackintosh in comparison with the other Crofter MPs a consideration of the final years of his political career, from 1886 to 1892, is necessary; the theme of this period is the consequences of his vote against Irish Home Rule for his career as a Highland politician.

---

[1] F.W.S. Craig (ed), *British Parliamentary Election Results, 1832-1885* (London, 1977), pp. 588, 623; F.W.S. Craig (ed), *British Parliamentary Election Results, 1885-1918,* (London, 1974), p. 543; F.W.S. Craig (ed), *British Electoral Facts, 1832-1987* (Aldershot, 1989), p.66.

[2] K. T. Hoppen, 'The Franchise and Electoral Politics in England and Ireland, 1832-1885', *History,* 70 (1985), pp.202-217; M. E. J. Chadwick, 'The Role of Redistribution in the Making of the Third Reform Act', *Historical Journal,* 19 (1976), pp.665-83; J. P. D. Dunbabin, 'Parliamentary Elections in Great Britain, 1868-1900: A Psephological Note', *English Historical Review,* 81 (1966), p. 83; M. Kinnear, *The British Voter: An Atlas and Survey since 1885* (2nd Edition, London, 1981), p.13; M. Dyer, *Capable Citizens and Improvident Democrats: The Scottish Electoral System, 1884-1929* (Aberdeen, 1996), pp. 13-18.

[3] Chadwick, 'The Role of Redistribution'; T. Lloyd, 'Uncontested Seats in British General Elections, 1852-1910', *Historical Journal,* 8 (1965), p. 262.

[4] J. F. McCaffrey, 'Political Reactions in the Glasgow Constituencies at the General Elections of 1885 and 1886', unpublished PhD thesis, University of

Glasgow, 1970, Chapter One.
[5] Hoppen, 'Franchise and Electoral Politics', p. 217.
[6] N. Blewett, 'The Franchise in the United Kingdom, 1885-1918', *Past and Present,* No 32 (1965), pp. 27-56; J. F. McCaffrey, 'The Irish vote in Glasgow in the later nineteenth century', *Innes Review,* 21 (1970), pp.30-36.
[7] *Times* 20 Oct 1885; *Scottish Highlander,* 16 Oct 1885.
[8] *Inverness Courier,* 16 September 1884; see also D. Ross, 'When townsfolk took to the streets', *Inverness Courier,* 21 July 1992.
[9] E. A. Cameron, *Land for the People? The British Government and the Scottish Highlands, c.1880-1925* (East Linton, 1996), pp. 28-36.
[10] K. T. Hoppen, *The Mid-Victorian Generation, 1846 to 1886* (Oxford, 1997), p. 681; J. F. McCaffrey, 'Political Issues and Developments', in W. H. Fraser & I. Maver (eds), *Glasgow, Volume II: 1830-1912* (Manchester, 1996), pp.210-11.
[11] Cameron, *Land for the People?,* pp. 36-38.
[12] I. M. M. MacPhail, *The Crofters' War* (Stornoway, 1989), p.167, refers to this period as a 'watershed in the political history of the Highlands and Islands.
[13] Cameron, *Land for the People?,* pp.106-7, 117-18; C. B. Levy, 'Conservatism and Liberal Unionism in Glasgow, 1874-1912', unpublished PhD thesis, University of Dundee, 1983, p. 101.
[14] *Ross-shire Journal,* 7Aug 1885; *Inverness Courier,* 6 Aug 1885; *Inverness Advertiser,* 4 Dec 1885.
[15] *Scottish Highlander,* 21 Aug 1885.
[16] J. Hunter, *The Making of the Crofting Community*(Edinburgh, 1976), p.161; J. Hunter, 'The Politics of Highland Land Law Reform, 1873-1895', *SHR,* 53 (1974), p.54; Cameron, *Land for the People,* p.36.
[17] MacPhail, *The Crofters' War,* p.155.
[18] A. Simon, 'Church Disestablishment as a Factor in the General Election of 1885', *Historical Journal,* 18 (1975), pp.791-820; J. G. Kellas, 'The Liberal Party and the Scottish Church Disestablishment Crisis', *English Historical Review,* 79 (1964), pp.35-7; D. C. Savage, 'Scottish Politics, 1885-6', *SHR,* 40 (1961), pp. 118-135; Levy, 'Conservatism and Liberal Unionism in Glasgow', pp.108-12.
[19] *Oban Times,* 6 Dec 1884.
[20] MacPhail, *Crofters' War,* pp.111-25, 154-5.
[21] *Oban Times,* 6 Dec 1884.
[22] Achnacarry Castle, Cameron of Lochiel MSS, William Harcourt to Cameron of Lochiel, 20 Jan 1885.
[23] Savage, 'Scottish Politics', pp.125-6.
[24] MacPhail, *Crofters' War,* p.155.
[25] *Nairnshire Telegraph,* 21 Jan 1885.
[26] MacPhail, *Crofters' War,* p.155.

[27] *Inverness Advertiser,* 17 Oct 1884.
[28] *Inverness Courier,* 15 Aug 1885.
[29] *Scottish Highlander,* 14 Aug 1885.
[30] NAS, Ivory Papers, GD 1/36/1/32/16, Davidson of Cantray to Ivory, 22 Nov 1885; NLS, Blackie Papers, MS 2636, f. 114, Eila J. MacKenzie, (Sir Kenneth's wife) to John Stuart Blackie, 9 Nov 1885.
[31] *Nairnshire Telegraph,* 14 Jan 1885.
[32] *Scotsman,* 9 Jan 1885.
[33] *Scottish Highlander,* 2 Oct 1885.
[34] *Crofter,* No 5, August 1885.
[35] MacPhail, *Crofters' War,* p. 155.
[36] *Northern Chronicle,* 4 Nov 1885.
[37] The complex but abortive attempt to buy up the *Highlander* can be followed in three fascinating bundles of correspondence, NAS, Innes and Mackay Papers, GD296/156-8, these contain letters from Charles Innes and Donald Cameron of Lochiel, respectively Conservative agent and member in Inverness-shire; further material on the origins of the *Northern Chronicle* can be found in NAS, Mackintosh Muniments, GD176/2390, The Mackintosh to Charles Innes, 12 Sept 1880; GD176/2398/1, Charles Innes to the Mackintosh, 14 Mar 1881.
[38] *Crofter,* No 1, March 1885, No 2, April 1885, No 3 May 1885, No 4 June 1885, No 5 August 1885; 'The Late Duke of Sutherland', *Celtic Monthly,* 1, (1892-3), pp. 21-2; D.W. Kemp, 'The Duke of Sutherland', *Celtic Monthly,* 3 (1895), pp. 101-3; *John O' Groat Journal,* 24 Jun, 22 Jul 1885; G. B. Clark, 'Rambling Recollections of an Agitator', *Forward,* 13 Aug, 20 Aug 1910.
[39] *Crofter,* No 1, March 1885.
[40] *Inverness Advertiser,* 14 Aug 1885.
[41] *Crofter,* No 1, March 1885.
[42] *Northern Chronicle,* 14 Oct 1885; for background on the Junior Carlton Club see; Sir Charles Petrie, Bt., *The Carlton Club* (London & New York, 1972), pp.89-90; R. Blake, *The Conservative party from Peel to Thatcher* (Revised edition, London, 1985), pp.138-9; H. J. Hanham, *Elections and Party Management: Politics in the Time of Disreali and Gladstone* (2nd edition, Hassocks, 1978), p. 100. I am grateful to Dr Iain Hutchison, of the University of Stirling, for discussing this topic with me.
[43] *Northern Chronicle,* 9 Sept, 7, 14, 21, 28 Oct, 4 Nov 1885.
[44] *Inverness Courier,* 6 Aug 1885.
[45] *Aberdeen Daily Free Press,* 21 Nov, 7 Dec 1885.
[46] *Highland News,* 23, 30 Nov 1885.
[47] *Inverness Courier,* 22, 29 Aug, 24 Sept, 6 Oct 1885.
[48] *Inverness Courier,* 6 Aug 1885.
[49] *Northern Chronicle,* 28 Nov 1885, 2 Dec 1885.

[50] HRA, KEP, AG/Inv/10/15, Fraser to Alexander Macdonald, 21 Nov 1885.
[51] H. R. Mackenzie, *Yachting and Electioneering in the Hebrides,* (Inverness, 1887), pp. 19, 49; *Inverness Courier,* 22 Sept 1885; *Scottish Highlander,* 11 Sept 1885.
[52] Mackenzie, *Yachting and Electioneering,* p. 47; *Scottish Highlander,* 2 Oct 1885.
[53] D. E. Meek (ed), *Tuath is Tighearna: Tenants and Landlords, An Anthology of Gaelic Poetry of Social and Political Protest from the Clearances to the Land Agitation (1800-1890),* (Scottish Gaelic Texts Society, Edinburgh, 1995), pp. 132-3, 243.
[54] Meek, *Tuath is Tighearna,* pp. 130-1, 242; see also, H. Barron, 'Verse, Fragments and Words from Various Districts', *TGSI,* 48 (1972-74), pp. 346-7.
[55] MacPhail, *Crofters' War,* p.115.
[56] Election Address, *Scottish Highlander,* 20 Nov 1885; see appendix I for the full text of the address.
[57] *Scottish Highlander,* 4 Sept 1885.
[58] *Scottish Highlander,* 11, 18, 25 Sept, 2, Oct 1885.
[59] *Scotsman,* 15 Aug, 6 Oct 1885, *Northern Chronicle,* 2 Dec 1885; *Inverness Courier,* 26 Nov 1885.
[60] HRA, KEP, AG/Inv/10/31,Fraser to Alexander Macdonald, 22 Nov 1885.
[61] *Scottish Highlander,* 2 Oct 1885; Mackenzie, *Yachting and Electioneering,* p.27; this odd event was the subject of a cartoon, see 'Lord Dunmore refusing Mr Fraser Mackintosh, M.P. admittance into the Cathedral of Rodel, October 1885', in Album of 12 cartoons by various artists, 9 on the 1874 Inverness Burghs election, 3 on the 1885 Inverness County Election', Inverness Public Library, Fraser Mackintosh Collections, FM 1074.
[62] F. W. S. Craig (ed) *British Parliamentary Election Results, 1885 -1918,* (London, 1974), p.543.
[63] *Scottish Highlander,* 18 Dec 1885.
[64] HRA, KEP, AG/Inv/10/31, Fraser to Alexander Macdonald, 5 Dec 1885.
[65] *Inverness Courier,* 8 Dec 1885.
[66] *Scottish Highlander,* 2 Dec 1885 (Special Election Edition); Meek, *Tuath is Tighearna,* pp. 141, 249.
[67] Meek, *Tuath is Tighearna,* pp. 22-3, 140-2, 248-9.
[68] *PD,* 3rd Ser, vol 304, cols 552, 768; on John Macdonald Cameron, see *Highlander,* 6 Feb 1875; *Inverness Courier,* 6 Sept 1912.
[69] *Scotsman,* 7, 12 Dec 1885.
[70] Levy, 'Conservatism and Liberal Unionism', p. 124.
[71] H. C. G. Matthew, *Gladstone, 1875-1898* (Oxford, 1995), p. 213.
[72] M. Barker, *Gladstone and Radicalism: The Reconstruction of Liberal Policy in Britain, 1885-94* (Brighton, 1975), pp. 47-8.

[73] Matthew, *Gladstone*, p.243.
[74] Cameron, *Land for the People*, p.37.
[75] Election Address, *Inverness Courier*, 29 Jun 1886.
[76] *PD*, 3rd Ser, vol 303, cols 180-1.
[77] Cameron, *Land for the People?*, p.55.
[78] *PD*, 3rd Ser, vol 303, col 181
[79] D. W. Crowley, 'The "Crofters' Party"', 1885-1892', *SHR*, 35 (1956), p.120.
[80] *PD*, 3rd Ser, vol 305, col 25.
[81] *PD*, 3rd Ser, vol 305, col 36.
[82] E. A. Cameron, 'The Scottish Highlands as a Special Policy Area, 1886 to 1965', *Rural History*, 8 (1997), pp. 196-200.
[83] *PD*, 3rd Ser, vol 305, col 680.
[84] *PD*, 3rd Ser, vol 304, cols 109-206, 458-566, 761-873, 918-975, 1716-1747; vol 305, cols 22-143; M. Stenton & J. Lees (eds), *Who's Who of British Members of Parliament* (4 Vols, Sussex, 1976-81), I, p. 323; II, pp. 55-6, 229, 234-5; Cameron, 'Special Policy Area', p. 198; The question of whether or not Fraser Mackintosh had acted as factor for Ramsden had been a minor controversy at the election of 1885 in Inverness-shire.
[85] Lord Ebrington, 'Liberal Election Addresses', *Nineteenth Century*, 19 (1886), pp.606-619; C. A. Cooper, *An Editor's Retrospect: Fifty Years of Newspaper Work* (London, 1896), p. 402.
[86] W. C. Lubenow, *Parliamentary Politics and the Home Rule Crisis: The British House of Commons in 1886*, (Oxford, 1988), p. 2.
[87] A. B. Cooke & J. R. Vincent, *The Governing Passion: Cabinet Government and Party Politics in Britain, 1885-86* (Brighton, 1974).
[88] G. D. Goodlad, 'Gladstone and his rivals: popular perceptions of the party leadership in the political crisis of 1885-86', in E. F. Biagini and A. J. Reid (eds), *Currents of Radicalism: Popular radicalism, organised labour and party politics in Britain, 1850-1914* (Cambridge, 1991), pp. 163-83; P. T. Marsh, 'Tearing the Bonds: Chamberlain's Separation from the Gladstonian Liberals, 1885-6', in B. L. Kinzer (ed), *The Gladstonian Turn of Mind: Essays Presented to J. B. Conacher* (Toronto, 1985), pp. 123-153.
[89] T. A. Jenkins, *Gladstone, Whiggery and the Liberal Party, 1874-1886* (Oxford, 1988), pp. 256-93; Lubenow, *Parliamentary Politics*; W. C. Lubenow, 'The Liberals and the National Question: Irish Home Rule, Nationalism, and their Relationship to Nineteenth Century Liberalism', *Parliamentary History*, 13 (1994), pp. 119-42.
[90] B. W. Rodden, 'Anatomy of the 1886 Schism in the British Liberal Party: A Study of the Ninety Four Liberal Members of Parliament who voted against the First Irish Home Rule Bill', unpublished PhD thesis, Rutgers University, 1968.
[91] Goodlad, 'Gladstone and his rivals'.

[92] Matthew, *Gladstone, 1875-1898,* pp. 211-258; Lubenow, *Parliamentary Politics,* pp. 3-4.
[93] Matthew, *Gladstone, 1875-1898,* p.248.
[94] Barker, *Gladstone and Radicalism,* p. 48.
[95] Matthew, *Gladstone,* p. 248-54.
[96] NLS, A. R. D. Elliot Papers, MS 19512, Diary, Jan 1886-87, p.51, 8 Apr 1886.
[97] *Times,* 13, 15, 28 May, 1, 2, Jun 1886; J. K. Lindsay, 'The Liberal Unionist Party until December 1887', unpublished PhD thesis, University of Edinburgh, 1955, pp. 145-166.
[98] Hoppen, *Mid-Victorian Generation,* p.687.
[99] J. B. Kinnear, 'The Coming Land Question', *Fortnightly Review,* 32 (1879), pp. 305-17.
[100] NLS, Blackie MSS, MS 2636, f. 227, Stafford to Blackie, 5 Jun 1886.
[101] Rodden, 'Anatomy of the 1886 Schism', pp. 81-9,304-311, 329-334, 475-84, 631-36, 719-20. I. G. C. Hutchison, *A Political History of Scotland, 1832-1924: Parties, Elections and Issues* (Edinburgh, 1986), p.163; I am grateful to my colleague, Mr Owen Dudley Edwards, for drawing my attention to the eccentricities of Boyd Kinnear.
[102] R. J. Akroyd, 'Lord Rosebery and Scottish Nationalism, 1868-1896', unpublished PhD thesis, University of Edinburgh, 1996.
[103] J. F. McCaffrey, 'The origins of Liberal Unionism in the west of Scotland', *SHR,* 50 (1971), pp. 49-51.
[104] Lubenow, *Parliamentary Politics,* p.14; P.T. Marsh, *Joseph Chamberlain: Entrepeneur in Politics* (New Haven & London, 1994), p. 233-4.
[105] G. D. Goodlad, 'The Liberal Party and Gladstone's Land Purchase Bill of 1886', *Historical Journal,* 32 (1989), p.641; Hutchison, *Political History,* p. 164; R. Quinalt, 'John Bright & Joseph Chamberlain', *Historical Journal,* 28 (1985), pp.640-1.
[106] *Scottish Highlander,* 1 Jul 1886.
[107] NLS, A. R. D. Elliot Papers, MS 19487, f.231, Napier to Elliot, 31 May 1886.
[108] *Scottish Highlander,* 24 Jun 1886.
[109] *Scottish Highlander,* 27 May 1886.
[110] *Scottish Highlander,* 27 May 1886.
[111] P. Jalland, 'U.K. Devolution 1910-1914: political panacea or tactical diversion', *English Historical Review,* 94 (1979), p.758.
[112] C. H. D. Howard, 'Joseph Chamberlain, Parnell and the Irish "Central Board" Scheme, 1884-5, *Irish Historical Studies,* 8 (1952-3), pp. 324-61; J. Loughlin, 'Joseph Chamberlain, English Nationalism and the Ulster Question', *History,* 77 (1992), pp. 207-212; Marsh, *Chamberlain,* p.192-3;NLS, Blackie

Papers, MS 2637, ff. 289-90, Chamberlain to Blackie, 2 Jul 1888
[113] Jalland, 'U.K. Devolution', p. 765; H. J. Hanham, *Scottish Nationalism* (London, 1969), p. 97.
[114] Matthew, *Gladstone, 1875-1898,* p.250.
[115] Election Address, *Inverness Courier,* 29 Jun 1886.
[116] NLS, A. R. D. Elliot Papers, MS 19487, f.273, Eliott to Alexander Craig Sellar, 16 Oct 1886.
[117] Lists of these Vice Presidents can be found on the covers of the SHRA pamphlets, see *The Union of 1707 Viewed Financially* (Edinburgh, 1887) or W. Mitchell, *Home Rule for Scotland and Imperial Federation* (Edinburgh, 1892) [N.L.S. pamphlets 3.2820].
[118] Hanham, *Scottish Nationalism,* p.93.
[119] R. J. Finlay, *A Partnership for Good? Scottish Politics and the Union Since 1880* (Edinburgh, 1997), p. 9.
[120] Hutchison, *Political History,* p.163; J. F. McCaffrey, *Scotland in the Nineteenth Century* (London, 1998), p. 76.
[121] *Times,* 2 Jun 1886.
[122] UBL, Joseph Chamberlain Papers, JC8/6/1, Irish Government Bill, Opinions of Members.
[123] R. Quinalt, 'Joseph Chamberlain: A Reassessment', in T.R. Gourvish & A. O'Day, (eds), *Later Victorian Britain, 1867-1900,* (London, 1988), pp. 76-8; Marsh, *Chamberlain,* p. 203; UBL, Joseph Chamberlain Papers, JC6/5/12, Notebook on Scottish Land Question and 1885 Campaign; JC5/16/108, Chamberlain to Jesse Collings, 20 Sept 1885; JC Letters Additional 36, Chamberlain to W. S. Bright MacLaren, 25 Apr 1885.
[124] Goodlad, 'Gladstone and his rivals', pp. 169-72.
[125] *Scottish Highlander,* 17 Jun 1886; Hutchison, *Political History,* p.165.
[126] *Northern Chronicle,* 21 Jul 1886.
[127] *Northern Chronicle,* 16 Jun 1886; Craig, *Election Results, 1885-1918,* pp.491-36; Lloyd, 'Uncontested Seats', p.263.
[128] Craig, *Election Results, 1885-1918,* p.543; J. Vincent & M. Stenton (eds), *McCalmont's Parliamentary Poll Book* (8th Edition, with introduction and Additional Material, Brighton, 1971); *Dod's Parliamentary Companion: Fifty-Fifth Year, 1887,* (London, 1887).
[129] Meek, *Tuath is Tighearna,* pp. 149-52, 253-55.

Chapter Seven

Political Twilight, 1886 to 1892

Introduction

The Conservative victory at the 1886 General Election, and their policy from that date until they lost office in 1892, saw the land issue slide down the political agenda. The government emphasised the development of the economy and the improvement of the transport infrastructure and communications network in the Highlands. The main aim of this policy, which in some ways mirrored their 'Constructive Unionism' projects in Ireland, was to break the mould of the crofting community. The Government felt that the part-time agriculture characteristic of the crofting districts was inefficient and meant that only desultory attempts were made to diversify the Highland economy. The neglect of fishing was held to be particularly culpable. After various investigations into the nature of the Highland economy and infrastructure in the late 1880s and early 1890s, minor changes were carried through in the late 1890s and early 1900s, but they were too limited to have anything other than a marginal impact.[1] These were uncontroversial initiatives which Fraser Mackintosh had always been broadly in favour of during the Napier Commission, for example, and it was not surprising that he supported the government on occasion, a fact which he did not deny.[2] His views on these issues would become clear in a series of newspaper articles in the *Scottish Highlander* which will be examined in greater depth below.

A further development in this period was the fracturing of the formerly highly disciplined Crofters' movement. Fraser Mackintosh's opposition to Irish Home Rule continued to cause problems for him as party political questions became increasingly important in the Crofters' movement. These issues will be considered below in an attempt to provide some background to the election of 1892, when Fraser Mackintosh was defeated by another Crofter candidate. The wider political context of these years was quite different from the period from 1880 to 1886. The Conservatives, supported by the Liberal Unionists, held office under the Premiership of Lord Salisbury throughout the period and this was an administration keen to emphasise stability and order, and reluctant to engage in any major reforming measures. This general outlook was reflected in their Highland policy.[3]

The Fracturing of the Crofters' Movement

This process began at the annual Conference of the HLLRA in 1886 at Bonar Bridge, in Sutherland. A proposal to unite the various factions of the HLLRA was proposed by Donald Murray of the London HLLRA. He denied that this was an attempt by London to 'usurp authority over the crofter question'. He noted that the HLLRA had been founded in Inverness in 1882 but had not flourished there because 'so many of its leading men lived upon the custom of sportsmen'. London, Murray declared, 'was beyond the range of landlord's shot and shell'. This motion was opposed by the Sutherland HLLRA, on whose behalf Angus Sutherland spoke, arguing that 'there had not been sufficient time given them to consider this matter'; this position was supported by John MacLeod of Gartymore, Angus Sutherland's successor as MP for the county. Roderick MacDonald, the MP for Ross-shire, and for long one of the leading lights in the London HLLRA, decried this position, asking: 'why should the people of Sutherland take a different view in this matter to the people of all the rest of the Highlands'.[4]

The Bonar Bridge conference considered a wide range of party political questions, such as Disestablishment and Irish Home Rule, upon which the movement was hardly united. The conference was an interesting moment in the history of land reform movements in the United Kingdom in that there was a concerted attempt to bring together representatives from Wales and Ireland as well as the Scottish Highlands. Unfortunately for the future prospects of this pan-Celtic land movement the Irish MPs were unable to be present due to House of Commons business, although G. B. Clark did read a fraternal greeting on their behalf. Perhaps the most interesting contribution to this so-called 'Celtic Parliament' came from the fundamentalist Welsh land reformer, Evan Pan Jones: his views were close to those of John Murdoch or Michael Davitt. In his speech at Bonar Bridge he derided traditional methods of land reform, such as the 'three Fs', which he referred to as the 'three frauds; the small holdings movement advanced by Joseph Chamberlain and Jesse Collings under the slogan 'three acres and a cow'; and peasant proprietorship, which Jones declared to be 'multiplying the disease in order to get rid of it'. Jones argued that contrary to all these nostrums, 'remedies of any kind short of clearing landlordism out of the country would be of no avail' and he concluded with the following peroration:

Let them have land nationalisation in some form or another, and let Highlanders, Irishmen, Welshmen and Cornishmen shake hands over the grave of landlordism.[5]

These sentiments were far in advance of anything demanded by the Crofters' movement. The Rev Donald MacCallum spoke on behalf of the HLLRA and delivered a speech which concentrated on lauding the contribution made by the Irish to the cause of land reform in the United Kingdom. There was also an apologetic tone to this speech, expressing regret for the frequent negative comments about Irish tactics which had been common in the early 1880s. MacCallum concluded:

The time was past when they regarded the Irish as mischief makers, and, thank God, they could look to them not only as brothers after the flesh but brothers in spirit and truth, and they were willing now to work with them for the restoration to the people of their rights.[6]

There was certainly a more positive view of the Irish in the late 1880s, whether it was merely rhetoric to suit the occasion, as may have been the case in 1886, or a tactical diversion to explain certain positions on Irish Home Rule, as in the case of Fraser Mackintosh - as will be noted below - it is certainly a noticeable trend.

It has been argued that these party political questions had the result of casting the 'Imperial idealist' Fraser Mackintosh into 'outer darkness' as far as the Crofters' movement was concerned.[7] This is something of a simplification, as we have noted; Fraser Mackintosh's position in 1886 was informed by a variety of factors and did not simply stem from Imperialism. Neither was his Unionism crude or atypical of many other Scottish and, indeed, Highland Liberals. Although other Crofter MPs had voted for the Irish Home Rule Bill their world view was not dissimilar from that of Fraser Mackintosh. Despite formerly sitting for an Irish constituency, Donald MacFarlane was also something of an imperial enthusiast and a supporter of Home Rule All Round. Fraser Mackintosh contrasted most obviously with G. B. Clark, the MP for Caithness, who was the most progressive of the Crofter MPs; nevertheless, as late as 1888 Clark stood up for Fraser Mackintosh arguing that he, along with the other Crofter MPs, had done 'his level best to represent his constituents'.[8]

The newly formed *Highland Land League* (*HLL*) was moribund for most of 1887, an important year for crofters, as the work of the *Crofters'*

Commission gathered momentum. The operation of the Commission was the focus of activity in 1887 as it turned its attention to areas of the Highlands which had been central to the Crofters' agitation, such as Skye and Tiree. The Commission had the noticeable effect of normalising relations between crofter and landlord in these formerly disturbed areas, which, of course, was exactly what the Conservative government hoped for. In the cases of Skye and Tiree, the Commission visited in the aftermath of the military and sought to deal with specific grievances after law and order had been restored. Despite initial opposition the *Highland Land League* could not be seen to criticise the Commission as it acquired great popularity among the crofters. Arguably, then, one reason why the *HLL* had such a quiet year was that there was now an alternative structure through which landlord-crofter relations could be mediated. Indeed, the procedures of the Commission were so straightforward and unintimidating that crofters did not even require the support or advice of the League in going before it with their fair rent applications. Just as landlords and factors found themselves frozen out of substantive input to tenurial relations, the Land League also found that one of its functions had been usurped as the relationship between the crofters and the Commission became more important.[9] This is only one indication of the extent to which the Crofters' Act, despite its limitations, had changed the nature of the Highlands in fundamental ways.

The 1887 conference of the League was held at Oban, and the proceedings reflected the lack of activity since Bonar Bridge the preceding year. It was reported that little had been done to carry out the union of the HLLRAs passed on that occasion, and the *Scottish Highlander* argued that Angus Sutherland should be replaced by Donald Murray.[10] At the 1887 conference, however, MacFarlane was elected chairman of the League. It was noted on this occasion that not only had very little been done to carry out the union proposals, but also that the fervid pan-Celticism evident at Bonar Bridge in 1886 had come to very little. The 1888 conference in Inverness saw considerable dissatisfaction that the *HLL* was controlled from London and that it ill-became an organisation which was supposedly in favour of Home Rule for Scotland not to hold more of its own meetings in the Highlands. The divisive influence of London control and issues such as temperance and Disestablishment were blamed for the strife in the *HLL*. There was also criticism of the Highland MPs' growing intimacy with the Gladstonian Liberal Party: Fraser Mackintosh, of course, was immune from this accusation. In a point of view which was in contrast to some of his statements earlier in the 1880s, Alexander Mackenzie argued that the *HLL* should look to the Irish M.P.s for an example of single mindedness, dedication to the crucial issue and an 'unwillingness to truckle to an political party'.[11] This period saw great pessimism among those who had been involved in the Crofters' movement since its origins in the 1880s. Many important figures from the early years of the struggle were distancing themselves from the movement, Fraser Mackintosh amongst them, but also John Murdoch, John Mackay, Hereford, Angus Sutherland and John MacDonald Cameron. The loss of these figures was lamented in organs such as the *Scottish Highlander,* and the blame was laid at the door of those who had introduced party political questions into the movement.[12] Alexander Mackenzie noted that both Home Rulers, such as John Murdoch, and Unionists, such as Charles Fraser Mackintosh and John Mackay, Hereford, had been driven out of the movement by the wider political agenda. Mackenzie went on to argue:

> It is perfectly obvious that a man may be a perfectly sound land law reformer although he may be a teetotaller or a publican, an Established Churchman, Free Churchman or Dissenter. A Member [of the League] is, very properly, never asked a question on any of these subjects, so long as he acts loyally to the constitution to which he has subscribed. Why, then, should a member be asked, as a Land Leaguer, whether he is in favour of or against Home Rule for Ireland?

Somewhat disingenuously, Mackenzie concluded that 'the people, if not their leaders, are perfectly sound, and they know exactly what they want'.[13] This seems wilfully to ignore the changes which had taken place in the Highlands since the passage of the Crofters' Act in 1886. The agitation had shifted focus in 1886 and 1887 and had died away altogether after heavy sentences were handed down to those involved in the Aignish riot in Lewis in January 1888. Improving economic conditions and the results flowing from the *Crofters' Commission* served to begin to build a loyalty to the tenurial regime established in 1886, and it seemed that the appetite for agitation in the crofting districts had been sated.[14]

The 1889 conference took place in Stornoway and some progress was made in restoring the primacy of Highland issues and reducing London influence. This had been presaged earlier in the year when the League had decided that meetings should be held in Scotland whenever possible and that a separate Parliamentary Committee be established in London. This, it was felt by the *Scottish Highlander,* would restore 'unity of action and vigorous advocacy' to the League . . . It is never too late to mend'.[15] The venue for the 1890 conference was Wick, partly in an attempt to reinvigorate the movement in Caithness and Sutherland.[16] The 9th Annual conference returned to Dingwall, where the HLLRA had met so successfully in 1884. This conference proved to be more discordant than the meetings at Stornoway or Wick, and activists from Skye, led by Myles Macinnes, attacked Fraser Mackintosh, in his absence, for his Unionist perspective. Myles Macinnes introduced a motion to the effect that no Unionist candidate should receive any support from the *HLL*. Fraser Mackintosh was defended by Gavin Clark and by a number of correspondents to the *Scottish Highlander* in the succeeding weeks, all of whom stressed that Highlanders should give primacy to Fraser Mackintosh's views and record on the Highland land issue rather than his vote in the House of Commons in 1886 on the Irish issue. The result of this activity was the formation of a breakaway Highland Land League in Inverness-shire led by Myles Macinnes and John Macleod, Gartymore.[17] It was this organisation which was used to promote a contest with Fraser Mackintosh at the 1892 election, an episode which will be returned to below.

Thus, it can be seen that the Crofters' movement endured a difficult period in the years immediately following the passage of the *Crofters' Act* in 1886, culminating in the division in the Land League in 1891 and the sponsorship of a candidate to contest Inverness-shire against Fraser Mackintosh at the General Election of 1892. Most explanations of this process have been rather introverted, concentrating on the divisions arising from the broader political agenda adopted by the League and the positions taken up by individuals. It is argued here that these were the symptoms of a changing political context with which the League found it difficult to cope. From the early 1880s the Crofters' movement had been swimming with the tide of political opinion. The Liberal government had demonstrated a willingness to grapple with land reform in Ireland. Once the agitation in the Highlands got under way in 1882 the government proved to be amenable to pressure to adopt a more sophisticated approach to the Highland land question, beginning with the appointment of the *Napier Commission* in 1883 and culminating in the Crofters' Bills of 1885 and 1886. The majority of the Crofter MPs elected in 1885 and 1886 were close to the Gladstonian Liberals in their political outlook, and although the specific political conditions of 1886 meant that the government were unable to take the views of the Crofter MPs on board in the passage of the *Crofters' Act*, they were not regarded as political outsiders. After 1886 the situation had changed dramatically: the government was Unionist, fundamentally opposed to further Highland land reform, despite claims of its necessity from the *HLL*, and in a wider sense opposed to the notion of dual ownership which underlay the *Crofters' Act*. They demonstrated this with legislation creating facilities for land purchase in Ireland - legislation which they would adapt to a Highland context in 1897. The Crofter MPs were now regarded as complete outsiders by a government which felt it could safely ignore them. The Crofters' movement also seemed to be distanced from its own members and adherents, the crofters themselves showing little appetite for the fight as conditions improved and some of the advantages of the 1886 act became evident. Thus, the movement, lacking a focus, drifted and divided.

The only possible sense of focus came with the first elections to the newly established County Councils in 1890; even here, however, the message from the electorate was mixed. Local government elections, in the shape of those for the School Boards, which had been in place since 1872, and for the newly established County Councils, have not been analysed as a component of the politics of the land question in the Highlands. In Ireland local politics were an arena which was fully exploited by the Land League. Alexander Mackenzie, however, was fully aware of the potential of local politics having spent so many years on the Town Council in Inverness. Prior to the establishment of the County Councils county affairs were the domain of the Commissioners of Supply, i.e landowners who contributed most of the income for the provision of the limited services which were available. Mackenzie clearly saw that the County Councils provided an opportunity to wrest control of crucial county affairs, such as policing, from the 'lairds and factors as Commissioners of Supply' who constituted a 'self elected autocratic body'.[18] Alexander Mackenzie, in particular, saw this new arena of politics as providing an opportunity for the Crofters' movement to re-establish contact with the grass roots. Further, it also provided an opportunity for the *HLL* to emphasise the political distance which existed between the landlords and the people and to establish its own anti-landlord credentials.[19] In Scotland as a whole the national press expressed the aspiration that politics would not intrude into the new

County Councils. The *Glasgow Herald* argued:

> ... it is men of business capacity, of clear heads, of shrewd sense, and of active public spirit, who are needed for the County Councils, and it matters not in the slightest how at Parliamentary contests they may give their votes.[20]

Sir George Trevelyan, the former Secretary for Scotland, had been one of the few politicians who had openly advocated a partisan approach to County Council politics, advice which was deprecated by the *Scotsman*.[21] Thus, those in the Highlands, such as Alexander Mackenzie, who took a more strident view were distinctive. The divisions in the Crofters' movement and the changing political focus in the Highlands, which have been examined above, are relevant here. The new elections gave an opportunity for the *HLL* to raise its profile once more. The politicisation of the County Councils was not something which had universal support in the Highlands, however. The *Northern Chronicle*, in particular, deprecated this tendency and emphasised the importance of economy in local politics and reminded voters that the new County Councils had 'no power whatever to initiate reforms of any kind, much less to distribute land among those who are now without it'.[22]

It is interesting to note that Mackenzie felt that the large number of candidatures by clergymen, of all denominations, was a positive feature of the new local politics. Candidates included the Rev John Macmillan of Ullapool, who had been the advocate of those evicted at Leckmelm in 1879-80, and Father Allan Macdonald of South Uist, who was a prominent folklorist.[23]

With the absence of clear party labels it is difficult to be clear about the perspectives of all the candidates, but a certain number can be identified. In Argyll, the Duke's factor Hugh MacDiarmid was elected for Tiree and the Marquis of Breadalbane was also successful, on the Land League side, the Rev Malcolm MacCallum, a future member of the Deer Forest Commission, was the representative for his parish, Muckairn. In Caithness, where there were an unusually high number of contests (26 out of the 30 divisions), J. N. M. Keith, factor to Sinclair of Ulbster, was elected for Pultneytown. In Ross and Cromarty the Earl of Cromartie was defeated on his own estate in Coigach, but his factor, William Gunn, was victorious in Fodderty. Other victorious landowners included Munro of Fowlis, R. C. Munro Ferguson and Kenneth Matheson of Lochalsh. Crofters were successful in Urquhart North and

South. In Inverness-shire Crofters were elected for Kirkhill and Kiltarlity, Alexander Mackenzie was returned for North Uist, Myles Macinnes for Sleat and Dugald Maclachlan for Portree. The Land League did not have it all their own way, however, with landowners such as Grant of Rothiemurchus, George Macpherson Grant of Ballindalloch and Lord Abinger being elected to the new Council.[24] The Highland press felt that the cause of the Crofters had been more successful in Inverness-shire than in the other northern counties, especially Ross-shire, where the Land reform candidates were 'routed'. Inverness-shire saw the return of approximately twenty-one reformers and ten orthodox Liberals, compared to twenty four Tories and Unionists. The *Scottish Highlander* enthusiastically summed up the result of the elections as the transfer of the government of the county 'from the classes to the people'.[25] As one would expect the Tory *Chronicle* took a different view of the results, denying that landlords and factors had been boycotted by the electorate and pointing out that the elections had resulted in 'highly conservative' councils in Argyll and Perth, 'good councils' in Inverness and Ross, whereas 'Sutherland alone has got a Land League council'.[26] The *Chronicle* was primarily concerned that the new County Councils should operate as unobtrusively as possible. The County Councils had few powers over controversial areas and certainly very little over the land issue. The passage of the *Allotments and Small holdings Act* in 1892 did give them limited responsibilities but this piece of legislation was hardly operative in the Highlands. Thus, the elections to the County Councils in 1890 give some interesting indications of the changes which took place in Highland politics in the period between the General Elections of 1886 and 1892. These changes were affected not only by the divisions in the Land League but also by the new contexts of politics, principally the operation of the *Crofters' Commission* and the formative stages of the policies which the Conservative government would implement with more vigour after they returned to office in 1895.

The Problematic Member
Fraser Mackintosh's activities in this period undoubtedly contributed to his political demise. In the aftermath of his vote against Irish home rule he resorted to increasingly implausible tergiversation on this matter, leading to his growing unpopularity with important elements of the Crofters' movement, especially in Skye. At Portree in 1886 he attempted to argue that the reason he had voted against Irish Home Rule was in

order to retain the Irish MPs at Westminster, as they had been the most faithful supporters of the Crofters; 'Do you think the Englishman would give us the Crofters' Bill unless we had the Irishmen at our backs?', he asked. This did not cut much ice in Skye, which was solidly in favour of Irish home rule; witness the reception given to Michael Davitt the following spring. J. G. Mackay, the Portree merchant and leading member of the HLLRA, responded to Fraser Mackintosh by pointing out;

> Mr Fraser Mackintosh has admitted that the Irish members were the best friends of the Highland people. Is he going to reward them by denying them justice?[27]

Not the least noteworthy aspect of his statement was the contrast which it provides with almost everything else which Fraser Mackintosh had ever said about Ireland, especially about the Irish MPs.

Disillusionment with the direction which the Crofters' movement was taking and poor health combined to induce Fraser Mackintosh to announce his retirement in April 1887. The Crofters' movement was well aware of the need to be careful about the selection of a 'good crofter candidate' to succeed him. There was no wish to repeat the mistakes which had been made prior to the 1885 election when both Duncan Cameron and Fraser Mackintosh came forward as Crofter candidates and the former had to be persuaded to withdraw. The announcement of his intending retiral was the occasion for some retrospectives on Fraser Mackintosh's political career. The *Scottish Highlander* was prepared to put aside differences on Ireland and other issues to accord respect for his contributions on behalf of Gaelic, on the *Napier Commission* and, as an independently minded member, on behalf of the Highlands generally.[28]

A period of uncertainty followed as to who was the best candidate to succeed him in the interests of the Crofters' movement. Donald MacFarlane, who had been defeated in Argyll in 1886, came forward as a candidate, as did Alexander Mackenzie, the proprietor of the *Scottish Highlander,* and Gilbert Beith, who had opposed R. B. Finlay in the Inverness Burghs in 1885. Beith had as long a track record as a proponent of Disestablishment as Finlay had as an opponent of the idea. He did, however, show signs of being able to adapt the arid details of Disestablishment to a Highland social context by arguing that the landlord patrons of the Church of Scotland were controlling an institution whose resources should be regarded as public property, to be used for the good of the whole community.[29] MacFarlane had a long pedigree as a friend of the Crofters, but had very little background in Inverness-shire and his candidature did not extend beyond the making of a few speeches in late 1887. Mackenzie's candidature was the most sustained in this curiously uncertain period. His thoughts on the land question were standard *HLL* propaganda; he declared that 'the Crofters want - and, in my opinion, they never will be satisfied until they get it - all the productive, arable and pasture of the Highlands'. Such a statement did not amount to serious politics in May 1888, when it was uttered. As we have seen the Unionist government viewed such statements with contempt, and the crofters showed little sign of agreement with such stridency.[30]

In March 1889 the *Northern Chronicle* suggested that Fraser Mackintosh should reconsider his retirement and come forward in the Tory-Unionist interest. The *Chronicle* approved of Fraser Mackintosh as a sound Unionist and as an opponent of Disestablishment. They felt that he was the exception in the group of Crofter MPs the rest of whom were written off as 'the draggled tail of the Parnellites in the House of Commons'.[31] The *Scottish Highlander* confidently stated that 'on no considerations whatever, personal or political, will Mr Fraser Mackintosh stand for re-election'. He was not, however, prepared to stand down from the seat before an election, but it was thought by some that he was keen to retire from politics to 'devote his well earned repose for the rest of his life to literary and antiquarian work, which has always been more congenial to his tastes than mere party politics'.[32] Reports of his health improved in 1888 and he steadily became more active in politics again. He had spent a long period at the spa town of Kissingen in Germany and when he arrived back in the Highlands in the autumn of 1888 he appeared to be in rude health.[33]

April and May 1889 saw the publication in the *Scottish Highlander* of a series of articles by Fraser Mackintosh entitled 'Opening Up the Highlands'. The ideas expressed in these articles about transport, industrial development and colonisation chimed closely with the thinking of the Conservative government of the day, and they are worthy of some scrutiny given our concentration on the themes in Fraser Mackintosh's rhetoric at earlier points in his political career. Whilst he was probably less active as a politician and public speaker in the years covered by this chapter, he did, for the first time, indulge in lengthy written exposition of his political views.[34] In the first of the articles he argued that the development of the Highland economy was not only 'essential to the localities' but also of 'great importance from a national point of view'. In his comments on the various railway schemes competing for the attention of parliament, he was critical of the way the railway companies who 'will neither give proper facilities nor permit others to do so'. At this time there were a variety of competing schemes to develop a terminus on the west coast in an attempt to stimulate the fishing industry by speeding up the marketing of fish.[35] In his second article Fraser Mackintosh argued that he was in favour of migration: 'I say shame to any who help to strangle a scheme which tends to the repeoplement of former habitations, and must increase their comfort and means of subsistence.' Migration was an understated theme in government policy in this period: it would become much more prominent from the later 1890s after the establishment of the *Congested Districts Board*. This theme was returned to in a later article which echoed themes which had informed the *Napier Commission* earlier in the decade. Fraser Mackintosh argued that the Highland problem was an amalgam of localised congestion alongside widespread desolation whilst overall 'it cannot be said that over the total Highland area the present population is excessive'.[36] As a policy prescription he argued that migration must go together with the extension of holdings and that any organised and direct migration must be voluntary and in family groups.

In the third article Fraser Mackintosh tackled some of the cultural background to common perceptions of the Highlands and the Highlanders. In particular, he attempted to counter the notion of the lazy Highlander by arguing that it was not indolence which prevented the crofter from becoming involved in the fishing industry, but the hazardous nature of that industry given the limited facilities and equipment available to crofters. Thus, as he had done during his time on the *Napier Commission*, he argued for the provision of better communication facilities, piers, harbours and breakwaters which would help to develop and make safe the fishing industry and thereby encourage Highlanders to become involved in it to a greater extent.[37] In the final article Fraser Mackintosh tackled the controversial subject of emigration, he acknowledged the controversy by noting that emigration had had a bad reputation in the past, due to what Fraser Mackintosh called 'forced emigration'. It should be remembered that the *Napier Commission* had included emigration as one of its recommendations for dealing with the Highland problem, but Fraser Mackintosh had dissented from this aspect of the Report. Further, he gave his approval to the experimental colonisation scheme which the Unionist government were currently implementing. This scheme involved providing facilities and finance for a number of Hebridean families to emigrate and establish themselves in Canada.[38]

The *Scottish Highlander,* commenting on these articles under the heading of 'A Common Sense Policy', argued that the ideas which they contained were not only valuable as a contribution to the debate on the Highland problem, but were impressive from a land law reform perspective. Further, their authorship demonstrated the error of division among Highland land law reformers on party political issues such as Irish Home Rule. It is interesting to note, however, that the *HLL* had opposed Lord Lothian's specific colonisation scheme in the late 1880s, as the very notion of emigration ran counter to their core idea that there was plenty of land available in the Highlands if it was only properly distributed. This was long standing opposition and the stance had included criticism of the *Napier Commission* for advancing the idea of emigration in the 1880s. Indeed, the most striking feature of these articles was the similarity with the recommendations of the *Napier Commission*. Fraser Mackintosh's conclusion was also noteworthy in the context of earlier examples of his rhetoric which have been examined here. He wrote:

> I ask for communications, for piers and harbours, for migration and for emigration, all to be going on, and at work simultaneously, a million as a beginning and to be divided equally. That would go much to solve the Highland question. Would it not be wise for government to grant a boon closing a sore and a danger, making happy and contented a loyal and deserving people.[39]

This was very close indeed, except in its financial demands, to the policy being implemented by the government at the time; especially in the emphasis on the need to integrate various approaches to the Highland problem.[40] The emphasis on the loyalty of the Highland people is a long running theme of Fraser Mackintosh's rhetoric, a theme which had been evident as he began to be vocal on the land question in the early 1880s, but one to which he paid less attention during the height of the land agitation when political necessity demanded that he pay more heed to the more advanced programme of the HLLRA. It is instructive that this theme recurred once the land agitation had died down; and atrophy in the organisational structure of the Crofters' movement meant that it was less able to keep Fraser Mackintosh 'on message'.

In a more wide ranging series of articles later in the year, Fraser Mackintosh reviewed a number of controversial political issues which he had encountered during his career, under the heading of 'Legislative Measures Recent and Prospective'. These included electoral registration, government funding for the Highlands, free education, the duration of parliaments, local government and land purchase. The three topics most worthy of comment here are electoral registration, free education, and land purchase. As we noted in looking at the electoral reforms of 1884/5 and the 1885 election, registration was something which Fraser Mackintosh had been concerned with for a time. He felt, as did many others, that the requirement that the elector be responsible for his own registration was a serious problem which partly defeated the object of the reforms. In particular, he argued that the requirement that electors should not be in arrears of poor rates was a particular problem for small tenants in the Highlands, especially when landlords were in control of the collection of such rates. He had raised this issue in parliament in 1884; although no progress was made on this occasion he looked back with 'satisfaction' to having identified and raised the question.[41] Free education was a core demand of radical Liberals in the 1880s and 1890s. It had been part of the so-called 'Unauthorised Programme' put forward by Joseph Chamberlain at the General Election of 1885. Charles Cameron, the radical member for the College Division of Glasgow, and an associate of Fraser Mackintosh in his advocacy of the cause of the Crofters, was a staunch advocate of free education; indeed, he had introduced a private member's bill on the subject in 1881. Fraser Mackintosh had made reference to the issue at various points in his political career. His position was that since 1872 education had been compulsory in Scotland therefore it should also be free. There was a particular Highland aspect to this issue. The long tradition of schooling by the Gaelic societies created what Anderson has called a 'deep rooted' tradition of free education. This also reflected reality in that the poverty of Highland society meant that fee income was low and was sometimes paid in kind; this, of course, meant that teachers in the Highlands were faced with low incomes thus depressing the quality of teaching. Free education was ultimately achieved in 1890 as a spin off from the fiscal recalculations consequent upon the creation of the Scottish County Councils.[42]

In considering the topic of land purchase Fraser Mackintosh was once again close to Conservative thinking on the subject, remarking that it would 'enhance the stability of the state' and that without it there would be 'no peace or settlement' in the Highlands.'[43] This is an important theme in Fraser Mackintosh's later rhetoric. He tended to emphasise the value of reform for the restoration of peace and stability rather than in the interests of justice or the settlement of grievances. Land Purchase was a classic Conservative (and conservative) idea, with the ultimate intention of creating a class of small landholders who would be less inclined to undertake land agitation if they had a stake in rural society, and Fraser Mackintosh's statement expresses this idea clearly. The conceptual difficulty with land purchase, which in principle was favoured by landlords, was bridging the gap between the price at which the landlords were willing to sell and the price which the tenants could afford to pay. Fraser Mackintosh pointed out:

> The situation then, is this; there are lands and proprietors willing to sell, on the one hand, while on the other there are people cribbed and confined, anxious to get lands or extended lands. Surely government is called upon in these circumstances to step in, and if by mere interposition of credit it enables the occupiers to become owners on fair terms, the transaction is beneficial all round.

Land purchase has been described as 'euthanasia' for landlords.[44] The arena in which the idea was most refined was Ireland; there had been land purchase clauses in the legislation which disestablished the Church of Ireland in 1869, and, as has been noted, land purchase was part of Gladstone's 1886 strategy for dealing with Ireland. The Conservatives found the idea more attractive and passed statutes over the period from 1885 to 1903 extending ever more generous terms to landlords.[45] In Scotland the idea proved to be less successful: the Conservative government passed the *Congested District Act* in 1897, but the advantages of the 1886 regime and the loyalty to it from within the crofting community was such that land purchase proved to be an unsuccessful policy in the Scottish Highlands.[46] Later in the article, however, Fraser Mackintosh showed that he was not ideologically hidebound in this matter. His priority was that crofters needed more land 'either as free owners or as occupants with fair rents, extended areas and fixity of tenure'.[47]

At first sight these articles appear to be a *pot pourri* of distantly related ideas on a variety of issues. The spectrum runs from a radical

Liberal idea, such as free education, to a Conservative idea, such as land purchase. If there is a theme running through these articles, however, it might be Fraser Mackintosh's willingness to go beyond the boundaries of traditional Liberalism, which emphasised the role of the individual. He was willing to embrace the notion of state intervention, whether it be in providing money to improve the Highland transport and communications infrastructure, taking the initiative on the land issue, or providing money to facilitate free education.

A third series of articles, on the 'Deer Forest Question' published in 1891, was more radical and demonstrated how far Fraser Mackintosh had come on this issue since the 1870s when, as we have noted, he defended commercialised sport as an important prop to the Highland economy. He emphasised the unique nature of this aspect of the Highland land system:

> The Highlands of Scotland are not of great area or extent compared with other countries, but where in the civilised world will be found such a proportion of the land exclusively devoted to sport, as with ourselves? The fact is most humiliating to us as a people.[48]

He emphasised this aspect in a later article, pointing out that despite the fact that Ireland had 'its great difficulty in the land question' the Highlands were in a 'worse position, for in addition to the question of land it has that of sport'.[49]

He went on to argue that the only solution to the problem was the total abolition of the game laws. He contrasted modern commercialised sport with traditional Scottish hunting, which he argued was once organised, partly at least, for the 'pleasure' and 'interest' of the people.[50] Whilst this may be a somewhat idealistic view, it does represent a notion which could have been drawn from the history of deer hunting based on materials which were available at the time, and which Fraser Mackintosh had in his library.[51] These articles constitute as strident an attack on the sporting economy as can be found anywhere in the Highlands in this period. He emphasised the depopulation, environmental degradation and restrictions of access which were an inevitable result of this form of land use. The steady encroachment of deer forest onto good, low lying land capable of supporting a human population was also identified as a problem arising from the excessive extension on sporting estates. The argument that deer forests were confined to high ground incapable of any other form of land use was the classic defence of the system put forward by its proponents, such as George Malcolm the factor for the Ellices of

Invergarry, who had very large deer forests on their estates.[52] Fraser Mackintosh went on from mere criticism of the deer forest system to recommend political action on the issue. Indeed, this formed the opening theme of the series of articles, when Fraser Mackintosh asked:

> Are the Highlanders then to permit their country to be drained year by year of its best and purest blood before their very eyes without using the most energetic efforts to prevent it? Impossible![53]

He rounded off the articles with a similar political declaration:

> It is not uninteresting to speculate as to what may be the fate of sport in the Highlands. When a strong and democratic government is formed one of its first measures must be a reform of the game laws. Will they be abolished forthwith or will a reasonable time be given to set the house in order? This may be done but there is not the slightest chance of compensation. [54]

This increasing journalistic activity presaged the moment when Fraser Mackintosh re-entered the political fray. In the absence of personal correspondence we cannot say what his motives were, nor whether he acted enthusiastically or reluctantly. He may have been motivated by the continuing muddle among the prospective Crofter candidates for the county. In June 1890 MacFarlane had decided to contest Argyll once again and in December of the same year Alexander Mackenzie announced his decision not to pursue his candidature in Inverness-shire. His publicly announced reasons for this decision had a disingenuous ring about them. He claimed that the current state of the House of Commons, with the Irish party in tatters over the O'Shea divorce,[55] meant that a Liberal majority was unlikely at the next election and that his efforts to 'effectually serve my fellow countrymen in the House of Commons would be of comparatively little use'. His retiral was the signal for Fraser Mackintosh to re-enter the fray. We might speculate that Mackenzie, not a wealthy man, did not relish the expense of a contest nor the prospect of unpaid service as an MP.[56] This was not a popular decision in Skye, where the Glendale crofters met to resolve that they could not support Fraser Mackintosh because of his record of voting with the Tories since 1886. On this occasion, however, John Macpherson, in many ways the conscience of the Crofters' movement, argued that Fraser Mackintosh should be supported on account of his consistent support for the cause of the crofters. Mackenzie responded to this resolution by suggesting that Fraser Mackintosh had only agreed to come forward again after he had retired and that they would not have opposed each other.[57] Fraser Mackintosh's return was welcomed by the *Northern Chronicle*, the Unionist newspaper in Inverness, which had earlier called for his return to end the political confusion in the County. The *Chronicle* lauded Fraser Mackintosh's virtues:

> a genuine Celt, a sound Unionist, and a supporter of a National Recognition of religion ... He is infinitely preferable to the many strangers who in these latter days, carpet bag in hand, so profusely tender their services to constituencies which are often taken in by their lavish promises and pledges.[58]

These factors combined to produce a challenge to Fraser Mackintosh at the 1892 election in the shape of Dr Donald MacGregor. Macgregor had been born in the Rannoch area of Perthshire and after medical training had spent most of his career in England.[59] He had been adopted for the Inverness Burgh seat in November 1890 in opposition to the Liberal Unionist MP, R. B. Finlay. When he stood down from the candidature in the Burghs he was replaced by Gilbert Beith who had been a prospective candidate in the County. MacGregor's candidature was supported by a faction of the Land League led by John MacLeod of Gartymore, the proprietor of the *Highland News* (which had run a campaign against Fraser Mackintosh since 1886) and Myles Macinnes, who was also strongly opposed to Fraser Mackintosh. They toured the Long Island detailing the reasons for opposing Fraser Mackintosh; mostly, they concentrated on his Unionism and his support for the government since 1886. Their activities were condemned by Alexander Mackenzie who labelled them the 'Portree clique': Mackenzie defended Fraser Mackintosh stoutly and poured scorn on the notion that MacGregor's candidature was realistic. Mackenzie went to considerable lengths in this argument: 'Dr Donald MacGregor against a man with such a record of magnificent and long continued services to the Highlands as Mr Fraser Mackintosh is too ridiculous even to be laughed at'. He attempted to engender some enthusiasm for Fraser Mackintosh's campaign by reminding the electors of the period in 1885 and 1886 when the Crofter MPs had an impact on opinion. They managed to do this, he argued, by maintaining their independence from either of the main political parties but that this position had been compromised of late as the Crofters' movement moved closer to the Liberal Party.[60]

The activities of Macleod and Macinnes led to the resignation of the President of the branch of the *HLL*,, Archibald MacDonald, Garafad, who informed Macinnes that he

> could not be party to the proceedings of such an insignificant coterie condemning the sitting member and foisting on the constituency an unknown nominee of their own. A more despotic action an eastern potentate could not be guilty of.

Macdonald admitted that he differed from Fraser Mackintosh on matters 'not directly affecting the Highlands', but that he considered his 'past and present services' to the Highlands to be 'great and valuable' and that he intended to do all he could to secure his return at the next General Election.[61] John Macleod's newspaper, the *Highland News,* regarded MacGregor as a 'Highlander of Highlanders' and the 'beau ideal' of a Highland candidate. More importantly, their conception of Highland politics was different to that of Alexander Mackenzie and other loyal supporters of Fraser Mackintosh. It was a more hard edged and partisan view, with less space for personal considerations. The *News* pointed out in early 1892:

> The struggle in Inverness-shire will in reality be, as elsewhere, a struggle between Liberalism and Toryism, whatever name the Tories may choose to call themselves. A man who calls himself a Liberal, yet votes steadily and invariably to keep a Tory government in power, is simply insulting the constituency. Tory is who Tory does.[62]

The *News* followed this up with a detailed examination of Fraser Mackintosh's record in parliament since his unopposed election in 1886, purporting to show that he was closely associated with the Tory party and that his voting record on Highland matters, and land reform more generally, was poor. His votes on other issues which he had espoused at various points during his career, such as Home Rule All Round and Temperance, were also subjected to scrutiny and found wanting.[63]

MacGregor explained his entry to the polls with reference to Fraser Mackintosh's support for the Conservative government.[64] The campaign, although keen, never reached the same heights as the famous campaign of 1885. This was as Alexander Mackenzie had predicted.[65] The *Highland News* was the main supporter of Dr MacGregor; he was presented not only as a land law reform candidate but also, in contrast to Fraser Mackintosh, as a sound Gladstonian. 'The question is not MacGregor or Fraser Mackintosh, but Gladstone or Salisbury. Freedom or Coercion. The olive branch or the scorpion'.[66] When the election result was announced there was some surprise at the outcome which saw MacGregor record a victory with 3,035 votes compared to Fraser Mackintosh's 2,706.[67] The turnout was substantially lower, and MacGregor's winning total in the two-sided contest was almost 500 fewer than Fraser Mackintosh's winning total in the three-cornered contest of 1885.

One commentator has ascribed the victory to Fraser Mackintosh's absence from the House of Commons and the constituency between 1886 and 1892: this claim, however, is unsubstantiated.[68] The local press put the defeat down to the religious feeling aroused over the Home Rule and Disestablishment issues.[69] One factor which may have reduced the turnout was that the election was held at a time of year when many crofter electors would have been away from home at the fishing. The 1885 election, by contrast, took place in the depths of winter when the maximum number of crofter electors would have been at home.[70] The *Northern Chronicle* was honest enough to refer to its earlier criticisms of Fraser Mackintosh in its comment on the election result, pointing out that his service to the Highlands had often been characterised 'with more zeal than wisdom', but it went on to accuse the electorate of Inverness-shire of acting with 'black ingratitude and a short-sightedness which deeply stain the honour and loyalty of the Highland race'.[71] Outside the Highlands there was general criticism of the crofters' ingratitude in their desertion of Fraser Mackintosh, who was perceived as their most genuine representative over a long period. The *Scotsman* commented:

> Less than seven years ago he was the idol of the people, and was returned to parliament by an overwhelming majority: now he finds an uncompromising, and too often and unscrupulous enemy in every petty village official of the Land League, and is rejected by the very voters who returned him in 1885, and whom he has never ceased to serve.[72]

The *Scotsman's* praise for Fraser Mackintosh in defeat, which contrasts strongly with earlier criticism of him, can be put down to that newspaper's consistent Unionism from 1886.[73]

Conclusion

The 1892 election was a much more direct contest between Home Rule and Unionism than the 1886 election: on the latter occasion the contest was muted by the fact that the Home Rule Bill had been recently defeated and there were a number of uncontested seats, including Inverness-shire. In 1892, however, the picture was very different: a number of so-called 'Radical Unionists' came forward to challenge the Crofter MPs; John Mackay in Sutherland, Sir William Bell of Scatwell in Caithness, and Provost Neil MacLean of Govan in Ross-shire.[74] The Liberal Unionists had been sufficiently astute to pick Gaelic speakers, some of whom (Mackay, for example) had substantial track records in the Crofters' movement.[75] In Ross-shire the sitting Crofter MP, Dr Roderick Macdonald, who was now regarded as a liability due to his utter inactivity, was persuaded to retire before the election and his place was taken by John Galloway Weir of Hampstead. In Argyll the situation was slightly different as the contest was once again between Donald MacFarlane and Colonel Malcolm of Poltalloch. Although the latter was a Unionist he certainly could not be described as radical.[76] This strategy was not successful, however, as all such candidates went down to defeats. Thus, Fraser Mackintosh's defeat in Inverness-shire was not an isolated example of Unionist failure in the Highlands; Angus Sutherland and Gavin Clark both defeated their Radical Unionist opponents as did John Galloway Weir.[77] In Argyll Donald MacFarlane retook the seat he had held between 1885 and 1886.[78] The Liberal strength in the Highlands (the 'Crofter' MPs, with the possible exception of Gavin Clark, were by now indistinguishable from orthodox Gladstonian Liberals) was part of a wider pattern. The 1892 election had resulted in a Liberal majority of 40, much less than Gladstone had hoped for. The two main parties were roughly balanced, the Liberals had won 272 seats, the Conservatives 268 (the share of the vote was almost identical: 40 per cent for the Conservatives and 40.6 per cent for the Liberals); the Liberal Unionists had been reduced in strength from 79 to 46, although they retained 11 Scottish seats. The 81 Irish Nationalists included nine Parnellites and there was one Independent Labour member in the shape of Keir Hardie. The Liberal strength was heavily concentrated in Scotland and Wales (81 seats); so much so, indeed, that despite the overall Liberal majority the Conservatives had a lead of over 40 in the English seats. The significance of this electoral geography was that the eighty-three year old Gladstone could govern with Irish support, but had insufficient nation-wide strength to triumph over the House of Lords on the issue of Irish Home Rule, which was the ultimate reason for his leadership of a fourth administration.[79]

Thus, Fraser Mackintosh was spared another parliament, the first part of which at least, was dominated by Irish Home Rule; Gladstone's second bill was defeated in 1894 precipitating the Grand Old Man's resignation and Rosebery's brief and ineffectual Premiership. This period saw the frustration of Highland expectations as the government failed to legislate on the land question. Another Royal Commission was established in December 1892, but it did not report until early 1895 and its proceedings were widely interpreted as a delaying tactic. Dr MacGregor was so frustrated by these events that he resigned his seat in 1895 and was defeated by a Tory landowner, Baillie of Dochfour, a kinsman of Henry J. Baillie, who had held the seat until 1868 and whom Fraser Mackintosh had supported in 1865.[80] We might speculate that these conditions might have been suitable for Fraser Mackintosh to rebuild his reputation among the Crofters, distanced, as he would have been, from the ineffectual Liberal government. Nevertheless, these must remain speculations, the former member for Inverness-shire now had a great deal more time to spend on antiquarian pursuits.

The perception that Fraser Mackintosh had been badly treated by those who were insufficiently appreciative of his efforts on behalf of the Highlands had a long afterlife. As late as 1917 a letter was published in the *Highland News* pointing out some of the inconsistencies in the recent publication by Joseph Macleod of *Highland Heroes of the Land Reform Movement*. It noted that Fraser Mackintosh was not identified as a 'Hero' and went on to point out

> Yet, because the late D. Fraser Mackintosh (sic) - a Federal Home Ruler and Hon Officer of the Scottish Home Rule Association - because he would not support Irish Home Rule first and before everything else, and because he would not declare for the Disestablishment of the Church of Scotland, he was stabbed in the back by those whom he had served so faithfully and so long. It was a great betrayal, and will always be regarded as such.[81]

The period from 1886 to 1892 had been a transitional one for the Highlands; crofters, landowners, estate managers and Land Leaguers accustomed themselves to the new conditions in the Highlands after the passage of the *Crofters' Act* and the operation of the *Crofters'*

Commission. Such intervention, as well as improving economic conditions, saw a distinct downturn in the frequency and intensity of land agitation in the Highlands. The essential grievance of the crofters and cottars - shortage of land - remained and would result in renewed agitation in the Edwardian period and the immediate post-war years.[82] In political terms, Fraser Mackintosh's defeat in 1892 can be seen as part of the general failure of Unionist candidates in the Highlands at that particular general election and as part of the fracturing of the Crofters' movement, as has been discussed above. We should not, of course, see Fraser Mackintosh merely as an unfortunate victim of these internecine disputes: his own opposition to Irish Home Rule, a position which was at variance with that of the other Crofter MPs and, it seems, with the views of the majority of his constituents, was an important contribution to the divisions. He was in this period, as in others, a very controversial figure, associated with, but not quite of, the Crofters' movement. It was, however, significant of the ways in which Highland politics had become less focused on the land question, that it was his opposition to Irish Home Rule and not his attitude to Highland questions, which caused the controversy. The *Highland News* did its best to argue that Fraser Mackintosh's attitude to Ireland was not an isolated blot on his record but part of a more general rightward drift in his politics. They noted his tendency to vote with the Conservative government on a host of issues. In the short term political knock-about this turned out to be a useful tactic, but it is interesting also in an overall consideration of Fraser Mackintosh's political career. Firstly, the Conservative government of the 1886 to 1892 period put forward many constructive proposals for the development of the Highlands, ideas which chimed with Fraser Mackintosh's own outlook, going back to his time on the *Napier Commission* and before. Secondly, Toryism was a strong feature of Fraser Mackintosh's political outlook in the early part of his career and it is not surprising that the political re-alignments which took place in 1886 over the Union should have brought this to the fore once again.

---

[1] E. A. Cameron, *Land for the People? The British Government and the Scottish Highlands, c.1880-1925* (East Linton, 1996), pp. 62-76.

[2] *Scottish Highlander*, 16 Jun 1892.

[3] Cameron, *Land for the People?*, pp. 81-2; M. Pugh, *The Making of Modern British Politics, 1867-1939* (Oxford, 1982), p. 59.

[4] *Scottish Highlander*, 30 Sept 1886.

[5] *Scottish Highlander*, 7 Oct 1886; P. Jones-Evans, 'Evan Pan Jones - Land

Reformer', *Welsh History Review,* 4 (1968-9), pp. 143-59, esp. 153.
[6] *Scottish Highlander,* 7 Oct 1886.
[7] J. Hunter, 'The Politics of Highland Land Law Reform, 1873-1895', *SHR,* 53 (1974), p.58.
[8] *Scottish Highlander,* 27 Sept 1888.
[9] Cameron, *Land for the People?,* pp. 41-51.
[10] *Scottish Highlander,* 25 Nov 1886, 22 Sept 1887.
[11] *Scottish Highlander,* 6, 13, 27 Sept 1888.
[12] *Scottish Highlander,* 6 Dec 1888, 3, 10 Jan, 25 Apr, 11 Jul 1889; Hunter, 'Politics of Highland Land Law Reform', pp. 58-61.
[13] *Scottish Highlander,* 6 Dec 1888.
[14] E. A. Cameron, ' "They will listen to no remonstrance": Land Raids and Land Raiders in the Scottish Highlands, 1886 to 1914', *Scottish Economic and Social History,* 17 (1997), pp. 43-49.
[15] *Scottish Highlander,* 3 Jan 1889.
[16] *Scottish Highlander,* 4 Sept 1890.
[17] *Scottish Highlander,* 20 Aug, 3 Sept, 17 Dec 1891.
[18] *Scottish Highlander,* 1 Aug 1889.
[19] *Scottish Highlander,* 14 Nov 1889.
[20] *Glasgow Herald,* 20 Jan 1890.
[21] *Scotsman,* 23 Jan 1890.
[22] *Northern Chronicle,* 8 Jan 1890.
[23] *Scottish Highlander,* 16 Jan 1890.
[24] *Glasgow Herald,* 22 Jan, 6 Feb, 8 Feb 1890.
[25] *Scottish Highlander,* 23, 30 Jan, 6, 13 Feb 1890.
[26] *Northern Chronicle,* 29 Jan, 12 Feb 1890.
[27] Quotes are from *Scottish Highlander,* 29 Jul 1886; for Michael Davitt in Skye see *Scottish Highlander,* 5 May 1886; J. Hunter, 'Irishman who won hearts and minds of Skye crofters', *West Highland Free Press,* 6 Jun 1997; I am grateful to my research student, Mr Andrew Newby, for discussing this topic with me.
[28] *Scottish Highlander,* 7 Apr. 1887.
[29] G. Beith. *The Crofter Question and Church Endowments in the Highlands, Viewed Socially and Politically* (Glasgow, 1884).
[30] *Scottish Highlander,* 15 Sept 1887, 10, 24, May, 2, 23, Aug, 13 Sept, 1888; I. G. C. Hutchison, *A Political History of Scotland 1832-1924: Parties, Elections and Issues* (Edinburgh, 1986), p. 157.
[31] *Northern Chronicle,* 26 Dec 1888, 6 Mar 1889.
[32] *Scottish Highlander,* 7 Mar 1889.
[33] *Scottish Highlander,* 11 Oct 1888.
[34] *Scottish Highlander,* 11, 18, 25 Apr, 2, 9 May 1889; Cameron, *Land for the People?,* pp. 62-82.
[35] *Scottish Highlander,* 11 Apr 1889; E. A. Cameron, 'Public Policy in the

2; M. Bentley, *Politics Without Democracy, 1815 - 1914: Perception and Preoccupation in British Government* (London, 1984), pp. 282-3; R. Shannon, *The Crisis of Imperialism, 1865 - 1915* (London, 1984), pp. 242-3.

[80] Hunter, 'Politics of Highland Land Law Reform', pp. 64-6; Cameron, *Land for the People?*, pp. 77-81.

[81] *Highland News*, 15 Sept 1917 (I am grateful to Andrew Newby for drawing my attention to this information); J. Macleod, *Highland Heroes of the Land Reform Movement*, (Inverness, 1917); I am grateful to Dr Catriona Burness for her kind gift of a copy of this volume and to Alison T. McCall for preparing a very useful index to this work.

[82] Cameron, 'Public Policy', Appendix No 1.

Chapter Eight

A Crofters' Party?

In a characteristically vivid phrase, T. C. Smout has argued that 'the Crofters' Party died young'.[1] It is the case, as we have seen, that the elections of 1892 and 1895 saw a very different atmosphere in Highland politics than that which had prevailed in 1885 and 1886. By the early 1890s the Crofters' movement had undergone a process of division and loss of focus.[2] By 1896 many of the original Crofter MPs who had been elected in 1885 and 1886 were no longer in parliament: Fraser Mackintosh had been defeated, as had his successor, Donald Macgregor; Angus Sutherland had been appointed as the Chairman of the Fishery Board for Scotland; Roderick MacDonald and Donald MacFarlane had retired. Gavin Clark was the only one of the original group still in circulation; he would remain in parliament until his defeat in 1900 and his political career continued in other forms until at least 1918, when he stood as a Labour candidate in Glasgow Cathcart.

This chapter will compare the career and outlook of Charles Fraser Mackintosh to that of the other Crofter MPs, especially Dr Clark, in an attempt to show just what a disparate group they were: so much so, indeed, that it is doubtful whether the appellation 'Crofters' Party' can be justified. Further, it has been suggested that the Crofter MPs were in some way forerunners of the Labour movement: certainly there was some crossover in personnel, most notably Dr Clark, but John Murdoch also showed an interest in the Scottish Labour Party. Other radicals, such as the flamboyant traveller and writer R. B. Cunninghame Graham, who were interested in the Crofting question, were also supporters of independent action by Labour candidates.[3]

A comparison between Fraser Mackintosh and Gavin B. Clark, MP for Caithness, the other long serving Crofter MP, can serve to emphasise the disparate nature of the group. Clark is also the other Crofter MP for whom there is the most information readily available; indeed, one recent writer has called for a biographical study.[4] Clark has left an impressionistic account of his career, 'Rambling Recollections of an Agitator', an appropriately entitled series of articles in *The Forward,* the

Glasgow based newspaper of the *Independent Labour Party* edited by that sometime land agitator, Thomas Johnston. What emerges from this account is the range of radical causes in which Clark had been involved from the late 1860s until his election to Parliament for Caithness in 1885. Republican agitation, the temperance movement, the Bulgarian Agitation of 1876, the *International Working Men's Association* and the *Social Democratic Federation*, were all movements which attracted Dr Clark's attention.[5] He was also a pacifist, he was a member of the Wounded Allies Relief Committee which established hospitals in France and Serbia, indeed he was decorated by the latter nation for his activities in this regard. He drew attention to the financial cost of the Great War and predicted 'a great commercial crisis at the end of the war'. On his death, the Prime Minister, Ramsay Macdonald, remarked that he would be remembered as much for his contribution to the peace movement as for his activities on the questions of land or the empire.[6]

In 1910 Clark remarked that he had 'always considered social reform to be more important than political reform'.[7] This was typical of many Victorian radicals who were influenced by such reformers as Alfred Russel Wallace and Henry George, proponents of the idea of land nationalisation. Clark records that a *Land Nationalisation Society* was begun in Glasgow in the late 1860s and a meeting was addressed by the veteran Chartist, Ernest Jones. The aim of the movement was to develop a holistic critique of the land system which would appeal to populations in both urban and rural Scotland. This was a difficult task: the question seemed rather remote to urban dwellers and the agricultural population were merely interested in more immediate gains, such as the reduction of rents. Clark's perception that the land question was not merely a rural question, and that land nationalisation was the ideal solution to the land question, remained central to his thinking throughout his career.[8] He also believed that the land question was fundamental to other types of social reform: Clark remarked in 1882 that through land reform

> we would ultimately be able to pay off our national debt, and defray all our local and national expenses from the income derived from the land . . . A large proportion of our crime and pauperism would soon disappear. The moral and physical degeneration caused by overcrowding would cease. Our fever dens would give place to comfortable homes, and the mass of the people would be elevated to a higher and better position - physically, intellectually and morally.[9]

Clark came to the Crofter question, not from a background of interest in the Highland past, or previous experience in the Highlands - as was the case with Charles Fraser Mackintosh - but from a fundamental belief that land reform was the vital first step in the radical transformation of society. Clark was to remark in 1910: 'as long as I can remember, I have held the views of the old Chartists on the land question, which I hold to be the most important of all economic problems'.[10] The contrast with Fraser Mackintosh, who at no point in his career expressed any interest in radical social thinking, could not be more stark.

Clark did, however, develop an interest in the Crofters and the Highland land question prior to his candidature for Caithness in 1885. In his 1882 pamphlet on land nationalisation he remarked on the 'atrocities' which took place during the clearances, and argued that they were 'equal to any perpetrated by the Russians in Poland, the Austrians in Italy, or the Turks in Bulgaria . . .'. In a further pamphlet in 1885 he condemned the *Napier Commission* as a landlord dominated body and its conclusions as 'unsatisfactory'.[11] Clark had spent his summer holidays in the Highlands for many years and in his lectures on land nationalisation he had often alluded to the Highland clearances, but it was not until the Battle of the Braes in 1882 and the formation of the HLLRA that he became actively involved as a member of the Executive Committee of the new organisation.[12] Clark did make the point in his memoir that Fraser Mackintosh also attended the first meeting and that he stood out from the other Highland MPs who 'belonged to the landlord class and were opposed to change'. Clark's interest in the Highland land question stemmed from his belief that conditions in the North of Scotland were symptomatic of the flaws and injustices which stemmed from the land laws. In this belief his views were closer to John Murdoch than Charles Fraser Mackintosh or Alexander Mackenzie, who came to the Highland land question from an engagement with Highland history and a supposition that the Highland land question was unique and self contained: they were not so well placed or widely connected within the broader radical movement to make the connections to other issues.

A further point of contrast between Charles Fraser Mackintosh and Gavin Clark concerned their attitude to Ireland. We have already seen how Fraser Mackintosh, along with other Highlanders, such as Alexander Nicolson, deprecated the assertiveness of the Irish MPs, the violence of the Irish land agitation and the fact that concessions were granted to Irish tenants prior to any treatment of the Highland land question. Donald MacFarlane, who represented both Irish and Scottish seats during his parliamentary career, was also of this view: he pointed out that 'great oppression may have been inflicted upon the Irish, but it was not endured without bursts of wild criminal resistance'.[13] Clark, was well informed about the Irish land question at an early stage and took a favourable attitude to the programme of the Land League. In 1881 he had visited Ireland as part of a deputation sent by the Social Democratic Federation. He remarked that 'the land system of Ireland was a disgrace to our system of civilisation'; but, he argued in a speech in Dublin, conditions in the West Highlands were 'as bad, if not rather worse than in the west of Ireland'. He went on to make the point, also made by Fraser Mackintosh in the early 1890s, that 'the formation of great sporting tracts for the amusement of the idle rich' added an extra dimension to the Highland land question. Clark concluded that he 'was glad to say that in the Island of Skye the people had begun to rebel against the evils under which they were suffering'.[14] Far from celebrating the passivity of the Highland crofters, Clark deprecated it, again marking him out from Fraser Mackintosh:

> I regretted that they had accepted their lot so patiently, and so uncomplainingly, and that so little had been done for them by those who had left the Highlands and had been successful in other parts of the world. In this respect the conduct of the Highlanders has always compared unfavourably with that of the Irish.[15]

Clark also took a contrasting position from the other Crofter MPs on the question of Irish Home Rule. As we have seen Fraser Mackintosh was in favour of the idea of 'Home Rule All Round'; D. H. MacFarlane was in favour of 'as much Home Rule as is consistent with the integrity of the United Kingdom and of all the other just claims of Ireland'.[16] In 1880 MacFarlane had published a pamphlet on Anglo-Irish relations in which he compared the histories of the Anglo-Scottish and Anglo-Irish Unions; he argued

> That England is a naturally richer country than Ireland, no one can fail to see. But is not England, in still greater degree, a richer country than Scotland? There can be no doubt that she is, but in prosperity they are nearly equal. Scotland has thriven because Scotland has been free and unfettered. Because Scotland has not been suppressed by oppressive legislation, but has been free to use the intelligent skill of her people in

the struggle against natural obstacles and an incongenial climate.[17]

The idea that the Anglo-Scottish Union of 1707 had benefited Scotland economically and had afforded sufficient space for Scotland to sustain and develop her national identity, especially through the survival of a Scottish civil society in the shape of the legal, ecclesiastical and education systems, was a commonly held idea in the late nineteenth century.[18] He believed that the demand for Home Rule had arisen from the way Ireland had been treated within the Union, from the perception that 'there is no genuine sympathy with their wants and aspirations'. He declared that he was a supporter of Home Rule for Ireland but he wished 'there had never been any justification for it' and he emphasised that he had no 'disloyal object'. MacFarlane believed that the English parliament is very far from being prepared for Home Rule' and his solution was that the Imperial parliament should hold a session every third year in Dublin and Edinburgh. He admitted that this would not 'fully meet the Irish demand, but it would certainly meet with less opposition'.[19] MacFarlane demonstrates the diversity of opinion which existed within the Irish Parliamentary Party in the early 1880s and the way in which that party kept the specifics of their demands to a minimum. By the mid 1880s MacFarlane had become disaffected by Parnell's overwhelming desire to control the activities of the Irish MPs; this hastened his transformation into a Crofter M.P.[20] MacFarlane's writings show this steady growth of interest in the Highland land question; like Clark he made the point that legislation which had granted tenurial rights, especially security of tenure, to Irish small tenants could usefully be applied to the Highlands.[21]

On constitutional questions, although most of the Crofter MPs showed an interest in the notion of Federal Home Rule, it was Clark who took the most sustained and active interest. He declared himself to be a 'Federal Home Ruler': indeed, he succeeded the Marquis of Breadalbane as the President of the *Scottish Home Rule Association* in 1887. He supported the notion of Home Rule for Ireland if it was part of a wider package of reform for the United Kingdom, in this position he was quite close to Fraser Mackintosh who adopted this position but in his case it stemmed from a much less positive attitude to the idea of Irish Home Rule, as we have seen. Clark was 'disappointed' with Gladstone's first Home Rule Bill in 1886 on the grounds that it did not adopt a federal approach, it excluded Irish MPs from Westminster, and the objectionable nature of the financial clauses. Clark, like many radicals, could not stomach the thought of public money being spent on land purchase: indeed, the idea of land purchase (the creation of a new class of private landowners) was anathema to those, like Clark, who advocated land nationalisation.[22] Nevertheless, he did not, like Fraser Mackintosh, vote against the third reading of the Irish Home Rule bill. Clark's attitude to Scottish Home Rule is also worthy of note. He does not seem to have been, like many Federal Home Rulers, a convenient convert to the idea. He laid out his ideas on this question in 1910:

> While I am an internationalist and a Cosmopolitan, I am (paradoxical as it may seem), at the same time, an ardent Scottish Nationalist, and, in the true sense, a patriot. The history of Scotland in the past shows that she, like other little countries, has done good work for human progress and the present generation is still in the van. If Scotland now had control of its own national affairs, she would be able to give a good lead to Conservative England in the solution of most of the pressing problems of the day . . . The study of Scottish history convinced me long ago that the incorporating Union was a serious calamity, and that it has had a most prejudicial effect.[23]

Clark had prepared a number of resolutions and bills on the questions of Scottish Home Rule and 'Home Rule All Round', which were presented to the House of Commons in the early 1890s. During these debates Clark emphasised a number of themes: the first was that the House of Commons would work more effectively if Scottish, Irish and Welsh affairs were devolved. Further, he denied that it was the Irish Home Rule question which was the cause of the congestion in the House. He went on to argue that federalism was the most sensible reform, this would not weaken the authority of the Imperial Parliament, nor would it involve the repeal of any Union. His final point was that in Scotland there was a growing demand for a greater measure of Home Rule: he pointed out that while the 'Scotch people were not hysterical on the question, they were calm and strong in their resolve to obtain the management of their local affairs'. The debates on these questions were not very well attended, nobody expected them to be successful, and Scottish Home Rulers had little impact in the 1890s, but they indicate Clark's commitment to the idea of federal home rule.[24]

Thus, on social and constitutional questions Gavin Clark's views were considerably more radical than of those of Charles Fraser

Mackintosh. It is also important to note that Clark came to the Highlands with a very different background from the other Crofter MPs. His interest arose not from personal or family background but from an ideological concern with the land question which led him to consider Ireland and Scotland as examples of areas which had suffered under unjust land laws. Clark was singularly unimpressed with the Government's attempts to provide ameliorative legislation for the crofters, although he did attempt to inform crofters, and others, on the issue.[25] He was highly critical of the *Crofters' Commission* which had been established by the 1886 Act to adjudicate on rent and other tenurial issues. As early as April 1887, when landlords were suing crofters for arrears of rent prior to the adjudication of the Commission, he condemned the *Crofters' Act* as a 'farce' and 'entirely useless for all practical purposes'.[26] Clark was equally harsh on the *Congested Districts Board*, the other government body with responsibility for the Highlands. This body had been established in 1897 by a Conservative government and had land purchase as part of its remit. In the early years of its existence it did not purchase any estates as none suitable for its purposes came onto the market, and it was permitted to allow its annual income of £35,000 to mount up. This was useful as the CDB was able to purchase two large estates in Skye when they came on the market almost simultaneously in 1904. Dr Clark, however, was critical of the fact that the Board was allowed to build up income without apparently doing anything with it: he also lamented the fact that the Board did not have any powers of compulsory purchase.[27]

We have seen that Fraser Mackintosh was an uncritical supporter of the imperial mission; on this question Clark also took a different view. Although he was not opposed to the empire he believed that imperialism had gone far enough and that Britain should be moving towards granting autonomy to those colonies which demanded it. In particular, Clark was deeply opposed to British attempts to retain control over the Boer Republics and expressed his opposition in a series of pamphlets.[28] His opposition to imperialism in South Africa was not an isolated view. He had also felt compelled to oppose the colonial policy of the second Gladstone administration and in 1910 he declared: 'It is time India should govern itself. She cannot make things worse than they are under our Rule'.[29] It was, however, the South African question which had the biggest impact on his political career. He was recognised in Britain and South Africa as one of the most active and fundamental of pro-Boers: the parliament of the South African Republic referred to him as 'that unwearied champion of truth and justice – that second knight without fear or blemish . . . his name is ingraved in shining letters on the grateful and tremulous hearts of the people of the South African Republic'.[30] The domestic reaction to his views on this question were slightly less congratulatory, and the position became especially serious with the outbreak of the Boer War in 1899. Conflict in South Africa meant that pro-Boer views were not merely unpopular but could be defined by opponents as open disloyalty.[31] Clark's views were well known and he made no attempt to hide them; supporting John Redmond's amendment to the address which called for the war to be ended, for example. This caused considerable controversy in Caithness, where a local newspaper referred to Redmond's Irish party as 'disloyal' and Clark as one of their 'true friends'.[32] This gave new impetus to a campaign against Clark which sought to persuade him that he no longer had the confidence of the local Liberal Committee and that he should stand down and face re-election. Clark steadfastly refused to do this, and argued that there was no evidence that he had lost the confidence of his constituency.[33] At the General Election of 1900 a Liberal Imperialist, R.L. Harmsworth, came forward as a candidate for Caithness.[34] Clark stood 'in the cause of Land reform and radicalism'· his election address outlined his opposition to the South African War, on the grounds that it was 'immoral and unjust', and emphasised his commitment to 'the interests of Labour and land reform which I have followed for the last fifteen years'.[35] When Harmsworth defeated Clark at the election in October one local newspaper remarked that there was 'universal satisfaction' at the result, and that 'the county had declared its patriotism so strongly'.[36]

He was the most left wing of the Crofter MPs, being involved in socialist organisations in London in the early 1880s and his last act was to stand as a Labour candidate in Glasgow Cathcart in the 1918 election, with land nationalisation at the top of his programme.[37] Thomas Johnston, in a retrospective article after Clark's death in 1930, emphasised his socialist credentials: 'all his life he remained a convinced and active Socialist and democrat'.[38] His ideas on the land question were probably the most advanced of all the Crofter MPs; he advocated land nationalisation, as we have seen. Thus, the range of contrasts with Charles Fraser Mackintosh are clear.

In his close and long-standing connections with the Highlands, although not with the crofting community, Fraser Mackintosh contrasts with Roderick MacDonald and Donald MacGregor who were accused of being 'carpet baggers'. MacDonald was probably the least voluble of the Crofter MPs, and probably also the most prosperous. His independent income earned from his coroners practice in London amounted to £1600 per year, and he left an estate of £28,000 on his death in 1894. The range of medico-legal positions which he held eventually helped to create the impression in Ross-shire that he was not a committed constituency member. This seems to lie behind his retiral from politics prior to the General Election of 1892, although the cancer which killed him in early 1894 and the loss of his wife that year may have been factors.[39] Before we reject Dr MacDonald as a dilettante a number of points should be made. Firstly, he was perhaps the classic example of the 'urban Gael', the creature supposedly behind the Crofters' movement, being born in Skye but becoming politically active through the London HLLRA in the early 1880s. Secondly, we should note that he was the first person to come forward as a 'Crofter candidate': at the Ross-shire by-election of 1884 he challenged the official Liberal candidate and future Conservative Secretary for Scotland, Ronald Munro Ferguson. A later account of the election described MacDonald as a 'hopelessly dull' platform performer and although MacDonald's manners were described as polished it was noted that his accent 'bore no trace either of his Highland or of his Scottish origin'.[40] This contest took place prior to the extension of the franchise and MacDonald was defeated: the *Scottish Highlander* later remarked that the 'educational value' of this 'courageous' election campaign was 'incalculable'. Dr Macdonald gained his revenge the following year when political conditions had altered fundamentally.[41]

Fraser Mackintosh can also be contrasted with Angus Sutherland in terms of their comparative relationship with the crofting community. It is fair to say that Fraser Mackintosh discovered the crofting community late in life. His background in the Highlands, as we have noted, was from the tacksman class and his career was mostly spent in the urban politics of Inverness and as a factor. Sutherland, by contrast, was firmly rooted in the crofting community; he had been born in Helmsdale, Sutherland, in 1848 and was educated in the parish school. While teaching in Glasgow in the 1870s Sutherland became involved in the activities of urban Gaels.[42] At a meeting of the *Glasgow Highland Association* in November 1880 he read a paper entitled 'Some Economic Aspects of Evictions'. The title of the paper underestimates the all encompassing view taken by Sutherland on this question: he compared the disruptive effects of evictions to those of civil war. The moral effect of eviction was also stressed, as he argued that the impact of eviction on the individual was to turn an 'honest and law-abiding and industrious citizen into the polar opposite'. Sutherland concluded by pointing to the cultural loss occasioned by clearance, although he was prepared to admit that the process of cultural change had begun to take place 'before the final breaking down of the patriarchal system in 1745'. The post-lecture discussion was rounded off by a ringing declaration of anti-landlordism by the lecturer, who declared: 'Every Highlander was a born agitator because he had suffered directly or indirectly from landlordism' and advocating land nationalisation as the way to prevent recurrences of episodes such as the Sutherland clearances.[43]

Sutherland did not arrive in parliament until after the passage of the *Crofters' Bill* and the failure of the *Home Rule Bill*: he had been defeated in 1885 by the Marquis of Stafford and did not reach Westminster until 1886 when the Marquis stood down after being horrified by Gladstone's Home Rule notions. Sutherland's later career is interesting in that he resigned his seat to became a government official in 1896; serving as the President of the *Fishery Board for Scotland*, a member of the CDB, and the *Royal Commission on Congestion* in Ireland, receiving a Knighthood for his services in 1907. Thus, Sutherland was more directly involved in the implementation of post-1886 crofting policy in a way that the other Crofter MPs were not. The *Congested Districts Board* ended up implementing a policy of land nationalisation by default in Skye and Vatersay after failing in its attempts to interest crofters in the idea of land purchase.[44]

Conclusion

As has been shown here there are two salient points which can be made about the Crofter MPs and the so-called Crofters' Party: the first is that they were a very diverse group of individuals, so disparate, indeed, that it is very doubtful if they can be called a 'Party'. If this label is justified, then it is so for only a very short time; namely that between the election of 1885 and the election of 1886, a period of only seven months. The election of 1885 was the crucial moment in the history of the Crofter MPs. This was the election at which they challenged and, on the whole defeated, the official Liberal candidates in the Highlands, a fact which encouraged the government to follow through with their plans to legislate on the Crofter question. This is not to argue that it was the

Crofter MPs who raised the issue, or the need for legislation. This had already been achieved, as the abortive *Crofters' Bill* of 1885 demonstrates. Their presence in the House of Commons, and Gladstone's need for support for his Irish Home Rule schemes helped to ensure that the Crofters' Bill was not entirely swallowed up by the Irish question. Beyond this the Crofter MPs had little impact on the content of the Bill. By the election of 1886 the process of bringing them within the broad folds of Liberalism had begun with the fact that they were not opposed by Liberal candidates and by the 1892 election it was difficult to distinguish them from orthodox Gladstonian Liberals, with the exception of Fraser Mackintosh, of course. The second point is the range of issues which influenced the Crofter MPs; they were not only motivated by the Highland land question, this can be clearly seen in the case of Gavin Clark, but also in the career of Angus Sutherland. Perhaps the individual who was most driven by the singularity of the Highland land question was Fraser Mackintosh, and it is significant that the limitations of his outlook induced conservatism, rather than radicalism, on this and many other issues.

[1] T. C. Smout, *A Century of the Scottish People, 1830-1950* (London, 1986), p.253. It is interesting that Professor Smout's discussion of the Crofters' Party comes not in the chapter on the Highlands but in that entitled 'The Working Class Radical Tradition'.

[2] G. B. Clark, 'Rambling Recollections of an Agitator', *Forward,* 8 Oct 1910

[3] D. Howell, *British Workers and the Independent Labour Party, 1888-1906* (Manchester, 1983), p. 148.

[4] I. F. Grigor, 'Crofters and the Land Question, (1870-1920), unpublished PhD thesis, two volumes, University of Glasgow, 1989, ii, p. 233; for a brief overview see, M. Espinasse, 'Gavin Brown Clark', in J.M. Bellamy & J. Saville (eds), *Dictionary of Labour Biography, vol iv* (London, 1981), pp. 59-61.

[5] M. S. Wilkins, 'The Non Socialist Origins of England's First Important Socialist Organisation', *International Review of Social History,* 4 (1959), pp. 199-207; R. Shannon, *Gladstone and the Bulgarian Agitation* (London, 1963); *Times,* 10 Oct 1876; it has been pointed out that many of the radicals who opposed the Boer War were veterans of the agitation over the Bulgarian atrocities; see, S. Koss, *The pro-Boers: The Anatomy of an Anti War Movement* (Chicago, 1973), p. xxii.

[6] G. B. Clark, *The Financial Revolution: counting the cost* (Glasgow, 1917), p. 11; *British Medical Journal,* 19 Jul 1930, pp. 126-7; *The Lancet,* 19 July 1930, p. 168.

[7] Clark, 'Rambling Recollections', *Forward,* 18 Jun 1910.

[8] Clark, 'Rambling Recollections', *Forward,* 18 Jun 1910; G. B. Clark, *The Land Question in Scotland* (Glasgow, 1911), p. 6; G. B. Clark, *A Plea for the Nationalisation of Land,* (Glasgow, 1882), p.6; G. B. Clark, *The Position of Farm Servants* (Glasgow, 1911); G. B. Clark, *The Land and the People: A Plea for Nationalisation* (Manchester, 1918), pp. 2-8.
[9] Clark, *Plea for the Nationalisation of Land,* pp. 39-40.
[10] Clark, 'Rambling Recollections', *Forward,* 13 Aug 1910.
[11] Clark, *Plea for the Nationalisation of Land,* p. 9; G. B. Clark, *The Highland Land Question* (London, 1885), p. 3.
[12] Clark, 'Rambling Recollections', *Forward,* 13 Aug 1910.
[13] D. H. MacFarlane, *The Highland Crofters versus Large farmers* (2nd edition, London, 1885), p. 5.
[14] Clark, 'Rambling Recollections', *Forward,* 16 Jul 1910.
[15] Clark, 'Rambling Recollections', *Forward,* 13 Aug 1910; see also Clark, *Plea for the Nationalisation of Land,* p. 12.
[16] *Oban Times,* 5 Sept 1885.
[17] D.H. MacFarlane, *Ireland versus England* (London, 1880), pp. 4-5.
[18] R. J. Finlay, 'Controlling the Past: Scottish Historiography and Scottish Identity in the 19th and 20th Centuries', *Scottish Affairs,* no 9 (Autumn 1994), pp. 131-34.
[19] D. H. MacFarlane, *Ireland versus England* (London, 1880), pp. 4-5, 19-22.
[20] *Oban Times,* 5 Sept 1885.
[21] D. H. MacFarlane, *The Depopulation of Rural Scotland* (London, 1882), p. 5; see also a letter from MacFarlane, *Spectator,* 29 Nov 1879, p. 1504.
[22] Clark, 'Rambling Recollections', *Forward,* 17, 24 Sept 1910.
[23] Clark, 'Rambling Recollections', *Forward,* 3 Sept 1910.
[24] *PD,* 3rd Ser., vol. 341, cols 677-84; 4th Ser., vol. 3, cols. 1684-1691; vol. 13, cols. 1828-33; A. C. I. Naylor, 'Scottish Attitudes to Ireland, 1880-1914', unpublished PhD thesis, University of Edinburgh, 1985, pp. 45-67.
[25] G. B. Clark, *The Crofters' Acts: With an introduction* (Glasgow, 1887).
[26] *PD,* 3rd Ser, vol. 313, col. 239; see also vol. 319, cols. 1700, 1720-21; G. B. Clark, *The Work of the Crofters' Commission* (Glasgow, 1911).
[27] E. A. Cameron, *Land for the People? The British Government and the Scottish Highlands, c.1880 - 1925* (East Linton, 1996), pp. 83-7; *PD,* 4th Ser., vol. 53, col. 1171-72; vol. 63, cols. 897-9; vol. 64, cols. 133-4; G. B. Clark, 'The Land Problem in the Highlands', *The Nineteenth Century and After,* 76 (1914), p. 136.
[28] G. B. Clark, *British Policy Towards the Boers: An Historical Sketch* (London, 1881); G. B. Clark, *Our Future Policy in the Transvaal; a defence of the Boers* (London, 1881); G. B. Clark, 'Our Boer Policy', *Fortnightly Review,* 14 (1885), pp. 278-89; G. B. Clark, *The Transvaal Crisis* (London, 1900); G. B. Clark (ed), *The Official Correspondence between the Governments of Great*

Britain, the South African Republic and the Orange Free State, which preceded the War in South Africa (London, 1900); Clark, 'Rambling Recollections', *Forward,* 23 Jul 1910.

[29] Clark, 'Rambling Recollections', *Forward,* 6, 20 Aug 1910.

[30] *Further Correspondence Respecting the Transvaal and Adjacent Territories,* PP 1884-85, LVII, pp. 4-5; R. Price, *An Imperial War and the British Working Class: Working Class Attitudes and Reactions to the Boer War, 1899-1902* (London, 1972), p. 82.

[31] Koss, *The pro-Boers,* p. xxiii; J. S. Galbraith, 'The pamphlet campaign on the Boer War', *Journal of Modern History,* 24 (1952), p. 116.

[32] *PD,* 4th Ser., vol. 78, cols. 843, 850-7; *John O' Groats Journal,* 9 Feb 1900.

[33] *Inverness Courier,* 3, 10, 17 Nov & 22 Dec 1899, 13 Feb 1900; *John O' Groat Journal,* 16, 23 Feb, 23, 30 Mar 1900; *Times,* 12 Feb 1900; S. J. Brown, ' "Echoes of Midlothian": Scottish Liberalism and the South African War, 1899-1902', *SHR,* 71 (1992), pp.164, 171.

[34] H.C.G. Matthew, *The Liberal Imperialists: The ideas and politics of a post-Gladstonian elite,* (Oxford, 1973), pp. 57, 300.

[35] *John O'Groat Journal,* 7, 21, 28 Sept.

[36] *John O'Groat Journal,* 12 Oct 1900; see also *Inverness Courier,* 12 Oct 1900.

[37] Hunter, 'Politics of Highland Land Law Reform', pp. 50, 67; MacPhail, *Crofters' War,* p. 162; *Forward,* 30 Nov, 21 Dec 1918.

[38] *Forward,* 12 July 1930.

[39] M. Stenton & J. Lees (eds), *Who's Who of British Members of Parliament, volume II* (Sussex, 1976-81) pp. 230-1; *Times,* 10 Mar 1894; *British Medical Journal,* 24 Mar 1894, p. 664; *The Lancet,* 24 Mar 1894, p.759; M. Espinasse, 'Roderick MacDonald', in Bellamy and Saville, *Dictionary of Labour Biography,* p. 117-18; *Ross-shire Journal,* 16 Mar 1894; *Inverness Courier,* 13, 16 Mar 1894.

[40] Senex, 'The Humours of a Highland Election: Memories of the Old Land League', *Ross-shire Journal,* 15, 22, 29 Nov 1929.

[41] *Scottish Highlander,* 15 Mar 1894.

[42] *Who Was Who, vol ii, 1916-1928* (5th ed London, 1992), p. 786.

[43] *Highlander,* 17 Nov 1880.

[44] Cameron, *Land for the People,* pp.106-8; C. Stewart, *The Highland Experiment in Land Nationalisation* (London, 1904).

Conclusion

History, Politics and Antiquarianism

The final area of Charles Fraser Mackintosh's career to be examined is his contribution to scholarship. In many ways this is his most enduring legacy: he is better remembered today as an historian or antiquarian than as a politician, and the works which he produced are still utilised by historians working on the Highlands in the medieval or early modern periods.[1] He was not, however, a pioneering historian, nor was his contribution to historical interpretation particularly original. Nineteenth century historiography in Scotland was strongly characterised by a willingness to approach history directly through primary sources, perhaps a reaction against the preceding century which had used the lens of conjecture and theory to perceive the past. Fraser Mackintosh asserted that 'facts are inexorable: theories are like the dark deceitful grass, which covers the rivulet's infant source'.[2] A host of clubs were established with the express purpose of publishing documents to get at the facts: the Roxburghe, Maitland, Bannatyne, Spalding and Grampian Clubs flourished in the mid-nineteenth century and brought a considerable amount of material into print. This was also the age when efforts were being made to systematically organise and publish the public records of Scotland, most notably the *Acts of the Parliaments of Scotland*.[3] Not very much of this activity was devoted towards the Highlands; the only club with this specific purpose, the Iona Club, published only one volume in 1847.[4] Fraser Mackintosh could be said to be a one man publishing club for Highland material. It was characteristic of the age, and of Fraser Mackintosh's outlook, that he should actually call for the establishment of a club devoted to Highland history. He proposed that this would reflect the growth of Inverness as the Capital of the Highlands and would help to illuminate the History of the Highlands which, he felt, was 'far from being known and, and cannot be satisfactorily elucidated except by the publication of authentic documents'.[5]

Fraser Mackintosh's chief contributions to antiquarian scholarship were his two volumes of *Antiquarian Notes,* published in 1865 and 1897, with a second combined edition issued in 1913. These volumes began life as weekly newspaper columns in the *Inverness Advertiser,* in the case of the first volume, and the *Scottish Highlander*, in the case of the second volume. In 1875 he produced *Invernessiana: contributions toward a history of the town and parish of Inverness from 1160 to 1599,* and in 1890 he followed this up with *Letters of Two centuries chiefly connected with Inverness and the Highlands from 1616 to 1815.* In addition to these more general collections of documents he was also interested in the history of the Mackintoshes and Clan Chattan. He was devoted, almost to the point of obsession, to the cause of proving that the Mackintoshes were the senior partners in the Clan Chattan; indeed, he suggested that the first volume of his proposed Highland Publishing Club should be a volume on *The Mackintoshes of that Ilk, Captains of Clan Chattan, 1160-1860.*[6] We should be careful, however, not to separate Fraser Mackintosh's politics from his scholarship to too great an extent. The first point which can be made is that Fraser Mackintosh displayed a type of sentimental Jacobitism which was not uncommon for a late nineteenth century Unionist. This aspect of his thinking surfaces in several areas: in a discussion of the History of the Clan Chattan, for example, he suffixed a remark on the Hanoverian army by declining to 'call it the Royal Army'.[7] In a fuller discussion of Jacobite history he argued that the failure of the risings of 1715 and 1745 was not due to any failure, lack of sagacity or shortage of skill on the part of the Highland chiefs; he felt that if, in 1745, the Jacobite army had pushed on to London with 'vigour and determination' the rebellion would have been successful. He remarked in conclusion that:

> The credit or discredit of failure in 1715, through weak and divided counsels; and in 1745, from want of support, lies at the door of England alone.[8]

This was a theme in Fraser Mackintosh's outlook which was recognised by contemporaries: one reviewer of *Letters of Two Centuries* protested against 'Mr Fraser Mackintosh's inherited and rather incongruous Jacobitism' and noted that he was 'perhaps too considerate of the feelings of remote descendants - unless their ancestors happened to be anti-Jacobites'![9] Fraser Mackintosh's sentimental support for the Stuart cause was not confined to his historical writings on the eighteenth century, however; he also expressed his loyalty to the Stuart cause by raising a monument to the seventeenth century Royalist poet Iain Lom. This ornamental stone slab, in the burial ground of Cille Choirill chapel in the Braes of Lochaber, was designed by the Inverness architect John

Conclusion: History, Politics and Antiquarianism

Rhind, who also designed the houses of Fraser Mackintosh and his associate Sir John Ramsden of Ardverikie. The idea of the monument was canvassed after a debate in the *Inverness Courier* in 1873 about the exact spot at which the poet's remains were buried: it seems unlikely, although the monument is placed on an impressive site, commanding fine views down Glen Spean, that it stands at the place where 'the Bard of Keppoch lies fast asleep', as the inscription has it.[10]

His obituary in the *Northern Chronicle* pointed to a possible reason for his lingering Jacobite sympathies when it remarked that Fraser Mackintosh had been 'born and brought up among people who had not divested themselves of clannish or Jacobite sympathies, and the bias he received when young to some degree remained with him to the last.'[11] This assertion is borne out by his genealogy: his father, Alexander Fraser of Dochnalurg, was born in 1764 and, therefore Fraser Mackintosh was only one stage removed from people who had lived through the Jacobite rebellion, although his father died in 1834 when Charles was only six years old.[12]

Underlying these views was a deeply idealistic and sentimental perspective on the Highland past which revealed itself in his political views, as we have seen. Fraser Mackintosh repeatedly argued that the traditional bonds between landlord and tenant had produced stability and good feeling in Highland social relations. This idea emerges in his historical work, much of which can be read as an elegy for the days of clanship, chiefly duty and tenurial deference. In such views Fraser Mackintosh also attached pivotal importance to the rebellion of 1745-6 in transforming the nature of Highland society, describing it as the occasion upon which Clanship received its 'death blow'.[13] Pre-1745 Highland society represented a golden age which was only disturbed by external events, such as the defeat of the Jacobite rebellion, rather than the internal stresses and strains which modern historians have identified.[14]

In *Dunachton Past and Present,* admittedly one of his first books, published in 1865, Fraser Mackintosh laments the effects of the clearances pointing out that in Badenoch 'where is now desolation, a people lived, herding their cattle, and enjoying existence in their simple way'. The lesson he drew from such an historical experience was that the resident gentry were 'now too few' and that if Dunachton was to be restored to its former glories it would be through the actions of 'the young chief, when he takes possession of his house'.[15] Even in one of his later works, published after the Crofters' agitation, *Letters of Two Centuries,* similar views can be found. In his comments on letters referring to the actions of men from Glengarry and Knoydart who refused to enlist in the British army in 1794, he drew a distinction between Highland militarism before and after the rebellion of 1745-6. He argued that the factor which produced the change was the *Disarming Acts* and 'other severe and repressive measures which cowed the spirit of the people' and induced them to emigrate rather than enlist. He deprecated both the process of enlistment - in which the 'screw of landlordism was unscrupulously used - and the deployment of Highlanders after enlistment, 'being nearly always sent to unhealthy climates without previous training'.[16] It has been argued that these views represented an overly optimistic view of pre-1745 'loyalty for clan solidarity'.[17] This may well be the case, and Fraser Mackintosh does, elsewhere, celebrate clanship as an almost ideal form of social organisation, something which can be seen in his constant praise for the Chieftainship of the Frasers of Lovat.[18] In his praise of the Frasers of Lovat he even went as far, in a speech to the Gaelic Society of Inverness, as trenchant criticism of Robert Louis Stevenson's portrayal of Simon Fraser of Lovat in his novel *Catriona,* published in 1893. As Andrew Lang pointed out in a letter to the *Inverness Courier,* it was unlikely that the author of *Catriona* would reply to the speech of Mr Fraser Mackintosh![19]

In these views we can see a number of interesting themes: the transformation of Highland society by the rebellion of 1745 and the government repression which followed in its wake; the transformation of Clan Chiefs to commercial landlords which wrecked the bonds between chief and people; and the British state's exploitative use of Highland regiments, although the 'bravery and good conduct' of these regiments could be celebrated.[20] The role of the Highlanders as soldiers in defence of the empire was often introduced into the debates on the land question in the 1880s as a reason for taking steps to prevent the further depopulation of the region. The origins of such a process, however, safely in the past, could be criticised without any seeming contradiction with the celebration of the current role of the Highland regiments.

Concluding Themes
After his enforced retiral from politics in 1892 Charles Fraser Mackintosh concentrated on antiquarian pursuits, publishing, as we have

Conclusion: History, Politics and Antiquarianism

seen, a number of books and papers in the mid-1890s. He presided at the Mod in Inverness in 1897 and once again in Oban the following year. By the late 1890s his health worsened and he spent increasing amounts of time in Bournemouth: he died there in January 1901 and was buried in Kensal Green Cemetery in West London. Due to his latter isolation in Bournemouth his last illness was not well known in the Highlands and his death was unexpected: the *Oban Times* commented that 'few persons knew of the funeral, and much disappointment has been expressed by many who wished to show their respect by attending'.[21] Obituaries and retrospectives of Fraser Mackintosh's career tended to elide political controversies and inconsistencies, and concentrated on his contribution to the history of Inverness and the Highlands. Even his arch enemy from the 1885 election, the *Northern Chronicle,* remarked that Fraser Mackintosh was a 'worthy man, a diligent rummager of old documents and a zealous friend of the Highland people' whilst referring obliquely to his anti-feudal and rather advanced Liberal principles'.[22]

There are different aspects to Fraser Mackintosh's career, the solicitor and factor, the politician and the antiquarian, for example; and different dimensions to his view of identity, Highland, Scottish, British and Imperial. The chronological approach adopted here has afforded insight into the way his views changed over time. A number of different periods of his career can be identified. In the 1850s and 1860s he was seeking to establish his political credentials and his status in the local arena, through his activities on the Inverness Town Council and through the construction of Union Street in the early 1860s. Although this period was not entirely free from financial stress, as we have seen, it was the time when he laid the basis for his later activities. The profits from the Union Street project seem to have afforded the financial independence which allowed him to contemplate a political career. His political identity in this period seems to have been at least as much drawn from the local Conservative circle as from Liberal contacts. His activities at the General Elections of 1857, 1859, and 1865, when he acted as the agent for Conservative leaning candidates is instructive in this regard. Further, his years in the employ of the young Mackintosh chief, from 1868 to 1873, can be seen in this light; his employer, after all, encouraged him to come forward as a 'moderate Conservative' at the 1874 General Election. Given Fraser Mackintosh's fealty to his adopted clan perhaps too much of a political nature can be read into his factorship. These years did have political consequences, however, as was demonstrated at the General Election of 1885, when Fraser Mackintosh came forward as a Crofter candidate and his factorial past was used against him by both his Conservative and Liberal opponents.

In parliament in the years from 1874 to 1882 he became known as the 'Member for the Highlands' by virtue of the fact that he was practically the only member sitting for a Highland constituency who was not a landlord or a patron of a landlord. His activities in support of the Gaelic language also helped to earn this epithet. As we have noted, he was active in raising the profile of Gaelic in the Scottish educational debate and was instrumental in ensuring that the Civil Census of 1881 included an enumeration of Gaelic speakers.

The outbreak of the Crofters' War in the early 1880s can be seen as a major turning point in the political career of Charles Fraser Mackintosh. In some ways he may have been trapped by the perception that he was the lone friend of the Highlander in parliament. As the Crofter issue emerged from the shadows he was in danger of being outflanked by others, such as Donald MacFarlane, or Charles Cameron. As our examination of issues such as the game laws and deer forests has shown, he was by no means a natural radical on the land question. Despite this he was vocal in support of the Crofters at the earliest stages of the campaign to draw attention to their grievances; notably at the meetings in Inverness about the Leckmelm evictions in 1880, and in parliament he was active in pressing for the appointment of a Royal Commission to investigate such grievances. His membership of that Commission and the perception that he was the 'friend of the Crofter' during its investigations, a perception largely fostered by the fact that he was the only member of the Commission remotely connected with the Crofters' movement, drew him more closely into the ambit of that movement: his note of dissent to the Napier Report and his appearance at the Dingwall Conference of the HLLRA confirmed this. This phase of his career culminated in the messy divorce from the Inverness Burghs and his appearance as the sole Crofter candidate for the County of Inverness at the General Election of 1885. His time at the centre of the Crofters' movement was short-lived, however, as he was the only one of the Crofter MPs to vote against Irish Home Rule in 1886. This was not the only reason for his marginalisation, the fracturing of the Crofters' movement after the formation of the Highland Land League in 1886 also played its part. In the final phase of his parliamentary career, down to his defeat in 1892, it could be argued that Fraser Mackintosh reverted to type

Conclusion: History, Politics and Antiquarianism 225

and his latent Conservatism came to the fore once again. This would be too simple an explanation: many of the themes to which he had pointed throughout his political career were prominent in his writings in this period, even if many of his policy prescriptions were close to ideas being advanced by the Unionist government of the day. The one area where his ideas had advanced considerably were on the subject of deer forests. There are a number of possible explanations for this: during the 1870s when Fraser Mackintosh was the MP for the Inverness Burghs, which profited from traffic to the Highland deer forests, he was limited in the extent to which he could criticise deer forests. It would also be fair to say that in the 1870s deer forests were neither so extensive, nor so controversial, as they became in the 1880s and 1890s. It was one of the main contributions of the Crofters' movement to put this extensive and exclusive form of land use on the political agenda to such an extent that they became the subject of a Royal Commission in 1892. Thus, Fraser Mackintosh's advancing views on this subject may have merely mirrored wider views of the game question.

Throughout the period of his career when he was most closely involved with the Crofters' movement the most important theme in Fraser Mackintosh's rhetoric is his continuing belief in the virtue and loyalty of the Highland people. These were the characteristics which marked them out from the violent and disloyal Irish: it was their patience and stoicism which ensured that they were deserving of government intervention. His involvement in the Crofters' agitation may have reflected this paternalistic, or even proprietorial, and certainly idealistic, view of the Highland people. He was not interested in the wider implications of social change in the Scottish Highlands, either for other rural areas of Britain, or for other comparable social groups. In many ways, although he was widely travelled, he had the most restricted world view of all the Crofter MPs: his frame of reference was the Highland past, with which he was intimately acquainted. It is in this area that his historical and his political views chime most closely. He certainly deprecated the depopulation of the Highlands and appreciated the grievances at the heart of the Crofters' agitation, but he had never fully come to terms with the decline of clanship. 1745 was the key date in his view of Highland history, commercialism and clearance were alien impositions, dating from the aftermath of Culloden.

There was a tendency in reviews of his career and in obituaries to resolve the apparent inconsistencies of Fraser Mackintosh's politics by noting that whatever his views on party political questions he had always been a loyal servant of the Highlands.[23] It might be argued, in final conclusion, that Fraser Mackintosh developed a view of the Highland land issue, expressed most clearly in his later career, which emphasised the need for peaceable settlement of grievances and the restoration of amicable relations between crofters and landowners above a recognition of the continuing problems which crofters faced.

Fraser Mackintosh went through a number of apparent political identities during his career. On some issues, such as the land issue or the game issue, his views underwent a considerable transformation over the course of his career. On other issues he remained remarkably consistent, these included issues such as Disestablishment, which he consistently opposed. Another important and consistent theme running through Fraser Mackintosh's career was that of imperialism. In 1884 he remarked in the course of a speech in Inverness that 'it has been intended by providence that this country should take a very important role in the civilisation of the world'.[24] It was his belief in the integrity of the Empire which caused him to oppose Irish Home Rule in 1886. He was typical of his period, however, in that he saw no contradiction between a Scottish national identity, Britishness and Imperialism.[25] In one of his final public speeches, to the Annual Assembly of the *Gaelic Society of Inverness* in 1897, he compared the Gaelic and Celtic Societies round the world to 'colonies and dependencies owing allegiance to Queen Victoria'. He expressed similar sentiments while presiding at the Mod in Inverness in the same year, remarking that 'as the closest advocates of a united and enlarging Empire, we love to think of ourselves as Highlanders, never forgetting this, and so acting in life.'[26]

Fraser Mackintosh was also something of a political outsider, never at his happiest in a recognisable political grouping. His emphasis on his 'independence' in 1874 was a successful use of that tactic. His reluctance to become a political insider probably contributed to his demise in 1892. By then he was distanced from the Crofters' movement but never really accepted by the Unionist coalition.[27]

A final concluding point can be made by comparing him to the other Crofter MPs; once again this serves to emphasise his individuality and the diversity of the group of Crofter MPs. His attitude on Home Rule was very different from that of MacFarlane, although it is important not to characterise MacFarlane as a Parnellite nationalist. In his election address of 1886, issued albeit when he was fighting for his political life against Malcolm of Poltalloch, he outlined his support for Home Rule in the context of the unity of the United Kingdom and referred to the 'complete supremacy of the United Kingdom'.[28] He did not have the range of contacts in urban Scotland, or London which characterised Angus Sutherland or Roderick MacDonald, and he certainly did not have the holistic radical outlook expressed by Gavin Clark or John Murdoch.

Fraser Mackintosh was an essentially circumscribed local politician who was propelled onto the national stage by the rise of the Highland land issue on the wider political agenda: by the projection of the local political culture of the Scottish Highlands onto a wider screen.. The fact that he was only really prominent on the wider stage during the mid-1880s has led to misrepresentations of him as a radical. His activities during the Crofters' War can only really be understood by considering his contributions to public life from his earliest involvement in politics in the 1850s and 1860s. The final point to make is that despite the localism of his political activities Charles Fraser Mackintosh was not immune from the wider political forces sweeping Britain in the 1880s. The prominence of the Highland land question in this period was part of this process, but so also were questions such as Irish Home Rule, which profoundly affected the shape of the *Crofters' Holdings (Scotland) Act* of 1886, and divorced Fraser Mackintosh from the other Crofters MPs. Thus, Highland history, as with the career of Charles Fraser Mackintosh, cannot meaningfully be explored in isolation. Wider questions and processes, at first sight tangential, must be central to the research strategy of the historian of the Scottish Highlands.

---

[1] A. I. Macinnes, *Clanship Commerce and the House of Stewart, 1603-1788* (East Linton, 1996); S. I. Boardman, *The Early Stewart Kings: Robert II and Robert III* (East Linton, 1996).

[2] Charles Fraser Mackintosh, *Dunachton, Past and Present: Episodes in the History of the Mackintoshes,* (Inverness, 1865), p. 31.

[3] M. Ash, *The Strange Death of Scottish History* (Edinburgh, 1980), C. Kidd '*The Strange Death of Scottish History* Revisited: Constructions of the Past in Scotland, c.1790-1914', *SHR,* 76 (1997), pp. 86-102; M. D. Young, 'The age of the Deputy Clerk Register, 1806-1928', *SHR,* 53 (1974), pp. 157-193.

[4] Fraser Mackintosh's library contained many volumes of club publications, including the Iona Club's single publication, *Collectanea De Rebus Albanicis,* (Edinburgh, 1847), see *Catalogue of the Library at Lochardil and London, belonging to Charles Fraser Mackintosh of Drummond, Inverness* (London, 1885), pp. 1, 6-7, 13, 39, 45, 64, 85.

[5] Charles Fraser Mackintosh, *Antiquarian Notes, A Series of Papers Regarding Families and Places in the Highlands,* (2nd edition, Stirling, 1913), p. 344.

[6] Charles Fraser Mackintosh, *Dunachton Past and Present: episodes in the history of the Mackintoshes* (Inverness, 1866); Charles Fraser Mackintosh, *An Account of the Confederation of Clan Chattan* (Glasgow, 1898); Charles Fraser Mackintosh, *Address on the History of Clan Chattan* (Oban 1895); Charles Fraser Mackintosh, 'Notes on the Arms and Crest of the Mackintoshes and Clan Chattan', *Celtic Monthly,* 1 (1892-3), pp. 83-4; see also, Charles Fraser Mackintosh, *The Last MacDonalds of Isla: chiefly selected from original bonds and documents, sometime belonging to Sir James MacDonald, the last of his race, now in the possession of Charles Fraser Mackintosh, F.S.A. Scot* (Glasgow, 1895); the contents of this volume were originally published in the *Celtic Monthly;* Fraser Mackintosh, *Antiquarian Notes* (2nd edition), pp. 344-45.

[7] Fraser Mackintosh, *Address on the History of Clan Chattan,* p.7.

[8] Charles Fraser Mackintosh, 'Incidents in the Risings of 1715 and 1745', *Transactions of the Gaelic Society of Glasgow,* 2 (1891-94), pp. 28-9; see also *Letters of Two Centuries,* p.158.

[9] *Northern Chronicle,* 9 Apr 1890.

[10] A. MacDonell & R. MacFarlane, *Cille Choirill, Brae Lochaber* (Spean Bridge, 1986), pp. 48-9; *Inverness Courier,* 20 Nov 1873; A. M. Mackenzie (ed), *Orain Iain Luim: Songs of John MacDonald, Bard of Keppoch,* (Scottish Gaelic Texts Society, Edinburgh, 1973); John Rhind designed many prominent buildings in Inverness and the North, including Crown School in Inverness (1879) and Fraser Mackintosh's own house at Lochardil (1876-8). Unfortunately, he died in 1889 during a court case over payments which he alleged were owed to him by Sir John Ramsden in connection with the construction of Ardverikie House on the shores of Loch Laggan; see, M. Glendinning, R. MacInnes & A. Mackechnie, *A History of Scottish Architecture: From the Renaissance to the Present Day* (Edinburgh, 1996), p. 591; *Inverness Courier,* 23 Jul, 2, 13 Aug, 1889; A. Stewart, *'Twixt Ben Nevis and Glencoe: the natural history, legends and folk-lore of the West Highlands* (Edinburgh, 1885), p. 11; there are bundles of correspondence in the Fraser Mackintosh Collection relating to Rhind's dispute with Sir John Ramsden, NAS, Fraser Mackintosh Collection, GD 128/1040, 1054-55.

[11] *Northern Chronicle,* 30 Jan 1901.

[12] A. Mackenzie, *History of the Frasers of Lovat,* (Inverness, 1896), p. 606; *Inverness Courier,* 19 Feb 1834.

[13] Fraser Mackintosh, *Address on the History of Clan Chattan,* p. 7.

[14] MacInnes, *Clanship, Commerce and the House of Stewart,* pp. 1-55; R. A. Dodghson, *From Chiefs to Landlords: Social and Economic Change in the Western Highlands and Islands, c. 1493-1820* (Edinburgh, 1998), pp. 31-122.

[15] Fraser Mackintosh, *Dunachton Past and Present*, pp. 33-5.
[16] Fraser Mackintosh, *Letters of Two Centuries*, pp. 327-8.
[17] E. Richards, *A History of the Highland Clearances: Agrarian Transformation and the Evictions, 1746-1886* (London, 1982), p. 151.
[18] Fraser Mackintosh, *Antiquarian Notes* (2nd edition), pp. 1-3; Fraser Mackintosh, *Letters of Two Centuries*, pp. 200-1, 258.
[19] *TGSI,* 19 (1893-4), pp. 145; *Inverness Courier,* 26 Jan, 2 Feb, 23, 30 Oct, 6 Nov 1894.
[20] Fraser Mackintosh, *Letters of Two Centuries,* pp. 327.
[21] *Oban Times,* 2 Feb 1901.
[22] *Northern Chronicle,* 30 Jan 1901; "Cona", 'Charles Fraser Mackintosh, F.S.A.Scot.', *The Celtic Monthly,* 1 (1892-3), pp. 81-2; K. D. Macdonald, 'Life of the Author', in Charles Fraser Mackintosh, *Antiquarian Notes.*
[23] For example, "Cona", 'Charles Fraser Mackintosh, F.S.A.Scot.', pp. 81-2.
[24] *Inverness Advertiser,* 17 Oct 1884.
[25] D. S. Forsyth, 'Empire and Union: imperial and national identity in 19th century Scotland', *SGM,* 113 (1997), pp. 6-12.
[26] *TGSI,* 20 (1897-98), pp. 2-3; *Inverness Courier,* 17 Sept 1897.
[27] Hatfield House MSS, 3M/E, Donald Cameron of Lochiel to Marquis of Salisbury, 28 Nov, 4 Dec, 11 Dec, 1890.
[28] *Scottish Highlander,* 1 Jul 1886.

Bibliography

1. Manuscript Sources
J.S. Blackie Papers (National Library of Scotland)
Cameron of Lochiel MSS (Achnacarry Castle)
Joseph Chamberlain Papers (Birmingham University Library)
Crofting Files (National Archives of Scotland)
Education Files (National Archives of Scotland)
A.R.D. Elliot Papers (National Library of Scotland)
Finlagan, Queen of the Hebrides, (National Library of Scotland)
Fraser Mackintosh Collection, (National Archives of Scotland)
Harcourt MSS, (Bodleian Library, Oxford)
Innes and Mackay Papers (National Archives of Scotland)
Inverness Burgh Valuation Rolls (National Archives of Scotland)
Inverness Town Council Minutes (Highland Regional Archive)
Ivory Papers (National Archives of Scotland)
Kilmuir Estate Papers (Highland Regional Archive)
Mackintosh Muniments (National Archives of Scotland)
Minute Book of the Royal Commission of Inquiry into the Condition of Crofters and Cottars in the Highlands and Islands of Scotland (National Archives of Scotland)
John Murdoch MS Autobiography (Mitchell Library, Glasgow)
Salisbury Papers (Hatfield House, Hertfordshire)

2. Other Collections
Charles Fraser Mackintosh Collections, (Inverness Public Library)
MacKinnon Collection, (Edinburgh University Library)

3. Newspapers and Periodicals
Aberdeen Daily Free Press
Bailie
British Medical Journal
Celtic Magazine
Celtic Monthly
Crofter
Forward
Glasgow Herald
Highlander
Highland Echo

Highland Monthly
Highland News
Invernessian
Inverness Advertiser
Inverness Courier
John O'Groat Journal
Lancet
Longman's Magazine
Nairnshire Telegraph
North British Daily Mail
Northern Chronicle
Oban Times
Quiz
Ross-shire Journal
Scotsman
Scottish Highlander
Spectator
Times

4. Parliamentary Papers

PP 1867, XXV, *Report on the State of Education in the Hebrides.*
PP 1872 (337) XI, *Select Committee on the Amendment of the Game Laws of the United Kingdom.*
PP. 1873 (285) XIII, *Select Committee on the Amendment of the Game Laws of the United Kingdom.*
PP 1883 LIX, *Reports as to the Alleged Destitution in the Western Highlands and Islands,*
PP. 1884, XXXIII-XXXVI, *Report of the Commission of Inquiry into the Condition of the Crofters and Cottars in the Highlands and Islands of Scotland.*
PP 1884-85, LVII, *Further Correspondence Respecting the Transvaal and Adjacent Territories,*

5. Printed Sources

Parliamentary Debates
Catalogue of the Library at Lochardil and London, belonging to Charles Fraser Mackintosh of Drummond, Inverness (London, 1885)
E. M. Barron (ed), *A Highland Editor: Selected Writings of James Barron of the "Inverness Courier"* (Inverness, 1927)
C. Byam Shaw (ed), *Pigeon Holes of Memory: the life of Dr John Mackenzie, 1803-86* (London, 1988)

J. Hunter (ed), *For the People's Cause: From the Writings of John Murdoch, Highland and Irish Land Reformer* (Edinburgh, 1986)
A. M. Mackenzie (ed), *Orain Iain Luim: Songs of John MacDonald, Bard of Keppoch* (Scottish Gaelic Texts Society, Edinburgh, 1973).
L. Mackinnon (ed), *Prose Writings of Donald Mackinnon, 1839-1914* (Scottish Gaelic Texts Society, Edinburgh, 1956)
D. E. Meek (ed), *Tuath is Tighearna: Tenants and Landlords, An Anthology of Gaelic Poetry of Social and Political Protest from the Clearances to the Land Agitation (1800-1890),* (Scottish Gaelic Texts Society, Edinburgh, 1995)

6. Reference Works

J. Baylen & N. J. Gossman (eds), *Biographical Dictionary of Modern British Radicals, Volume 3: 1870-1914, L-Z* (London, 1988)
J. M. Bellamy & J. Saville (eds), *Dictionary of Labour Biography, vol iv* (London, 1981)
F. W. S. Craig (ed), *British Parliamentary Election Results, 1832-1885* (London, 1977)
F. W. S. Craig (ed), *British Parliamentary Election Results, 1885 -1918* (London, 1974)
F. W. S. Craig (ed) *British Electoral Facts, 1832-1987* (Aldershot, 1989)
Dod's Parliamentary Companion: Forty Fourth Year, 1874 to *Sixtieth Year, 1892* (London, 1874 - 92)
S. Lee (ed), *Dictionary of National Biography* (London, 1909)
D. Mackinnon (ed), *A Descriptive Catalogue of Gaelic Manuscripts in the Advocate's Library, Edinburgh, and elsewhere in Scotland* (Edinburgh, 1912)
M. Stenton & J. Lees (eds), *Who's Who of British Members of Parliament,* (4 Vols, Sussex, 1976-81)
J. Vincent & M. Stenton (eds), *McCalmont's Parliamentary Poll Book* (8th Edition, with introduction and Additional Material, Brighton, 1971)
Who Was Who, vol ii, *1916-28* (5th ed, London, 1992)

7. Works by Charles Fraser Mackintosh

Charles Fraser Mackintosh, *Dunachton, Past and Present: Episodes in the History of the Mackintoshes* (Inverness, 1865)
Charles Fraser Mackintosh *Invernessiana: contributions toward a history of the town and parish of Inverness from 1160 to 1599* (Inverness, 1875)
Charles Fraser Mackintosh, 'A Plea for Planting in the Highlands', *Celtic Magazine,* 1, no 1, Nov 1875
Charles Fraser Mackintosh, 'The Depopulation of Aberarder in Badenoch, 1770', *Celtic Magazine,* 2, no 23, Sept 1877

Charles Fraser Mackintosh, 'The Gaelic Census of the Counties of Inverness, Ross and Sutherland', *Celtic Magazine,* 6, no 71, Sept 1881

Charles Fraser Mackintosh, *Letters of Two centuries chiefly connected with Inverness and the Highlands from 1616 to 1815* (Inverness,1890)

Charles Fraser Mackintosh, 'Notes on the Arms and Crest of the Mackintoshes and Clan Chattan', *Celtic Monthly,* 1 (1892-3)

Charles Fraser Mackintosh, 'Incidents in the Risings of 1715 and 1745', *Transactions of the Gaelic Society of Glasgow,* 2 (1891-94)

Charles Fraser Mackintosh, *Address on the History of Clan Chattan* (Oban 1895)

Charles Fraser Mackintosh, *The Last MacDonalds of Isla: chiefly selected from original bonds and documents, sometime belonging to Sir James MacDonald, the last of his race, now in the possession of Charles Fraser Mackintosh, F.S.A. Scot* (Glasgow, 1895)

Charles Fraser Mackintosh, *An Account of the Confederation of Clan Chattan* (Glasgow, 1898)

Charles Fraser Mackintosh, *Antiquarian Notes, A Series of Papers regarding Families and Places in the Highlands* (2nd edition, Stirling, 1913)

8. Contemporary Commentaries

'The Caledonian Bank Disaster', *Celtic Magazine,* 4, no 60, Feb 1879

'Gaelic in Highland Schools', *TGSI,* 7 (1877-78)

'Great Celtic Demonstration', *TGSI,* 7 (1877-78)

'The Gaelic Census', *TGSI,* 10 (1881-83)

'The Late Duke of Sutherland', *Celtic Monthly,* 1 (1892-3)

'Sheriff Nicolson', *Highland Monthly,* 4 (1892-3)

Report of the so-called Bernera Rioters at Stornoway, on the 17 and 18th July 1874 (n.p. 1874; reprinted facsimile edition, Edinburgh, 1985)

Testimonials in Favour of Donald Mackinnon, MA, (formerly Hamilton Fellow of the University of Edinburgh) Candidate for the Chair of Celtic Languages, History, Literature and Antiquities in the University of Edinburgh

Testimonial to George Malcolm, Esq J.P., F.S.I., Factor, Invergarry on the occasion of his retirement from the Factorship of the Glengarry and Glenquoich Estates Inverness-shire, (Edinburgh, 1911)

G. Douglas Campbell, 8th Duke of Argyll, 'A corrected picture of the Highlands', *Nineteenth Century,* 26 (1884)

G. Douglas Campbell, 8th Duke of Argyll, *Autobiography and Memoirs* (2 vols, London, 1906)

A. H. Beesly, 'The Game Laws and the Committee of 1872', *Fortnightly Review,* 19 (1873)

A. H. Beesly, 'Deer Forests and Culpable Luxury', *Fortnightly Review,* 19 (1873)
G. Beith, *The Crofter Question and Church Endowments in the Highlands, Viewed Socially and Politically* (Glasgow, 1884)
D. Cameron of Lochiel, 'A Defence of Deer Forests', *Nineteenth Century,* 18 (1885)
W. Chambers, ' The Gaelic Nuisance', *Chambers Journal,* no 723, 3 Nov 1877 & no 740, 2 Mar 1878
G. B. Clark, *British Policy Towards the Boers: An Historical Sketch* (London, 1881)
G. B. Clark *Our Future Policy in the Transvaal; a defence of the Boers* (London, 1881)
G. B. Clark, *A Plea for the Nationalisation of Land* (Glasgow, 1882)
G. B. Clark, *The Highland Land Question* (London, 1885)
G. B. Clark, 'Our Boer Policy', *Fortnightly Review,* 14 (1885)
G. B. Clark, *The Crofters' Acts: With an introduction* (Glasgow, 1887)
G. B. Clark *The Transvaal Crisis* (London, 1900)
G. B. Clark (ed), *The Official Correspondence between the Governments of Great Britain, the South African Republic and the Orange Free State, which preceded the War in South Africa* (London, 1900)
G. B. Clark, 'Rambling Recollections of an Agitator', *Forward,* Jun - Oct 1910.
G. B. Clark, *The Land Question in Scotland* (Glasgow, 1911)
G. B. Clark, *The Work of the Crofters' Commission* (Glasgow, 1911)
G. B. Clark, *The Position of Farm Servants* (Glasgow, 1911)
G. B. Clark, 'The Land Problem in the Highlands', *The Nineteenth Century and After,* 76 (1914)
G. B. Clark, *The Financial Revolution: counting the cost* (Glasgow, 1917)
G. B. Clark, *The Land and the People: A Plea for Nationalisation* (Manchester, 1918)
"Cona", 'Charles Fraser Mackintosh, F.S.A.Scot.', *The Celtic Monthly,* 1 (1892-3)
C. A. Cooper, *An Editor's Retrospect: Fifty Years of Newspaper Work* (London, 1896)
H. Craik, *A Century of Scottish History: From the Days Before the '45 to Those Within Living Memory* (Edinburgh & London, 1901)
B. Disraeli, *Sybil; or, The Two Nations* (1845, reprinted Harmondsworth, 1980)
Lord Ebrington, 'Liberal Election Addresses', *Nineteenth Century,* 19 (1886)
"Fionn" (Henry Whyte), 'Sheriff Nicolson', *Celtic Monthly,* 1 (1892-3)
"Fionn" (Henry Whyte), 'The Late Colin Chisholm, Inverness', Celtic Monthly, 4 (1896)
"Fionn" (Henry Whyte), 'John Murdoch, *The Highlander*', Celtic Monthly, 8 (1899-1900)

G. Hartley, 'Moors and Forests of the North', *Cornhill Magazine,* 46 (1882)
D. W. Kemp, 'The Duke of Sutherland', *Celtic Monthly,* 3 (1895)
J. B. Kinnear, 'The Land Question', *Fortnightly Review,* 32 (1879)
K. D. Macdonald, 'Life of the Author', in Charles Fraser Mackintosh, *Antiquarian Notes: A series of papers regarding families, and places in the Highlands* (2nd edition, Stirling, 1913)
R. MacDonald, *The Crofters' Bill, With an anlysis of its Provisions: and the Crofters Commissioners' Report, With Copious Index* (Aberdeen, 1885)
D. H. MacFarlane, *Ireland versus England* (London, 1880)
D. H. MacFarlane, *The Highland Crofters versus Large farmers* (2nd edition, London, 1885)
D. H. MacFarlane, *The Depopulation of Rural Scotland* (London, 1882)
G. G. Mackay, *On the Management of Landed Property in the Highlands of Scotland* (Edinburgh, 1858)
G. G. Mackay, *The Land and the Land Laws* (Inverness, 1882)
J. G. MacKay, 'Dr Donald MacGregor, M.P.', *Celtic Monthly,* 1 (1892-93)
A. Mackenzie, *A History of the Highland Clearances* (Inverness, 1883, reprinted Edinburgh, 1994)
A. Mackenzie, *History of the Mathesons with genealogies of the various families,* (2nd ed, Stirling and London, 1900), A. Macbain (ed)
A. Mackenzie, *History of the Frasers of Lovat* (Inverness, 1896)
A. Mackenzie, 'Report of the Royal Commission: an analysis', *Celtic Magazine,* 10, no 104, Jun 1884
A. Mackenzie, *Guide to Inverness, Historical, Descriptive and Pictorial* (Inverness, 1893)
A. MacKenzie, *Storming the Ramparts: The Crofters' Bill in Parliament or the Independent Highland members of 1885 and 1886 and What they attained* (Inverness, 1892)
H. R. Mackenzie, *Yachting and Electioneering in the Hebrides* (Inverness, 1887)
D. Mackinnon, *University of Edinburgh, Celtic Chair, Inaugural Address* (Edinburgh, 1883)
A. M. Mackintosh *The Mackintoshes and Clan Chattan* (Edinburgh, 1903)
N. Maclean, *The Former Days* (London, 1945)
J. Macleod, *Highland Heroes of the Land Reform Movement,* (Inverness, 1917)
G. Malcolm, *The Population, Crofts, Sheep-Walks, and Deer Forests of the Highlands and Islands* (Edinburgh, 1883)
J. Mitchell, *Reminiscences of my Life in the Highlands (1883) volume 1* (reprinted, Newton Abbot, 1971)
Lord Napier, 'The Highland crofters: a vindication of the report of the crofters' commission', *Nineteenth Century,* 27 (1885)

J. S. Nicholson, *Examination of the Crofters' Commission Report* (Edinburgh, 1884)

J. Noble, *Miscellanea Invernessiana: with a bibliography of Inverness newspapers and periodicals* (Stirling, 1902)

Senex, 'The Humours of a Highland Election: Memories of the Old Land League', *Ross-shire Journal*, 15, 22, 29 Nov 1929.

A. Stewart, *'Twixt Ben Nevis and Glencoe: the natural history, legends and folk-lore of the West Highlands* (Edinburgh, 1885)

C. Stewart, *The Highland Experiment in Land Nationalisation* (London, 1904).

9. Books and Articles

'New M.P. Kept cartoonists busy' *Inverness Courier*, 9 Feb 1993.

C. M. Allan, 'The genesis of British urban redevelopment with special reference to Glasgow', *Economic History Review*, 18 (1965)

R. D. Anderson, *Education and the Scottish People, 1750-1918* (Oxford, 1995)

M. Ash, *The Strange Death of Scottish History* (Edinburgh, 1980)

M. Barker, *Gladstone and Radicalism: The Reconstruction of Liberal Policy in Britain, 1885-94* (Brighton, 1975)

E. Barron, 'The Printed Word', in L. Maclean (ed), *The Hub of the Highlands: The Book of Inverness and District* (reprinted, Edinburgh, 1990)

H. Barron, 'Books belonging to a Highland Tacksman', *Scottish Gaelic Studies*, 12 (1971)

H. Barron, 'Verse, Fragments and Words from Various Districts', *TGSI*, 48 (1972-74)

H. Barron, 'Notes on the Ness Valley', *TGSI*, 43 (1960-63)

J. N. Bartlett, 'Investment for survival: Culter Mills Paper Company Limited, 1865-1914', *Northern Scotland*, 5 (1982-83)

M. Bentley, *Politics Without Democracy, 1815-1914: Perception and Preoccupation in British Government* (London, 1984)

P. Bew, *Conflict and Conciliation in Ireland, 1890-1910* (Oxford, 1989)

E. F. Biagini, 'Popular Liberals, Gladstonian Finance, and the debate on taxation, 1860-1874', in E. F. Biagini and A. J. Reid (eds), *Currents of Radicalism: Popular radicalism, organised labour and party politics in Britain, 1850-1914* (Cambridge, 1991)

R. Blake, *Disraeli* (London, 1966)

R. Blake, *The Conservative party from Peel to Thatcher* (Revised edition, London, 1985)

N. Blewett, 'The Franchise in the United Kingdom, 1885-1918', *Past and Present*, No 32 (1965)

S. I. Boardman, *The Early Stewart Kings: Robert II and Robert III* (East Linton, 1996)

D. Brooks, 'Gladstone and Midlothian: the background to the first campaign', *SHR,* 64 (1985)

S. J. Brown, '"Echoes of Midlothian": Scottish Liberalism and the South African War, 1899-1902', *SHR,* 71 (1992)

J. Buchanan, *The Lewis Land Struggle: Na Gaisgich* (Stornoway, 1996)

P. Bull, *Land Politics and Nationalism: A Study of the Irish Land Question* (Dublin, 1996)

A. D. Cameron, *Go Listen to the Crofters: The Napier Commission and Crofting a Century Ago* (Stornoway, 1986)

E. A. Cameron, 'Politics, ideology and the Highland land issue, 1886 to the 1920s', *SHR,* 72 (1993)

E. A. Cameron, 'The political influence of Highland landowners: a reassessment', *Northern Scotland,* 14 (1994)

E. A. Cameron, *Land for the People? The British Government and the Scottish Highlands, c.1880-1925* (East Linton, 1996)

E. A. Cameron, 'The Scottish Highlands as a Special Policy Area, 1886 to 1965', *Rural History,* 8 (1997)

E. A. Cameron, ' "They will listen to no remonstrance": Land Raids and Land Raiders in the Scottish Highlands, 1886 to 1914', *Scottish Economic and Social History,* 17 (1997)

E. A. Cameron, 'Embracing the Past: The Highlands in Nineteenth Century Scotland', in D. Broun, R. J. Finlay & M. Lynch (eds), *Image and Identity: The Making and Re-making of Scotland Through the Ages* (Edinburgh, 1998)

E. A. Cameron, 'The construction of Union Street, Inverness, 1863-65', *Scottish Local History Journal,* 44 (Winter, 1998).

E. A. Cameron, 'The Political Career of Charles Fraser Mackintosh, 1874-1892', *TGSI,* 60 (1996-98)

E. A. Cameron, 'Minister was a blunt instrument of God', *Inverness Courier,* 5 Jan 1999

J. L. Campbell, 'The Crofter's Commission in Barra, 1883', in J. L. Campbell (ed), *The Book of Barra,* (Reprinted, Stornoway, 1998)

F. Capie and G. Wood, 'Money in the economy, 1870-1939', in D. Floud and D. McCloskey (eds), *The Economic History of Britain since 1700, second edition, volume 2, 1860-1939),* (Cambridge, 1994)

E. F. Carter, *An Historical Geography of the Railways of the British Isles* (London, 1959)

I. Carter, *Farm Life in Northeast Scotland, 1840-1914: The Poor Man's Country* (Edinburgh, 1979)

M. E. J. Chadwick, 'The Role of Redistribution in the Making of the Third Reform Act', *Historical Journal,* 19 (1976)

M. Chase, 'Out of Radicalism: The Mid-Victorian Freehold Land Movement', *English Historical Review*, 106 (1991)

M. Collins, 'The banking crisis of 1878', *Economic History Review*, 42 (1989)

A. B. Cooke & J. R. Vincent, *The Governing Passion: Cabinet Government and Party Politics in Britain, 1885-86* (Brighton, 1974)

B. L. Crapster, 'Scotland and the Conservative Party in 1876', *Journal of Modern History*, 29 (1957)

D. W. Crowley, 'The "Crofters' Party", 1885-1892', *SHR*, 35 (1956)

J. Dawson, 'The Gaidhealtachd and the emergence of the Scottish Highlands', in B. Bradshaw & P. Roberts (eds), *British consciousness and identity: The making of Britain, 1533-1707* (Cambridge, 1998)

T. M. Devine, 'Scottish Farm Labour in the Era of Agricultural Depression, 1875-1900', in T. M. Devine (ed), *Farm Servants and Labour in Lowland Scotland, 1770-1914*, (Edinburgh, 1984)

T. M. Devine, *The Great Highland Famine: Hunger, Emigration and the Scottish Highlands in the Nineteenth Century* (Edinburgh, 1988)

T. M. Devine, *Clanship to Crofters' War: The social transformation of the Scottish Highlands* (Manchester, 1993)

R. A. Dodghson, *From Chiefs to Landlords: Social and Economic Change in the Western Highlands and Islands, c. 1493-1820* (Edinburgh, 1998)

J. S. Donnelly, *The Land and the People of Nineteenth-Century Cork: The Rural Economy and the Land Question* (London, 1975)

J. S. Donnelly, 'The Irish Agricultural Depression of 1859-64', *Irish Economic and Social History*, 3 (1976)

J. P. D. Dunbabin, 'Parliamentary Elections in Great Britain, 1868-1900: A Psephological Note', *English Historical Review*, 81 (1966)

V. E. Durkacz, *The Decline of the Celtic Languages: A Study of Linguistic and Cultural Conflict in Scotland, Wales and Ireland from the Reformation to the Twentieth Century* (Edinburgh, 1983)

V. E. Durkacz, 'Gaelic Education in the Nineteenth Century', *Scottish Educational Studies*, 9 (1977)

M. Dyer, *Capable Citizens and Improvident Democrats: The Scottish Electoral System, 1884-1929* (Aberdeen, 1996)

M. Espinasse, 'Gavin Brown Clark', in J. M. Bellamy & J. Saville (eds), *Dictionary of Labour Biography, vol iv* (London, 1981)

R. J. Finlay, 'Controlling the Past: Scottish Historiography and Scottish Identity in the 19th and 20th Centuries', *Scottish Affairs*, no 9 (Autumn 1994)

R. J. Finlay, *A Partnership for Good? Scottish Politics and the Union Since 1880* (Edinburgh, 1997)

D. S. Forsyth, 'Empire and Union: imperial and national identity in 19th century Scotland', *SGM*, 113 (1997)

R. F. Foster, *Modern Ireland, 1600-1972* (London, 1988)

A. Gailey, *Ireland and the Death of Kindness* (Cork, 1987)
J. S. Galbraith, 'The pamphlet campaign on the Boer War', *Journal of Modern History*, 24 (1952)
W. Gillies, 'A Century of Gaelic Scholarship', in W. Gillies (ed), *Gaelic and Scotland, Alba agus a' Ghaidhlig* (Edinburgh, 1989)
M. Glendinning, R. MacInnes & A. Mackechnie, *A History of Scottish Architecture: From the Renaissance to the Present Day* (Edinburgh, 1996)
G. D. Goodlad, 'The Liberal Party and Gladstone's Land Purchase Bill of 1886', *Historical Journal*, 32 (1989)
G. D. Goodlad, 'Gladstone and his rivals: popular perceptions of the party leadership in the political crisis of 1885-86', in E. F. Biagini and A. J. Reid (eds), *Currents of Radicalism: Popular radicalism, organised labour and party politics in Britain, 1850-1914* (Cambridge, 1991)
J. S. Grant, *A shilling for your scowl: The history of a Scottish legal mafia* (Stornoway, 1992)
I. F. Grigor, *Mightier than a lord: the Highland crofters' struggle for the land* (Stornoway, 1979)
A. M. Hadfield, *The Chartist Land Company* (Newton Abbot, 1970)
H. J. Hanham, *Elections and Party Management: Politics in the Time of Disraeli and Gladstone* (2nd edition, Hassocks, 1978)
H. J. Hanham, 'The Problem of Highland Discontent, 1880-85', *Transactions of the Royal Historical Society*, 5th Series, 19 (1969)
H. J. Hanham, *Scottish Nationalism* (London, 1969)
K. T. Hoppen, 'The Franchise and Electoral Politics in England and Ireland, 1832 -1885', *History*, 70 (1985)
K. T. Hoppen, *The Mid-Victorian Generation, 1846 to 1886* (Oxford, 1998)
C. H. D. Howard, 'Joseph Chamberlain, Parnell and the Irish "Central Board" Scheme, 1884-5, *Irish Historical Studies*, 8 (1952-3)
D. Howell, *British Workers and the Independent Labour Party, 1888-1906*, (Manchester, 1983)
J. Hunter, *The Making of the Crofting Community* (Edinburgh, 1976)
J. Hunter, 'The Politics of Highland Land Law Reform, 1873-1895', *SHR*, 53 , (1974)
J. Hunter, 'Irishman who won hearts and minds of Skye crofters', *West Highland Free Press*, 6 Jun 1997
I. G. C. Hutchison, *A Political History of Scotland, 1832-1924: Parties, Elections and Issues* (Edinburgh, 1986)
P. Jalland, 'U.K. Devolution 1910-1914: political panacea or tactical diversion?', *English Historical Review*, 94 (1979)
T. A. Jenkins, *Gladstone, Whiggery and the Liberal Party, 1874-1886* (Oxford, 1988)

P. Jones-Evans, 'Evan Pan Jones - Land Reformer', *Welsh History Review,* 4 (1968-9)
J. G. Kellas, 'The Liberal Party and the Scottish Church Dis-establishment Crisis', *English Historical Review,* 79 (1964)
R. Kelley, 'Midlothian: a study in politics and ideas', *Victorian Studies,* 4 (1960-61)
M. Keswick (ed), *A Celebration of 150 Years of Jardine Matheson and Company: The Thistle and the Jade* (London, 1982)
C. Kidd, 'Teutonist Ethnology and Scottish Nationalist Inhibition, 1780-1880', *SHR,* 73 (1995)
C. Kidd '*The Strange Death of Scottish History* Revisited: Constructions of the Past in Scotland, c.1790-1914', *SHR,* 76 (1997)
M. Kinnear, *The British Voter: An Atlas and Survey since 1885* (2nd Edition, London, 1981)
S. Koss, *The pro-Boers: The Anatomy of an Anti War Movement* (Chicago, 1973)
M-L. Legg, *Newspapers and Nationalism: The Irish Provincial Press, 1850-1892* (Dublin, 1999)
T. Lloyd, 'Uncontested Seats in British General Elections, 1852-1910', *Historical Journal,* 8 (1965)
T. O. Lloyd, *The General Election of 1880* (Oxford, 1968)
J. Loughlin, 'Joseph Chamberlain, English Nationalism and the Ulster Question', *History,* 77 (1992),
W. C. Lubenow, *Parliamentary Politics and the Home Rule Crisis: The British House of Commons in 1886* (Oxford, 1988)
W. C. Lubenow, 'The Liberals and the National Question: Irish Home Rule, Nationalism, and their Relationship to Nineteenth Century Liberalism', *Parliamentary History,* 13 (1994)
J. MacAskill, 'The Chartist Land Plan' in A. Briggs (ed), *Chartist Studies* (London, 1959)
J. F. McCaffrey, 'The Irish vote in Glasgow in the later nineteenth century', *Innes Review,* 21 (1970)
J. F. McCaffrey, 'The origins of Liberal Unionism in the west of Scotland', *SHR,* 50 (1971)
J. F. McCaffrey, 'Political Issues and Developments', in W. H. Fraser & I. Maver (eds), *Glasgow, Volume II: 1830-1912* (Manchester, 1996)
J. F. McCaffrey, *Scotland in the Nineteenth Century* (London, 1998)
L. J. McCaffrey, 'Home rule and the general election of 1874 in Ireland', *Irish Historical Studies,* 9 (1954-55)
O. MacDonagh, *O'Connell: The Life of Daniel O'Connell, 1775-1847* (London, 1991)

I. Macdonald, 'Alexander Nicolson and His Collection', in A. Nicolson, *A Collection of Gaelic Proverbs and Familiar Phrases* (Edinburgh, 1996)

S. Macdonald, 'Crofter Colonisation in Canada, 1886-92: the Scottish Political Background', *Northern Scotland*, 7 (1986-7)

A. MacDonell & R. MacFarlane, *Cille Choirill, Brae Lochaber* (Spean Bridge, 1986)

A. I. Macinnes, *Clanship, Commerce and the House of Stewart, 1603-1788* (East Linton, 1996)

J. N. MacLeod, 'Charles Fraser Mackintosh M.P. - A True Friend of the Highlands', *Northern Chronicle*, 5 Aug 1953

J. MacNaughton, 'Burgh M.P. went on to champion the causes of the crofters in the Highlands', *Inverness Courier*, 19 Jan 1993.

I. M. M. MacPhail, 'The Napier Commission', *TGSI*, 48 (1972-4)

I. M. M. MacPhail, *The Crofters' War* (Stornoway, 1989)

G I. T. Machin, *Politics and the Churches in Great Britain, 1832 to 1868* (Oxford, 1977)

W. H. Maehl, 'Gladstone, the Liberals, and the election of 1874', *Bulletin of the Institute of Historical Research*, 36 (1963)

P. T. Marsh, *Joseph Chamberlain: Entrepeneur in Politics* (New Haven & London, 1994), p. 233-4

P. T. Marsh, 'Tearing the Bonds: Chamberlain's Separation from the Gladstonian Liberals, 1885-6', in B. L. Kinzer (ed), *The Gladstonian Turn of Mind: Essays Presented to J. B. Conacher* (Toronto, 1985)

H. C. G. Matthew, *The Liberal Imperialists: The ideas and politics of a post-Gladstonian elite* (Oxford, 1973)

H. C. G. Matthew, *Gladstone, 1809-1874* (Oxford, 1986)

H. C. G. Matthew, *Gladstone, 1875-1898* (Oxford, 1995)

D. E. Meek, 'Gaelic Poets of the Land Agitation', *TGSI*, 49 (1974-76)

D. E. Meek, 'The Land Question Answered from the Bible; The Land Issue and the development of a Highland Theology of Liberation', *SGM*, 103 (1987)

D. E. Meek, 'The Role of Song in the Highland Land Agitation', *Scottish Gaelic Studies*, 16 (1990)

D. E. Meek, 'The Catholic Knight of Crofting: Sir Donald Horne MacFarlane, M.P. for Argyll, 1885-86, 1892-95', *TGSI*, 58 (1992-94)

G. Moran, 'Escape from Hunger: The Trials and Tribulations of the Irish State Aided Emigrants in North America in the 1880s', *Studia Hibernica*, 29 (1995-97)

G. Moran, 'Near Famine: The Crisis in the West of Ireland, 1879-82', *Irish Studies Review*, No 18 (Spring 1997)

R. J. Morris, 'Urbanisation and Scotland', in W. H. Fraser & R. J. Morris, eds, *People and Society in Scotland, Volume II, 1830-1914* (Edinburgh, 1990)

R. J. Morris, 'Death, Chambers Street and Edinburgh Corporation', *History Teaching Review Year Book,* 6 (1992)

N. Newton, *The Life and Times of Inverness* (Edinburgh, 1996)

W. Norton, 'Malcolm MacNeill and the emigrationist alternative to Highland land reform, 1886-1893', *SHR,* 70 (1991)

A. O'Day, *The English Face of Irish Nationalism: Parnellite Involvement in British Politics, 1880-1886* (Dublin, 1977)

A. O'Day, 'Defining Ireland's Place in Parliamentary Institutions: Isaac Butt and Parnell in the 1870s', in A. O'Day (ed), *Government and Institutions in the post - 1832 United Kingdom* (Lewiston, N.Y., 1995)

W. Orr, *Deer Forests, Crofters and Landlords* (Edinburgh, 1982)

Sir Charles Petrie, Bt., *The Carlton Club* (London & New York, 1972)

R. Price, *An Imperial War and the British Working Class: Working Class Attitudes and Reactions to the Boer War, 1899-1902* (London, 1972)

M. Pugh, *The Making of Modern British Politics, 1867-1939* (Oxford, 1982)

R. Quinalt, 'John Bright & Joseph Chamberlain', *Historical Journal,* 28 (1985)

R. Quinalt, 'Joseph Chamberlain: A Reassessment', in T.R. Gourvish & A. O'Day, (eds), *Later Victorian Britain, 1867-1900* (London, 1988)

D. Read & E. Glasgow, *Feargus O'Connor: Irishman and Chartist* (London, 1961)

E. Richards, *A History of the Highland Clearances: Agrarian Transformation and the Evictions, 1746-1886* (London, 1982)

E. Richards, *A History of the Highland Clearances: Emigration, Protest, Reasons* (London, 1985)

E. Richards & M. Clough, *Cromartie: Highland Life, 1650-1914* (Aberdeen, 1989)

D. Ross, 'Inverness Bank even had Gaelic on notes!', *Inverness Courier,* 10 Sept 1991

D. Ross, 'When townsfolk took to the streets', *Inverness Courier,* 21 July 1992.

D. C. Savage, 'Scottish Politics, 1885-6', *SHR,* 40 (1961)

R. Saville, *Bank of Scotland: A History, 1695-1995* (Edinburgh, 1996)

R. Shannon, *Gladstone and the Bulgarian Agitation* (London, 1963)

R. Shannon, *The Crisis of Imperialism, 1865-1915* (London, 1976)

R. Sharpe, *Raasay: A Study in Island History* (London, 1982)

A. Simon, 'Church Disestablishment as a Factor in the General Election of 1885', *Historical Journal,* 18 (1975)

T. C. Smout, *A Century of the Scottish People, 1830-1950* (London, 1986)

J. Thomas & D. Turnock, *A Regional History of the Railways of Great Britain, Volume XV, The North of Scotland* (Newton Abbot, 1989)

D. A. Thornley, 'The Irish Home Rule Party and Parliamentary Obstruction, 1874-87', *Irish Historical Studies,* 12, (1960-61)

D. A. Thornley, *Isaac Butt and Home Rule* (London, 1964)

W. E. Vaughan, *Landlords and Tenants in Mid-Victorian Ireland* (Oxford, 1994)
M. S. Wilkins, 'The Non Socialist Origins of England's First Important Socialist Organisation', *International Review of Social History*, 4 (1959)
C. W. J. Withers, *Gaelic in Scotland, 1698 -1981: The Geographical History of a Language* (Edinburgh, 1984)
C. W. J. Withers, 'On the geography and social history of Gaelic', in W. Gillies (ed), *Gaelic and Scotland, Alba agus a' Ghaidhlig* (Edinburgh, 1989)
C. W. J. Withers, *Urban Highlanders: Highland-Lowland Migration and Urban Gaelic Culture, 1700-1900* (East Linton, 1998)
A. S. Wohl, *Endangered Lives: Public Health in Victorian Britain* (London, 1984)
J. D. Wood, 'Transatlantic Land Reform: America and the Crofters Revolt, 1878-1888', *SHR*, 63 (1984)
M. D. Young, 'The age of the Deputy Clerk Register, 1806-1928', *SHR*, 53 (1974)

10. Theses

R. J. Akroyd, 'Lord Rosebery and Scottish Nationalism, 1868-1896', unpublished PhD thesis, University of Edinburgh, 1996
E. A. Cameron, 'Public Policy in the Scottish Highlands: Governments, Politics and the Land Issue, 1886 to the 1920s', unpublished PhD thesis, University of Glasgow, 1992
I. F. Grigor, 'Crofters and the Land Question, (1870-1920)', unpublished PhD thesis, 2 volumes, University of Glasgow, 1989
I. G. C. Hutchison, 'Politics and Society in mid-Victorian Glasgow, 1846-1886', unpublished PhD thesis, University of Edinburgh, 1974
C. B. Levy, 'Conservatism and Liberal Unionism in Glasgow, 1874-1912', unpublished PhD thesis, University of Dundee, 1983
J. K. Lindsay, 'The Liberal Unionist Party until December 1887', unpublished PhD thesis, University of Edinburgh, 1955
J. F. McCaffrey, 'Political Reactions in the Glasgow Constituencies at the General Elections of 1885 and 1886', unpublished PhD thesis, University of Glasgow, 1970
A. M. McCleery, 'The Role of the Highland Development Agency: with particular reference to the work of the Congested Districts Board, 1897-1912', unpublished PhD thesis, University of Glasgow, 1984
J. Mackenzie, 'The Highland community in Glasgow in the nineteenth century: a study of non assimilation', unpublished PhD thesis, University of Stirling, 1987
M. K. MacLeod, 'The interaction of Scottish educational developments and socio-economic factors on Gaelic education in Gaelic speaking areas, with

particular reference to the period 1872-1918', unpublished PhD thesis, University of Edinburgh, 1981
A. C. I. Naylor, 'Scottish Attitudes to Ireland, 1880-1914', unpublished PhD thesis, University of Edinburgh, 1985
B. W. Rodden, 'Anatomy of the 1886 Schism in the British Liberal Party: A Study of the Ninety Four Liberal Members of Parliament who voted against the First Irish Home Rule Bill', unpublished PhD thesis, Rutgers University, 1968
C. Whyte, 'William Livingstone/Uilleam Macdhunleibhe (1808-1870): a survey of his poetry and prose', unpublished PhD thesis, University of Glasgow, 1991
J. C. Williams, 'Edinburgh Politics, 1832 -1852', unpublished PhD thesis, University of Edinburgh, 1972
J. D. Wood, 'Land Reform in the Atlantic Community, 1879-90: towards a comparative approach', unpublished M.Litt thesis, University of Edinburgh, 1981

Index

Aberdeen 99
Aberdeenshire 161
Aberdeen Free Press, The 149, 152
Abinger, Lord 185
Acts of the Parliaments of Scotland 219
Aignish 181
Allotments and Small Holdings (Scotland) Act, 1892, 185
Alvie (Strathspey) 152
Ardverikie, 161, 164, 221
Argyll, duke of 78, 119, 123, 128, 134, 146, 184
Armagh 47
Arrears of Rent (Ireland) Act 1882, 131
Australia 101

Baillie of Dochfour, Edward 121, 198
Baillie, Henry 35, 36-8, 198
Ballifeary Estate, 27
Bank of Scotland 75
Bannatyne Club 219
Barclay J.W. 73, 164, 167
Barra 97, 122
Beith Gilbert 186, 194
Bell, George 29
Bell of Scatwell, Sir William 197
Ben Lee (Skye) 108
Benbecula 97
Berlin 117
Bernera Riot 65-6, 92-95
Biggar, Joseph 77
Blackie, Professor John Stuart 81, 130, 164
Board of Agriculture for Scotland 128
Boer War (1899-1902) 211-12
Bonar Bridge, 178-9, 180
Bournemouth 223
Boyd Kinnear, John 164
Braes (Skye) 104, 106, 112, 120
Braes, Battle of (1882) 92, 108
Breadalbane, marquis of 184, 209

Bulgarian agitation (1876) 206
Butt, Isaac 77

Caithness 101, 134, 182, 212
Calcutta 101
Caledonian Bank, 75
Cameron, Sir Charles 3, 100-2, 142, 190, 225
Cameron, Duncan 107, 145-6, 149, 186
Cameron of Lochiel, Donald 38, 50, 66, 79, 80, 83, 97, 119-20, 128, 132, 145-7, 149
Cameron of Fassifern, Sir Duncan 17
Campbell of Monzie, Alexander, 9, 15-19, 23, 36, 42
Campbell, Lord Colin 78
Campbell, Sir George 102, 161
Campell, John Francis 46, 119
Campbell, Walter Frederick 46
Canada 131, 166
Carlow 101
Carlton Club (see also Junior Carlton Club) 53, 59, 152
Celtic, campaign for Chair of at Edinburgh University 69, 71, 119
Chamberlain, Joseph, 153, 163-4, 165, 166, 167-8, 178, 190
Chambers, William 29, 69
Chambers Street, Edinburgh, construction of 29
Chartism 47
Cille Choirill 220
Clark, Dr Gavin B 4, 47, 109, 134, 150, 157-8, 160-1, 178, 179, 182, 197, 205-11, 215, 227
Coigach 184
Collings, Jesse, 153, 178
Colonsay 119
Congested Districts Board 128, 188, 211, 214
Congested Districts (Scotland) Act, 1897, 191
Conservative Party 43, 44, 53, 57, 79-80, 142-3, 149, 152-3, 158, 169, 197, 199
Cook, John 21
Cooper, Charles 162
County Councils 183-5
Craik, Henry 130
Crofter candidates 78, 100, 150, 152, 155, 182
Crofter, The 148, 150
Crofters' Holdings (Scotland) Act, 59, 134, 142-3, 155, 158-9, 163-4, 167, 180, 181, 183-3, 198-9, 211, 215
Crofters' movement, 46, 108-112, 131, 133-4, 143, 148, 155, 178-85
Crofters' Commission 160, 179-80, 181, 185, 198-9, 211

Crofters' Party 205-15
Crofters' War, 59, 74, 75, 85, 91-112, 148
Cromartie, earl of 123, 184
Cromartie estate 121
Culloden, Battle of (1746) 225
Cunninghame Graham, R.B. 205

Davidson, Donald 15, 24
Davis, Thomas 48
Davitt, Michael 47, 77, 109, 178, 186
Deer Forests 74-5, 126, 131-2, 192-3, 224
Deer Forest Commission 74, 184
Dillon, John 77
Dingwall 74, 76, 133-4, 182, 224
Disestablishment, 39, 101, 159, 180, 186, 191, 196, 226
Disraeli, Benjamin 16, 35, 81
Disruption of 1843, 46
Drummond Estate, 26-7, 150-1
Dublin 47-8, 161, 164, 166, 208
Dumfriesshire 161
Dunmore, Lord 157
Dunvegan, 157
Dunvegan Castle 157

Edinburgh, University of 119, 134
Education (Scotland) Act, 1872, 68, 69, 128, 190
Elcho, Lord 37
Electoral reform 141-2
Eliott, Arthur, 166
Ellice, Sir Edward 36, 121, 132, 192
emigration 126, 131, 133
Emigration Advances Act, 1851, 131
Esslemont, Peter 161

Falkirk 164
Farquharson, Dr Robert 161
Fasach (Skye) 157
Finlay, Robert, B. 5, 145, 164, 186, 194
Fintan Lalor, James 48
Fishery Board for Scotland 128, 214
Fishing 112, 126-8, 131, 188
Federation of Celtic Societies 3, 71, 108
Fodderty 184

Forward, The 205-6
France, George, 19
Fraser of Kilmuir, Captain William, 36, 80, 105-6, 122, 154, 157
Fraser of Dochnalurg, Alexander (Father of CFM) 9, 221
Fraser Mackintosh, Charles
    antiquarianism of 11, 54, 84, 219-22
    Ballifeary Estate, purchase of, 27
    Battle of the Braes and 109
    Caledonian Bank, 75
    Cameron of Lochiel and 83
    cartoons relating to, 52, 54
    Clan Chattan, views on 220
    Clanship, views on 220-2, 225
    Clark, G.B., contrast with, 206-11
    Conservatism of 15-19, 32, 35, 40, 43, 52, 53, 59, 84, 152-3, 156, 191, 195, 199, 223, 224-5
    Crofters' War 92-112, 225
    death of 223
    debts 41
    deer forests, views on 110, 192-3, 224
    disestablishment, opposition to 226
    Drummond Estate, purchase of, 26-7
    education, views on 66-73, 190
    electoral reform, views on 190
    emigration, views on 100, 133, 188
    evictions, views on 100
    factor for Mackintosh of Mackintosh 39, 41, 42, 44, 152-3, 223
    family background 9-10
    funeral of 223
    Gaelic, 3, 9, 58, 66-73, 100-1, 128-9. 154, 158, 186, 224
    game laws 55-6, 73-6, 192
    general elections, (1857) 17-18, 223; (1859) 18-19, 223; (1865) 35-8, 223; (1868) 38-42; (1874) 42-5, 52-8. 148-9, 156, 223; (1885) 142-58, 160, 224; (1886) 168-70; (1892) 144, 168, 182, 194-6
    health of 187, 223
    Highland economy, views on 187-90
    Highlander and 53-4
    'Home Rule All Round' 165-6, 179, 195
    Inverness Courier and 54-5, 58
    Imperialism 66, 77, 97, 166, 211, 226
    Inverness Town Council and 19-23, 223
    Ireland, views on 3, 76-8, 110, 133-4, 158-69, 177, 179, 185-6, 225, 226-7
    Jacobitism 9-10, 67, 220-1

Index 251

journalism of 187-94
land purchase, views on 190-1
Leckmelm evictions 85, 95-100
landlord 120, 150-1
Liberalism of 40, 44, 52, 53, 84, 120, 192, 223
Liberal Unionism of 56, 84, 120, 144, 164-5, 166-70, 179, 182, 194
London Inverness-shire Association and 102
MacKay, George G. and 121
Macpherson, Mary (Mhairi Mhor nan Oran) and, 50-2
Napier Commission 4, 117-35, 143-44, 149, 224
obituaries of 223
parliamentary career 66-85, 100-112, 141-70, 177-99, 224-5
retiral from business (1867) 31
retiral from politics 186
sources relating to 6-9
student at University of Edinburgh 9
Union Street, construction of 15-16, 24-6, 28-31, 121, 223
Free Church of Scotland, 46, 96, 109, 122, 145
Free Trade, 44

Gaelic, 3, 9, 51, 58, 66-73, 94, 119, 128, 154, 158, 160, 186, 197, 224
Gaelic Society of Inverness, 66, 68, 69, 72, 84, 109, 222, 226
Gair, John 9
Gair, Walter 9
Game Laws 37, 39, 55-6, 73-6, 192, 224
Gavan Duffy, Charles 48
general elections (1857) 15, 17-18, 223; (1859) 15, 18-19, 223; (1865) 35-8, 81, 223; (1868) 38-42; (1874) 15, 42-5, 52-8, 76, 148-9. 156, 223; (1880) 38, 78, 79-84, 161; (1885) 15, 78, 79, 93, 142-58, 160, 162, 186, 190, 224; (1886) 168-70, 177, 185; (1892) 169, 182, 185, 104-6, 205, 213; (1895) 205; (1900) 212
George, Henry 47, 206
Germany 187
Gladstone, Herbert 163
Gladstone, William 2, 6, 42-3, 44, 82, 146, 158-9, 161, 163-5, 166, 196, 197, 209, 215
Glasgow,
    City Improvement Trust 29
    City of Glasgow Bank 29, 75
    Glasgow Herald, The, 184
    Highland Association 95, 213-14
    Highland Society 51
    Inverness-shire Association 96, 133
Glengarry, 132, 222

Glendale (Skye) 104, 106, 112, 157
Glenquoich 132
Gordon Cathcart, Lady Emily 97, 119, 123
Grampian Club 219
Grant of Rothiemurchus 185
Greenock 155
Gunn, William 121, 123, 184

Hague, The 117
Hardie, J. Keir 197
Harmsorth, R.L. 212
Hartington, marquis of 164, 167-8
Harris, 157
Harcourt, Sir William 96, 101, 117, 146
Helmsdale 213
Hope of Fenton Barns, George 37, 73
Highland Heroes of the Land Reform Movement, (1917) 198
Highland Land Law Reform Association 5, 109-10, 133-4, 144, 146, 148, 155, 160, 178, 189, 213, 224
Highland Land League 179-83
Highland News, The 8, 152, 194, 195, 199
Highland Society of Glasgow 51
Highlander, The 1, 7, 45-50, 51, 53-4. 79, 105-7, 149
Home Rule League 77
Hypothec 37

Independent Labour Party, 206
India 101, 117-18, 211
Innes, Charles 7, 27, 32, 35, 37, 53, 59, 80, 93, 149
International Working Men's Association, 206
Inverness
    burgh politics, 16-19, 52-8, 145-9, 186
    campaign on Leckmelm evictions 97-9
    commercialised sport and 39, 74
    Farmers' Society 76
    Highland Land Law Reform Association of 109
    railways 23-4, 31
    Land League Conference, 1888 180
    Town Council 15, 19-23, 45
    Union Street, construction of 24-6, 28-31
Invernessian, The 76
Inverness Advertiser, The 7, 17, 18, 23, 24, 27, 28, 30, 37, 39, 45, 52, 75, 83, 145, 157, 219-20

Index

Inverness Courier, The 7, 17, 18, 23, 24, 27, 31, 36, 37, 45, 52, 53, 57,. 58, 76, 79, 81, 84, 102, 111, 142, 147, 152, 157, 221, 222
Inverness Farmers' Society 75
Inverness-shire,
    county council 185
    politics in, 35-42, 79-84, 142-58
    landownership 36
Iona Club, 219
Ireland 47-9, 76-9, 91, 103-4, 108, 120, 125. 131, 143, 158-69. 177, 179, 181, 189, 191, 193, 208, 214
Irish Home Rule 3, 48, 158-69, 178, 185-6, 197-8, 199, 209-10, 227
Irish Land Act, 1881 78, 102, 134
Irish Land League 98, 104
Irish World, The 107
Islay, 164
Ivory, William 108, 145-6, 156

Jardine Matheson and Company 16
Johnston, Thomas 206, 212
Jones Ernest 206
Jones, Rev Evan Pan 178-9
Junior Carlton Club (see also Carlton Club) 53, 152

Keith, J.N.M. 184
Kensal Green Cemetery (London), 223
Kilmuir (Skye) 102, 105-6, 108, 112, 145-6
Kilsyth 46
Kiltarlity 185
Kirkcudbright 120
Kirkcaldy 161
Kirkhill 185
Kissingen (Germany) 187
Knoydart 222

Lancashire 47
Land nationalisation 207
Land Nationalisation Society 206
Lang, Andrew 222
Leckmelm evictions 3, 5, 65-6, 92, 93, 94, 95-100, 104, 108, 122, 184
Leverhulme 95
Lewis, 16, 92-5, 112, 181
Liberal Party, 45, 55, 76-7, 79, 142-3, 149, 158, 161, 169, 180, 197
Lindsay Act (1862) 29

Littlejohn, Dr James 29
Lochaber 82, 121, 152
Lochardil 142
Lochend 152
Lochinver 119
Loch Laggan (Inverness-shire) 161
Lom, Iain 220-1
London Inverness-shire Association 102, 110
Lovat, Lord 79, 83, 121
Lyell, Leonard 158
Lyon-Mackenzie, Colin 20

Macauley, Thomas B. 17
MacCallum, Rev Malcolm 184
MacCallum, Rev Donald 179
MacDiarmid, Hugh (factor to duke of Argyll) 184
Macdonald, Fr Allan 184
Macdonald, Archibald 195
MacDonald, Donald 154
MacDonald, Kenneth D. 22, 109, 149
MacDonald, J.H.A. 164
MacDonald, Lord, 105, 108
Macdonald, James Ramsay 206
MacDonald, Ranald 122
MacDonald, Roderick 66, 98, 109, 150, 157-8, 161, 165, 168, 178, 197, 205, 212-13, 227
Macdonald Cameron, John 150, 158, 165, 181
Macecharn, Rev Charles 6
Macgregor, Rev Alexander 70
Macgregor, Dr Donald 194-6, 205, 212-13
MacFarlane, Donald H. 3, 4, 100-1, 150, 154-5, 157-8, 161, 165, 168-70, 179, 180, 186-7, 193, 197, 205, 208-9, 224, 226-7
Macinnes, Myles 182, 185, 194-5
Mackay, Rev Dr (Free North Church, Inverness) 103
MacKay, George G. 15, 20, 21, 24, 26, 30, 121-2
Mackay, John 181, 197
Mackay, John Gunn 186
Mackenzie, Alexander 5-6, 8, 9, 75, 76, 96, 109, 117, 120, 122, 123-6, 134, 145, 149, 156, 157, 168, 181, 183, 184, 185, 186-7, 193, 195, 207
Mackenzie of Gairloch, Sir Kenneth 38, 66, 79, 81-3, 85, 105, 119-20, 125, 142, 145-9, 153, 157
Mackinnon, Charles 121
Mackinnon, Professor Donald 119-20

Index

Mackinnon, Rev. of Strath, Skye, 103
Mackintosh of Borlum, Captain Alexander (Grandfather of CFM) 9
Mackintosh of Holme, Angus 1, 35, 37
Mackintosh of Mackintosh, Aneas, 40-42, 43, 80, 123
Mackintsh of Raigmore, Aneas 1, 5, 38-41, 45, 52, 54, 57, 79
Mackintosh, Marjory (Mother of CFM) 9
Maclachlan, Dugald 156, 185
MacLaren, Charles 161
MacLaren, Duncan 161
Maclauchlan, Thomas 119
Maclean, John 121, 157-8
Maclean, Neil 197
Macleod of Gartymore, John 178, 182, 194-5
Macleod, Joseph 198
MacLeod, Murdo 94
MacLeod, Reginald 8, 144-5, 153
Macmillan, Rev John 96, 97-8, 122, 184
MacNeill, Sir John 131
Macpherson, George 19-20, 23, 52
Macpherson 193
Macpherson, Mary (Mhairi Mhor nan Oran), 50-2, 94, 154
Macpherson Grant of Ballindalloch, George 36, 73, 185
Mactavish, Rev John 6, 96, 109
Madras 117
Maitland Club 219
Malcolm, George 44, 121, 132, 192
Malcolm of Poltalloch, Colonel 66, 78, 168-9, 197, 227
Matheson of Ardross, Sir Alexander 5, 15, 16-19, 23, 26, 28, 30, 38, 45, 52, 58, 66, 74, 82
Matheson, Sir James 16, 38, 92, 93-4, 99, 122
Mayo, earl of 117
McCombie, William 37, 73
McCulloch, John 161
McNeill, Malcolm 123
Mid-Lothian Campaign 81
Mitchell, Joseph 18, 40
Mollison James 121
Muckairn 184
Munro of Fowlis 184
Munro, Donald 93-4
Munro Ferguson, Ronald 142, 146, 157, 184, 213
Murdoch, John 5, 7, 45-50, 51, 53-4, 71, 79, 80, 81, 93-4, 95, 97, 104, 106-7, 117, 122, 123-6, 130, 178, 207, 227

Murray, Donald 146, 178, 180

Nairn 54, 55, 58, 78, 105, 147
Nairnshire Telegraph, The 57, 58
Nation, The 48
National Association for the Promotion of Social Science 118
Napier and Ettrick, Lord 3, 117-19, 127, 165
Napier Commission, 74, 91, 100. 112, 117-35, 150, 177, 182, 186, 188, 189, 207, 224
Newton House, Nairn 105
Nicholson, Professor J.S. 134
Nicolson, Sheriff Alexander 119-20, 128-31, 207
North British Daily Mail, The 101
North Uist 124
Northern Chronicle, The 7, 149, 152-3, 157, 184, 185, 187, 194, 196, 221, 223

Oban 74, 180
Oban Times, The 107, 145-6, 155
O'Connell, Daniel 35, 48
O'Connell, Morgan 35
O'Conner, Feargus 47

Parnell, Charles Stewart 77, 101, 143, 148, 158, 161, 170
Peddie, J. Dick 102
Peel, Sir Robert 44
Peter, John 121
Pirie, Alexander 95, 98, 104, 106
Plymouth 118
Portree 106, 185, 186, 194
Pultneytown 184

railways 23-4, 31, 188
Raasay 121-2, 148
Ramsay, John 164
Ramsden, Sir John 161, 164, 221, 228
Redmond John 212
Reid, Donald 147
Rhind, John 220-1, 228
Reidhaven, Lord 80
Rodel (Harris) 157
Rothiemurchus 185
Rose, Hugh 15, 24
Rosebery, earl of 161, 164, 198

Index 257

Rosehall (Sutherland) 122
Ross-shire 82, 146
Ross-shire Journal, The 145
Roxburghe Club 219
Russia 118-19, 127

St Clement's Chapel, Rodel, (Harris) 157
St Petersburg 117-18
St Rollox (Glasgow) 161
Stornoway 181
Salisbury, Marquis of 143, 162, 163, 177, 196
Scottish Education Department, 69, 70, 128-31
Scotsman, The 147-8, 156-7, 196
Scottish Office 162
Scottish Highlander 1, 7, 8, 107, 145, 147, 156, 157, 180, 181, 182, 185, 186, 187-94, 220
Scottish Home Rule Association 167, 209
Serbia 206
Simpson, James 22
Sinclair of Ulbster, Clarence, 157, 184
Skye 102, 105-6, 112, 124, 145-6, 180, 186, 208, 211, 214
Skye Vigilance Committee 108
Sleat (Skye) 156, 185
Smith John 94
Social Democratic Federation 206, 208
South Africa 211-12
South Uist 97, 124, 184
SSPCK 119
Spalding Club 219
Stafford, 161
Stafford, marquis of 150, 157, 164, 214
Stevenson, Robert Louis 222
Strathspey 152
Sutherland 121, 150, 157, 164, 178, 180, 182, 213
Sutherland, Angus 95, 109, 150, 157, 178, 181, 205, 213-14, 215, 227
Sutherland Association 109
Sutherland, Rev David 30
Sutherland, duke of 74

Tain 76
Tiree, 180, 184
Torbreck 9
Tramways and Public Companies (Ireland) Act, 1883 131

Transactions of the Gaelic Society of Inverness 1, 68
Trevelyan George Otto 163, 184
Trevelyan, Charles Edward 131
Tuke, James Hack 131

Uig 105-6, 146

Vatersay, 214
Vienna 117

Wales 178-9, 197
Wallace, Alfred Russel 206
Waterston, Charles 31
Weir, John Galloway 197
Western Isles 146
Whyte, Henry 95, 109
Whyte, John 109
Wick, 182
Wounded Allies relief Committee 206